# *Community Colleges*

## ●◦ A REFERENCE HANDBOOK

CONTEMPORARY EDUCATION ISSUES

# *Community Colleges*

## A REFERENCE HANDBOOK

David L. Levinson

A B C  CLIO

Santa Barbara, California • Denver, Colorado • Oxford, England

Library of Congress Cataloging-in-Publication Data
Levinson, David L., 1954–
    Community colleges : a reference handbook / David L. Levinson.
        p.    cm. — (Contemporary education issues)
    Includes bibliographical references and index.
    ISBN 1-57607-766-7 (hardback : alk. paper) — ISBN 1-57607-767-5 (eBook)
    1. Community colleges—United States—Handbooks, manuals, etc.
I. Title.    II. Series.

    LB2328.15.U6L49 2005
    378.1'543'0973—dc22

                                                2005001842

08    07    06    05            10   9   8   7   6   5   4   3   2   1

This book is also available on the World Wide Web as an eBook. Visit abc-clio.com for details.

ABC-CLIO, Inc.
130 Cremona Drive, P.O. Box 1911
Santa Barbara, California 93116-1911

This book is printed on acid-free paper ∞.
Manufactured in the United States of America

*For my wife, Evan*

# ☙ Contents

*Series Editor's Preface*     *xiii*
*Preface*     *xv*
*Acknowledgments*     *xxi*


*Chapter One: Introduction*     1

**Defining Community Colleges**     2
  *The Community Aspect of Community Colleges*     5
  *Creating Community*     6
**The Knowledge Economy**     8
**The Comprehensive Community College**     9
  *Governance*     12
  *Faculty*     13
  *Accreditation*     15
**The Promise of Higher Education**     16
  *Community Colleges and Expanding Access to
    Higher Education*     16
  *Community Colleges and the Growth of
    Higher Education*     17
**Challenges**     18
  *Bifurcated Student Populations*     18
  *Community College Students as First-
    Generation Learners*     20
  *International Students*     21
**The Benefits of the Community College**     22
  *Community Colleges and Workforce Training*     22
  *Community Colleges as Cultural Institutions*     22
  *Economic Impact and Economic Return of a
    Community College Education*     23
  *Community Colleges as Bastions of Democracy*     24
**The "Crisis in Education" and the Contemporary
  Importance of Community Colleges**     26
  *Boosters and Detractors*     28

Understanding the Student Experience in
    Community Colleges   *31*
Expanding the Mission of Community Colleges   *34*
Conclusion   *35*
    *References*   *35*


*Chapter Two: The Growth of Community Colleges*
*in the Twentieth Century*   *43*

Chronology   *43*
The Development of Community Colleges in the
    United States: An Interpretive Essay   *47*
Conceptualizing Historical Change   *50*
Review of Models for Explaining the Development
    of Community Colleges   *51*
Factors Influencing Community College
    Development   *53*
    *Population Change and Immigration*   *53*
    *Schooling for Acculturation and Assimilation*   *54*
The Development of Community Colleges and the
    Professionalization of Higher Education during
    the Twentieth Century   *56*
    *Institutionalism*   *58*
    *Politics versus Markets*   *59*
Tensions Surrounding Local versus Federal Control   *61*
    *The Ideological "Promise" of Schooling for*
        *Upward Mobility*   *64*
    *Immigration, Acculturation, and Citizenship*   *65*
    *Bureaucratization, Professionalization,*
        *and Control*   *66*
The Emergence of the Research University and Higher
    Education Segmentation   *68*
Conclusion   *69*
    *References*   *69*


*Chapter Three: Community Colleges and Access*
*versus Excellence*   *75*

Access versus Excellence: The Conundrum of
    Democratic Liberalism   *78*
    *The Promise of Equality and Persistence of*
        *Inequality*   *79*

**The Complexity of Measuring Community College**
  **Effectiveness** *82*
    *The Dilemma Facing Community Colleges* *83*
    *Accountability and High-Stakes Testing* *84*
    *Measuring Success* *86*
    *Assessing Outcomes* *90*
    *Meritocracy* *93*
    *Market-Based Reforms* *96*
**The Affordability of Higher Education** *97*
**Challenges of Attaining and Maintaining Excellence** *98*
    *Learning Communities and Peer Mentoring* *100*
    *The Learning College* *101*
    *Service Learning* *103*
    *Supplemental Instruction* *103*
**Online Learning** *103*
    *The Digital Divide* *105*
**The City University of New York: Balancing**
  **Access and Equity** *107*
**Developmental Education** *109*
**Conclusion** *110*
    *References* *111*


*Chapter Four: The Curriculum: Transfer versus Career* *117*

**The Historic Curriculum Divide** *117*
**Responding to Workforce Needs** *121*
    *Vocational Education* *122*
    *Determining Career Trajectories* *125*
**Community College Curricula** *126*
    *General Education* *126*
    *Cross-Functional Skills* *128*
    *Vocational Clusters* *130*
    *Absence of Clear Career Pathways* *131*
**Is There a Shortage of Skilled Workers?** *132*
    *Wage Inequality* *133*
    *Is College for All?* *134*
**Antipathy toward Vocational Education** *136*
    *Changing the Context of Undergraduate Education* *137*
    *Workforce Training* *141*
    *Separating Technical from Liberal Arts* *141*
**Conclusion** *143*
    *References* *143*

*Chapter Five: Community Colleges and Lifelong Learning*   149

Educational Inequality throughout the Life Span   *153*
Human Capital, Lifelong Learning, and
   Economic Development   *155*
Workforce Training and Workforce Intermediaries   *158*
Lifelong Higher Education Enrollment Patterns   *161*
   *Creating a Foundation for Lifelong Learning*   *162*
   *Factors That Inhibit Lifelong Learning*   *163*
Increase in Continuing and Professional
   Education Enrollments   *163*
   *Perfecting Adult Learning: CAEL and Adult*
      *Learning–Focused Institutions*   *164*
   *University Extension and Continuing*
      *Education Programs*   *165*
   *Learning Competencies*   *167*
Community College and Community Building   *167*
Recent Growth in Adult Education   *168*
   *Proprietary and For-Profit Institutions*   *168*
   *Distance Learning and Cyberschools*   *169*
Institutes for Learning in Retirement   *170*
Conclusion   *170*
   *References*   *170*


*Chapter Six: The Future of the Community College*   177

The Vision of Community College Leaders   *177*
   *Additional Prospects and Challenges*
      *Facing Community Colleges*   *193*
Mission and Finances   *195*
   *Practicing an Engaged Pedagogy*   *195*
   *Organizational Challenges Facing*
      *Community Colleges*   *197*
   *Certifications and Credentials*   *199*
   *Corporatization of Higher Education*   *200*
   *Distance and Online Learning*   *201*
   *Entrepreneurialism*   *203*
Community Colleges and the American Dream   *204*
   *The Challenge of Serving Diverse Populations*   *204*
   *Forging Closer Linkages to K–12*   *206*

    *Competition from For-Profit Providers*   **208**
    *Cultivating Human, Social, and Cultural Capital*   **208**
  **Conclusion**   **209**
    *References*   **209**

**Chapter Seven: Organizations, Associations, and Government Agencies**   **215**

**Chapter Eight: Selected Print and Nonprint Resources**   **227**

  **Print Resources**   **227**
  **Nonprint Resources**   **231**
    *Web Sites*   **231**
    *Online Periodicals and Publications*   **233**

  *Glossary*   235
  *Index*   241
  *About the Author*   255

# ✒ Series Editor's Preface

The Contemporary Education Issues series is dedicated to providing readers with an up-to-date exploration of the central issues in education today. Books in the series will examine such controversial topics as home schooling, charter schools, privatization of public schools, Native American education, African American education, literacy, curriculum development, and many others. The series is national in scope and is intended to encourage research by anyone interested in the field.

Contemporary education can be conceived of in the broadest sense of the term and encompasses a multitude of issues as they pertain to education, from kindergarten to secondary school and college. Because education is undergoing radical if not revolutionary change, the series is particularly concerned with contemporary controversies in education and how they affect both the organization of schools and the content and delivery of curriculum. Authors will endeavor to provide a balanced understanding of the issues and how they affect teachers, students, parents, administrators, and policymakers. Because education has recently undergone and continues to undergo intense changes in both conceptual orientation and organization, the intent of this series is to confront these changes in a way that will illuminate and explicate them. In this regard, the aim of the Contemporary Education Issues series is to bring excellent research, by some of the finest scholar-practitioners in the field, to today's educational concerns while at the same time pointing to new directions. In this vein, the series promises to offer important analyses of some of the most controversial issues facing society today.

—*Danny Weil*
**Series Editor**

# ↔ Preface

Community colleges have played an important role in the expansion of access to higher education, yet they are often dismissed and marginalized as institutions of last resort. Lacking the prestige that is associated with competitive baccalaureate-granting institutions and omitted from popular rankings of higher education institutions—such as the *U.S. News and World Report's* ratings of universities and colleges—community colleges are often considered to be in the hinterlands of academe. Similarly, the lay public and the scholarly community alike often fail to understand the mission and purpose of community colleges, obscuring the critical role these institutions play in contemporary higher education.

This book provides an analytical entry into institutions whose open access has ironically precluded a clear understanding of their effectiveness as they enter their second century of existence. An important subtext that runs throughout this analysis is that community colleges are at the crossroads of a number of larger social, political, and cultural tensions affecting U.S. society today. Understanding community colleges is important not only for appreciating the promise they offer and the pitfalls they face but for gaining a window of understanding concerning the multitude of policy choices facing the United States in terms of economic development, educational access, equity, mobility, and achievement.

Chapter 1 presents a general overview of the community college by discussing the structure of community colleges and also the changing demographics of college students in the United States. Chapter 2 provides a more detailed historical analysis, rooting the growth of community colleges within the larger context of K–12 educational developments in the United States. Chapter 3 discusses the difficulties of attempting to balance the competing and often contradictory demands of access versus excellence. A case study of open admissions in the City University of New York (CUNY) system is presented. Chapter 4 looks at the transfer versus career function of community colleges, which constitutes a resource allocation problem that affects higher education throughout the United States. Chapter 5 provides a discussion of lifelong learning by analyzing the rise of cradle-to-grave education in the United States. Chapter 6 articulates twenty-one trends in community colleges, emanating from a plenary session held at the 2001 annual meeting of the American Association of Community Colleges (AACC) to celebrate the hundredth anniversary of community colleges in the United States. Chapter 7 presents an annotated listing of organizations, associations, and federal and state agencies that are involved with community colleges. Chapter 8 provides a set of print and web-based resources on community colleges.

## EXISTING MONOGRAPHS ON COMMUNITY COLLEGES

A number of existing single-volume treatises on community colleges have certainly influenced this work, although, as I will suggest below, they are quite different in their approach to community colleges. (Additional monographs are described in Chapter 8 of this volume.)

Perhaps the most authoritative contemporary work is *The American Community College,* by Arthur M. Cohen and Florence B. Brawer, whose fourth edition was released in 2003. In this and previous editions, Cohen and Brawer provide a textbook presentation of the subject. They begin with a discussion of the origins of community colleges, cover various organizational aspects of their operations in ensuing chapters, and conclude with a discussion of the future prospects of these institutions.

Steven Brint's and Jerome Karabel's *The Diverted Dream: Community Colleges and the Promise of Educational Opportunity in America, 1900–1985* (1989) is a seminal critical work, which argues that community colleges are essentially institutions that house students who were displaced from higher-level academic tracks. According to Brint and Karabel, the vocational turn that community colleges took in the twentieth century essentially directed a substratum of the population to vocational ambitions that were less desirable than the life chances afforded to students in the academic tracks. This "sorting-out" function of community colleges, which has occurred under the guise of vocational terminal career tracks, are for Brint and Karabel the defining hallmark of community colleges.

Kevin Dougherty's *The Contradictory College: The Conflicting Origins, Impacts and Futures of the Community College* (1994) is perhaps the most formidable existing analytical work on community colleges. Dougherty does an excellent job of capturing the contradictory imperatives facing community colleges. Community colleges are "people's colleges" in the best inclusionary and democratic sense of the term, offering a myriad of educational programs to many who have traditionally been excluded from higher education. However, Dougherty raises some critical questions regarding the efficacy of these institutions, especially in terms of their students' persistence toward completion of baccalaureate degrees. Using longitudinal data sets from the National Center for Education Statistics (NCES), Dougherty shows that a student entering a baccalaureate institution and completing his or her first two years of study has a better chance at degree completion than does a student who earns a degree at a community college and then transfers to a four-year college. In fact, Dougherty concludes his book by suggesting that community colleges would be better off if they simply became branch campuses of existing universities, similar to the configuration of public higher education in Pennsylvania.

## UNIQUE FEATURES OF THIS VOLUME

Grounded in a detailed examination of current research on community colleges, this book examines community colleges in the context of the larger domain of higher education and developments in K–12. Many of the nuances of community colleges are explainable as a result of their being "squeezed" between K–12 below and baccalaureate institutions above. Although students who matriculate in a community college must have a high school degree or equivalent (GED), they often come to the school with significant developmental needs. An ongoing problem in many states is the lack of articulation between the proficiency exam that students take at the conclusion of their high school years and the incoming placement exams they are given upon entry into higher education.

This volume also views community colleges within larger political and economic contexts. Some of the critical dimensions include the following:

1. *The globalization of the U.S. economy and consequent shifts that have occurred in manufacturing and other U.S. industries.* Globalization has resulted in the restructuring of the labor market (Bluestone and Harrison 1982; Osterman 2000) and the steady internationalization of information technology (IT) workers, who have been a critical niche for community college workforce training programs since the later decades of the twentieth century.

2. *The growing social inequality in the United States, as seen in an increasingly stratified distribution of wealth and segmentation in residential patterns.* The latter has important implications for education because property taxes continue to be the primary way that municipalities

finance K–12 education. Differential resources accompany the growing segmentation of communities and hence increase the polarization between communities with well-supported schools and those with poor fiscal support.

3. *The increasing stratification of higher education, so that more students now compete for the relatively few slots available at a small number of select, high-status colleges.* This competition for admission to these schools has resulted in the rise of a cottage industry that markets services to anxious parents who are concerned that their son or daughter will not be admitted into a prestigious higher education institution. This phenomenon is also a driving force behind parental desires to save sufficient resources for their daughter or son to attend college.

4. *Recent fiscal and demographic developments in the late twentieth and early twenty-first centuries that have resulted in profound changes in public higher education.* The growing fiscal crisis faced by municipalities and states has resulted in lagging appropriations to higher education. These fiscal constraints coincide with the coming-of-age of a baby boomlet, straining current K–12 school capacity within many communities. Beside needing to address this problem, states are experiencing low tax revenues from a sluggish economy. As a result, public higher educational systems throughout the country are challenged by an overcapacity of students, with community colleges finding it difficult to serve all those who arrive at their doorsteps. For example, California and Florida—two states that have robust community college systems—were not able to serve all those who desired entry in the fall of 2003. In addition, community colleges throughout the nation had to increase tuition by an average of 11 percent between the 2002 and 2003 academic years just so that they could operationally compensate for reduced per capita support.

5. *The role of immigration and growing diversity in the United States.* Over 9 million immigrants entered the United States in the 1990s, averaging about 900,000 a year (Martin and Midgley 2003). This is the highest number of immigrants arriving in the United States since the early 1900s, and the influx has posed significant educational and workforce challenges for receiving communities. Community colleges continue to play a major role in providing English as a second language (ESL), Adult Basic Skills, and postsecondary education to this population.

The discussion that ensues in this book is grounded in a number of primary and secondary sources. The longitudinal research of the National Center for Education Statistics; reports written by research organizations such as the Community College Research Center at Columbia

University and Jobs for the Future in Boston; work from the Organization for Economic Cooperative Development (OECD), Brookings Institution, American Enterprise Institution, Rand Corporation, League for Innovation in the Community College, American Association of Community Colleges, and others—all constitute an important basis for analysis. In addition, a number of seminal works—such as those already cited and additional volumes as listed in Chapter 8—provides the basis of the work that follows.

Finally, this volume is informed by practice. As the president of a comprehensive community college, I have embedded within this book an insider's understanding of life in a community college and a knowledge of what information from the outside is helpful to guide decision making within community colleges.

### References

Bluestone, Barry, and Bennett Harrison. 1982. *The Deindustrialization of America: Plant Closings, Community Abandonment, and the Dismantling of Basic Industry.* New York: Basic Books.

Brint, Steven, and Jerome Karabel. 1989. *The Diverted Dream: Community Colleges and the Promise of Educational Opportunity in America, 1900–1985.* New York: Oxford University Press.

Cohen, Arthur M., and Florence B. Brawer. 2003. *The American Community College.* 4th ed. San Francisco: Jossey-Bass.

Dougherty, Kevin J. 1994. *The Contradictory College: The Conflicting Origins, Impacts, and Futures of the Community College.* Albany: State University of New York Press.

Martin, Philip, and Elizabeth Midgley. 2003. *Immigration: Shaping and Reshaping America.* Washington, DC: Population Reference Bureau, vol. 58, no. 2.

Osterman, Paul. 2000. *Securing Prosperity: The American Market: How It Has Changed and What to Do About It.* Princeton, NJ: Princeton University Press.

# ❧ Acknowledgments

It was Marie Ellen Larcada, initial editor of my previous book—*Education and Sociology: An Encyclopedia* (2002) who while at ABC-CLIO asked if I would be interested in writing this volume on community colleges. As she convincingly argued, it would be a beautiful fit with what I do in my everyday life. It is with much gratitude that I thank her for this edifying suggestion.

My colleagues at Bergen Community College and my compatriots in the New Jersey Academic Officers Association (AOA) provided plentiful inspiration for this book. My new Norwalk Community College associates, along with fellow Connecticut community college presidents and central office personnel extraordinaire, underscore the ways that community colleges nurture transformation in the lives of our students. Danny Weil, series editor, Alicia Merritt, and Carla Roberts, production editor at ABC-CLIO, were incredibly patient and supportive throughout what unfortunately became a longer ordeal than anticipated.

The lives of my daughters—Shana and Emily—provided a bounty of inspiration for this work. And finally, most of all, my wife Evan has been a soul mate throughout this project and my life. I recently reread the acknowledgments that accompanied my doctoral dissertation; they contained a disclaimer that although I may not have always acknowledged her importance, she was integral to seeing it completed. I also promised her in *Education and Sociology* that the next project would be less arduous—ha! Given her ability to forgive, I hope that this is not held too much against me when I embark on my next intellectual venture! Most of all, it is to her that I dedicate this book, with all of my love.

*Chapter One*

# ✏ Introduction

Since their creation at the turn of the twentieth century, community colleges have provided pathways to higher education for those excluded from the restrictive, medieval-based university structure that had been the hallmark of U.S. higher education since its founding. Although there is considerable debate over whether this enhanced access to higher education was an act of democratization (Parnell 1985) or a way of channeling students to peripheral educational institutions, thereby allowing a small group of elite universities to maintain their exclusivity (Pedersen 2000), it is an indisputable fact that community colleges have steadily increased their enrollment share and enhanced access to higher education throughout the past century.

Although community colleges are a major segment of U.S. higher education, they are typically dismissed as institutions of the last resort. Community colleges play an increasingly important role in providing advanced educational opportunities for a growing number of students. Especially now at the beginning of the twenty-first century, when state appropriations to community colleges are being cut—forcing community colleges to dramatically raise tuition and fees to compensate for these cutbacks (there has been an average increase of 11 percent in tuition from the fall of 2002 to the fall of 2003 ([American Association of Community Colleges [AACC] 2003])—many people are beginning to realize the centrality of community colleges for procuring an educated workforce in an increasingly knowledge-intensive economy. For example, in *Toward a National Workforce Education and Training Policy,* the National Center on Education and the Economy (NCEE), Jobs for the Future (JFF), and the Council for Adult and Experiential Learning (CAEL) assert that the nation's existing community college system constitutes the foundation for a revitalized workforce education and training system in the United States (Uhalde, Seltzer, Tate, and Klein-Collins 2003, 8):

> In most states, there is high quality, inexpensive training to be found in the community college system. Many community colleges cater to the needs of working adults by providing evening and weekend courses, self-paced degree completion, and strong ties to local employers.

Changes to the Higher Education Act can help to promote more progress, particularly in serving the needs of incumbent workers. The infrastructure that already exists provides a strong foundation on which to build new models for workforce education and training.

Community colleges are poised to be the linchpin for a new training and workforce system in the United States. As articulated in the just-quoted passage, community colleges are where the rubber meets the road with respect to providing workers with the skills necessary to embark on an upwardly mobile career pathway.

Throughout much of the twentieth century, there was a steady increase in the number of students attending community colleges in the United States. Although there were no students in community colleges before 1900—Joliet College, widely acknowledged to be the first community college, was not created until 1901—47 percent of all students in U.S. higher education were enrolled in a community college by 2003 (Community College Survey of Student Engagement 2003).

The development and dramatic growth of community colleges during the twentieth century occurred in an era when college attendance increasingly became the norm in the United States. In 1900 approximately 4 percent of high school graduates went directly to college upon graduation; this figure had increased to approximately 57 percent by 2000 (Callan and Finney 2003).

This introductory chapter begins with a description of the typical organizational structure of community colleges and the nuances that differentiate them from other sectors in higher education. Then "the promise" of community colleges is reviewed, followed by a discussion of their shortcomings and challenges as raised by critics. The chapter concludes with an overview of issues that will be raised in subsequent chapters.

## DEFINING COMMUNITY COLLEGES

One way of categorizing community colleges is to view them within the context of the Carnegie Classification of Institutions of Higher Education (Carnegie Foundation for the Advancement of Teaching 2000). In this scheme, community colleges make up the category of Associate's Colleges, one of ten categories of higher education institutions in the United States. This category includes 1,669 institutions representing 42.3 percent of all higher education institutions in the United States (Carnegie Foundation for the Advancement of Teaching 2000).

A more comprehensive and nuanced way of analyzing community colleges comes from the NCES, the research arm of the U.S. Department of Education, which finds 2,068 two-year institutions in the United States (NCES 2001). Of these, 1,029 are public two-year colleges, the group of institutions that constitute the object of the analysis presented in this book. NCES breaks down this group into three different types of institutions: 258 community development and career institutions, 505 community connector institutions, and 251 community mega-connector institutions (15 colleges are excluded from this typology because incomplete data was reported to NCES). Size of institutional enrollment is the most distinguishing characteristic of public two-year institutions. Community development and career institutions are those with an unduplicated headcount—that is, counting each student only once, no matter how many courses he or she is taking—of fewer than 2,000 students and primarily offer degrees and programs that are directly linked to workforce needs and job readiness. Community connector institutions are institutions with an unduplicated headcount of 2,000–9,999 students; in addition to workforce training, they offer general education courses and academic programs oriented toward facilitating student transfer to baccalaureate institutions. Community mega-connector institutions are colleges of 10,000 or more students, typically located near urban areas, that provide a full composite of workforce readiness, career, and transfer programs. (Figure 1.1 displays the classification system of two-year institutions.)

The analysis contained in this book is based on a composite view of these three types of public two-year colleges. In addition, many practices embedded within these institutions are also found at proprietary institutions, and the for-profit sector is a burgeoning player in higher education. In recognition of the increasing market share of this sector, these institutions will be referenced throughout the book.

It is important to note that community colleges differ extensively from the proprietary, for-profit institutions that flourished after World War II. Whereas those institutions were largely created to teach a relatively narrow skill, community colleges, especially those that call themselves "comprehensive," are more involved in providing some modicum of the general education typically included in many of the other higher education institutions. The rise of correspondence schools is an important part of the history of adult learning. Yet, as will be noted in Chapter 4, the rise of distance learning has meant that some of the problems associated with correspondence learning must be revisited.

*Figure 1.1*

**Classification System of Two-Year Institutions**

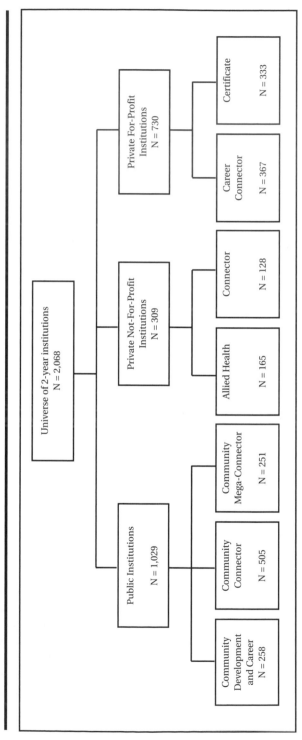

*Source:* U.S. Department of Education, National Center for Education Statistics, Integrated Postsecondary Education Data System (IPEDS), 1997 Full Collection Year.

*Note:* The sum of the number of institutions in each category does not add to the total number of institutions owing to missing data in the variables chosen for categorization. In the universe of 2,068 institutions analyzed in this report, 61 institutions could not be placed in a final category: 15 public two-year institutions, 16 private not-for-profit institutions, and 30 private for-profit institutions.

### *The Community Aspect of Community Colleges*

Although the concept of *community* is solidly embedded within the nomenclature of these institutions, there has been relatively little scholarly appreciation of how community colleges provide an important "sense of place" for millions throughout the United States. Although much has been written on the diminution of civic engagement, little has been written about the role of community colleges in reversing these trends (Levinson 2004). Community colleges in the twenty-first century have emerged as civic institutions whose breadth of mission and demographic scope are correctives to the social disintegration discussed by Robert Putnam (2000) and others. The National Center for Postsecondary Improvement underscores the severity of this issue: "Higher education's performance for the most part has fallen short of fostering an engaged citizenry. Despite pockets of extraordinary activity and a growing commitment to service learning, recent evidence indicates that today's college graduates are actually less engaged in the civic life of the nation than were preceding generations" (National Center for Postsecondary Improvement 2002, 3).

A number of treatises on the importance of instilling a sense of civic engagement in undergraduates has appeared (for example, Colby, Ehrlich, Beaumont, and Stephens 2003), and higher educational organizations such as the American Association of Higher Education (AAHE) and the American Association of Colleges and Universities (AAC&U) have spearheaded efforts to foster civic involvement through service learning and the formation of learning communities. It is worthwhile to note that some baccalaureate institutions, such as Trinity College in Hartford, Connecticut, have made their responsiveness to community needs a key point in their marketing. Trinity's Community Learning Initiative (CLI) promotes service learning and research through their courses. This initiative encourages communication and collaboration among students, faculty, and community residents. Community outreach workers are able to link students to service sites as part of one hundred courses that have been developed through CLI.

One way of appreciating the community college's comprehensive role is to consider it an important part of what Clark Kerr called "the multiversity": "The university is being called upon to educate a previously unimagined number of students; to respond to the expanding claims of national service; to merge its activities with industry as never before; to adapt to and re-channel new intellectual currents" (Kerr 1972, 86). This transformation, continued Kerr, is strengthened by the emergence of a "knowledge industry," and given that "knowledge production is growing at about twice the rate of the rest of the economy . . . knowledge has certainly never in history been so central to the conduct of an entire society" (88).

In many ways, Kerr's concept of the multiversity was a prophetic statement about the comprehensive community college at the turn of the twenty-first century. Community colleges provide access to a population formerly excluded from higher education. Certainly, when one examines the historical origins of higher education in the United States and looks at the way access to college is tightly regulated in most advanced industrial societies, the U.S. community college stands out as a cauldron of opportunity to students for whom education historically has been out of reach.

At the time when Clark Kerr originally coined the term "multiversity" in the early 1960s, the United States was undergoing a tremendous social transformation. The nation emerged in the post–World War II period as the dominant economic power in the world, and many of the military-related technological advances made during the war were finding domestic applicability through such agencies as the Defense Advanced Research Projects Agency (DARPA). Technological advances were filtering into an array of domestic applications, such as in commercial aviation, the developing field of information technology, and the expanding automobile industry. The Massachusetts Institute of Technology (MIT) and the California Institute of Technology (CalTech) represented the zenith of these developments within higher education.

As returning GIs populated U.S. higher education institutions as never before and later as their children became the baby boomers of the 1960s, the role of the university in U.S. life was being radically transformed. The number of public community colleges tripled between the end of World War II and the early 1970s (Cohen and Brawer 2003, 15).

### Creating Community

The growing importance of academe in the life of the nation also stems from its community-building potential. *Building Communities: A Vision for a New Century* was the title of a 1988 report released by the Commission on the Future of Community Colleges. Written as a follow-up, forty years later, to the report of the President's Commission on Higher Education, *Higher Education for American Democracy* (President's Commission on Higher Education 1947; commonly known as the Truman Commission Report)—which many acknowledge set the stage for a dramatic expansion of community colleges in that it underscored the importance of expanding access to higher education (Berger 2002)—

*Building Communities* provided a manifesto for what community colleges should look like in the twenty-first century. At the core of the commission's report was an affirmation of the importance of creating an inclusive learning community that would provide equal educational opportunity for all: "The nation's community colleges should vigorously reaffirm equality of opportunity as an essential goal. Every college should declare, with pride and conviction, its determination to serve all ages and racial and ethnic groups" (Commission on the Future of Community Colleges 1988, 10). This was especially important, argued the commission, in that community colleges educate the majority of Hispanic Americans and Native Americans who enroll in higher education.

Building a "curriculum through coherence," the commission asserted, would create a learning community whose reach would extend throughout the life span, and a common core of learning would unite these diverse constituents as community colleges invigorated their linkages to K–12, baccalaureate institutions, employers, and other community players.

The role of the community college in providing access to this new knowledge economy, and in the process in engaging communities, was part of a project called "New Expeditions" that was jointly sponsored by the W. K. Kellogg Foundation in partnership with the AACC and the Association of Community College Trustees (ACCT). In a report released in 2000 titled *The Knowledge Net*, they offered the following recommendations to foster civic engagement on the part of community colleges (American Association of Community Colleges and Association of Community College Trustees 2000, 4):

- "Community colleges should use their widespread community prominence and accessibility to help forge positive relationships among diverse segments of society."
- "Community colleges should assess their community's needs and assets and implement appropriate programs to cultivate and enhance current and future community leaders."
- "Community colleges should provide learners with an array of experiences to help them gain civic awareness and skills that will enhance their participation in a democracy."
- "Community colleges should be exemplary institutional citizens and leaders in their communities."
- "Community colleges should encourage staff and students to become active participants in community activities."
- "Community colleges should support the arts in their communities, foster partnerships that support cultural events, and

strengthen programming when the college serves as the community's cultural focus."

## THE KNOWLEDGE ECONOMY

Community colleges represent a growing universality in higher education, which is associated with the rise of the knowledge society. The creation of knowledge-based industries is inextricably tied to the nation's economic growth during the post–World War II era. Fueled by the application of military technology to domestic production, the rise of information technology and the growing technological sophistication of many aspects of production became the sine qua non of national prosperity. In the 1980s, the United States wrested dominance in technological innovation away from such emerging economies as that of Japan, providing the basis of U.S. economic dominance into the twenty-first century. At the heart of this change was the increasing technological sophistication of the U.S. workforce, which brought unprecedented productivity gains while service-sector employment also expanded.

The rise of the knowledge economy has made it incumbent upon the workforce to remain current with new ideas and technological innovation. The steady growth of information technology after World War II, which often occurred in the context of military-industrial development, accelerated the pace of changes at the workplace. The need to "[think] for a living" (Marshall and Tucker 1992) and the development of cognitive skills that could allow workers to "think symbolically" (Reich 1991) have made it paramount for workers to keep abreast of breaking developments in their fields.

The rise of the knowledge-based society is linked to a number of macroeconomic changes that occurred during the last decades of the twentieth century. These changes included the demise of traditional manufacturing industries in the United States and the concomitant flight of capital overseas, evidencing a phenomenon described by Barry Bluestone and Bennett Harrison as the "de-industrialization of America" (Bluestone and Harrison 1982). As a result, there was a significant reduction in the number of what had been well-paying jobs in industries such as the automotive industry.

Accompanying this reduction was the precipitous increase in service-sector employment, jobs in which wages were lower and benefits were scarcer than had been offered by jobs in traditional manufacturing entities. Accompanying this shift in the job market were a number of developments associated with the economic downturn of the late 1970s and early 1980s. The U.S. standard of living, which had increased steadily since World War II, declined from best in the world in 1960 to tenth place by the late 1970s. After 1978, there was an actual decline in the standard of living for U.S. citizens. Japan, Korea, France, Germany, and Great Britain surpassed the United States in productivity increases during this time. In addition, the U.S. share of world manufacturing declined from 25 percent to 17 percent from 1960 to 1980 (Levinson 1987).

Another important aspect of the development of the knowledge economy was the rise of information technology as an industry where technological prowess proliferated throughout the economy. The rise of the IT sector became the economic success story of the late twentieth century, resulting in impressive productivity gains in many segments of the economy. In some areas of the country, IT became the foundation for statewide economic rejuvenation. For example, what was known as the "Massachusetts miracle," a development that provided the basis for then governor Michael Dukakis's nomination as the democratic candidate for president in 1988, stemmed from impressive gains in employment within IT that fueled a statewide economic resurgence (Levinson 1987).

The ability to respond to these rather abrupt occupational changes became the forte of community colleges. An increase in part-time enrollments during this period reflects another aspect of this trend: the need for increasing on-the-job skills training, which was in part ushered in by dramatic expansion in community colleges. This increase also reflected the development of a tertiary part-time workforce, whose growth was in part fueled by an attempt by corporations to hold down labor costs by eliminating provision of the benefits associated with full-time employment. It also paralleled the increasing weakening of unions, whose share of the U.S. labor force began a dramatic decline at this time. These changes led to the growth of extension services and "continuing education" programs, which occurred as women entering the labor force increased and the number of dual career families grew.

## THE COMPREHENSIVE COMMUNITY COLLEGE

The community college is at the intersection of a myriad of developments within the larger society. Its diverse purposes and functions reflect the way higher education has taken on a new centrality in the knowledge-based economy. The comprehensive community college is usually made up of a wide variety of programs, offering both credit and noncredit courses. Those students desiring college credit or a degree are typically offered three types of degree programs: associate of arts (AA), associate of science (AS), and associate of applied science (AAS). In addition, community colleges are increasingly offering an associate of fine arts degree. Earning any of these degrees usually requires taking a modicum of general education or distribution courses, which typically span writing, mathematics, natural and social sciences, and communication. These aspects of the curriculum emulate the hallmarks of a liberal arts education. A solid general education foundation is an important part of the credit programs found in a comprehensive community college. General education, tantamount to what many consider to be the "core curriculum," includes courses in English, mathematics, social and natural sciences, history, and communications.

Increasingly, general education requirements are expressed in terms of demonstrating various competencies, which represents a focus on outcomes assessments that have emanated from the "crisis in education" circa 1983. The six regional accrediting bodies in the United States—the Middle States Commission on Higher Education; the New England Association of Schools and Colleges; the North Central Association of Colleges and Schools; the Northwest Association of Accredited Schools (earlier called the Northwest Association of Schools, Colleges, and Universities); the Southern Association of Colleges and Schools Commission on Colleges; and the Western Association of Schools and Colleges—have placed a special emphasis on this. In addition, there has been some convergence in applied and transfer programs as the focus is increasingly on the importance of "soft skills" and communicative competencies and on higher-order thinking and critical-thinking skills, all of which are transferable between occupations. For example, Bergen Community College in Paramus, New Jersey, defines nine core competencies that each student must achieve prior to graduation (shown in Table 1.1). These constitute general education competencies that all students need to demonstrate before graduating from the institution.

It is also common for community colleges to offer one-year certificates and other similar programs. Approximately 60 percent of community college students were enrolled in occupational or technical programs, leading either to a certificate or to an AAS degree (American Council on Education [ACE] 2001, 6–8). The growth of certificate programs has been noted both by Clifford Adelman and by Anthony Carnevale. Observing trends in employment and thus in the credentials that will be needed by future employees, community colleges work closely with industry and government to provide training for specialized occupations (Carnevale 2001). However, some observers point out that certificate programs are not always greeted with enthusiasm by faculty.

*Table 1.1*

**Bergen Community College Core Competencies**

| | |
|---|---|
| Communication | Students will read, write, speak, and listen effectively. |
| Quantitative reasoning | Students will compute accurately, correctly apply mathematical concepts and reasoning, and correctly interpret, analyze, organize, and display numerical data. |
| Critical thinking | Students will actively reflect on, reason about, and form independent judgments on a variety of ideas and information and will use these skills to guide their beliefs and actions. |
| Civic responsibility | Students will demonstrate an awareness of the responsibilities of intelligent citizenship in a diverse and pluralistic society and will demonstrate cultural, global, and environmental awareness. |
| Technological and information fluency | Students will demonstrate computer fluency and will be able to retrieve, organize, analyze, and evaluate information using both technological and traditional means. |
| Personal skills | Students will demonstrate an awareness of ethics, values, and personal responsibility and an ability to understand and manage themselves and their commitments. |
| Interpersonal skills | Students will demonstrate an ability to maintain personal and professional relationships, engage in meaningful teamwork, and resolve conflicts. |
| Applied knowledge | Students will demonstrate an understanding of and apply bodies of knowledge within and across disciplines. |
| Creativity and aesthetic appreciation | Students will demonstrate an understanding and appreciation of the creative process and an ability to think and express ideas creatively. |

*Source:* Bergen Community College. Learning Outcome Assessment Plan. http//www.bergen.edu/facultyhome/loaplan.asp. Accessed January 30, 2005.

They evolve, in part, because of the decrease in state funding for community colleges and are looked upon as an alternate source of revenue (Hanks and Williamson 2002).

Community colleges may also offer a number of noncredit programs, which often fall under the aegis of a division of continuing education.

Of growing importance are programs that respond to specific workforce or contract training needs, which are offered by over 90 percent of community colleges (Dougherty and Bakia 2000). Industry partnerships with community colleges provide employers with trained employees at a reasonable cost. Often these programs are subsidized by grants from the local Workforce Investment Boards (WIBs) and similar public funds.

### Governance

There is great variance among community colleges in their structure, form, and processes of governance. For example, whereas some have a faculty senate, which provides recommendations to the president concerning various aspects of academic policy, others have a more loosely federated system in which different constituents provide input to the president and other administrative officials.

Public community colleges come in two basic forms: Some are single or multicampus institutions governed by a board of trustees; others are components of a community college district that is governed by a chancellor to whom campus presidents report. Single or multicampus institutions have a CEO who is held accountable by the board for a college's entire operation. Each college typically has an executive staff or cabinet consisting of a chief fiscal officer (CFO), a chief academic officer, a chief student affairs officer, and a head of student affairs.

The tension between localized and centralized modes of educational organization is reflected in the diverse way states organize their community college systems (Tollefson, Garrett, and Ingram 1999). Rick Garrett (1999) finds the following distribution of state community college systems along the axis of centralization versus decentralization: 50 percent of state systems are characterized as highly to moderately decentralized, whereas 50 percent are characterized as moderately to highly centralized. This bifurcation reflects the pluralistic amalgamation of organizational structures found when examining the ways community colleges are organized in the United States.

Not only is there diversity among community colleges in their levels of centralization, but the funding formulas that drive community college budgeting also vary widely (Education Commission of the States 2000, 3–4):

⚫➤ Twenty-nine states use a funding formula for appropriations; fifteen states do not.

→ Twenty-four states have a single consolidated appropriation for all community colleges.
→ Twelve states allocate appropriations to individual institutions.
→ Eight states include community college allocations in a consolidated appropriation for moneys for all postsecondary institutions.

### Faculty

There is a substantial divide in higher education among the working conditions found in various segments (Levinson 2003). Faculty at community colleges are more likely than those in other sectors of higher education to be nontenured and to work in an institution that does not have a tenure system; to be part-time; to have a larger teaching load (fifteen credit hours is the norm for full-time faculty); and not to possess a terminal degree in their discipline. Community college faculty constitute a more temporary workforce than their counterparts at baccalaureate institutions (Parsad and Glover 2002).

Among community college faculty there is considerable variance with respect to collective bargaining representation. Reviewing the state of union representation at community colleges, F. R. Annunziato (1995) finds that two-year colleges represent a stronghold of union representation within higher education:

→ Two-year colleges accounted for 349 (69 percent) of the 502 faculty higher education collective bargaining agents.
→ Two-year college faculty accounted for 43 percent of the 242,221 faculty members represented by bargaining agents at all institutions.
→ Of the 432 public-sector two- and four-year faculty collective bargaining agents, 339 were established at two-year colleges.
→ Unions bargained for 587 faculty members at exclusively private two-year institutions, representing only 5.5 percent of all the private-sector faculty members covered by collective bargaining agreements.
→ Collectively, the ten largest states account for 87.5 percent of all unionized faculty at two-year colleges in all states.
→ The three largest unions were the National Education Association (accounting for 191 agents with contracts covering 43,692 faculty of 376 campuses), the American Federation of Teachers

(accounting for 116 agents with contracts covering 41,734 faculty on 218 campuses), and the American Association of University Professors (accounting for 9 agents covering 2,425 faculty on 17 campuses).
- Between 1966 and 1994, there were ninety-five faculty strikes at two-year colleges, representing 58 percent of all faculty strikes during the same period.
- Although the number of faculty strikes has declined since the 1970s, the proportion of two-year faculty strikes has declined at a faster rate.

Comparing the proportion of part-time and full-time faculty at community colleges with that at four-year institutions: 35.3 percent of faculty at public two-year colleges are employed full-time, compared to 72.6 percent at four-year colleges (NCES 2001, 69). Although some analysts argue that this has the advantage of providing community colleges with the benefit of a flexible workforce, others suggest that a primarily part-time labor force deprives students of the in-depth mentoring provided by a full-time faculty and lessens the quality and state-of-the-art nature of the curriculum because part-time faculty typically fall outside the curriculum-development process; in general, these critics argue, part-time faculty represent a transitory workforce whose impermanence is problematic for the institution. John Roueche, Suanne Roueche, and Mark Milliron (1995) find that community colleges also know relatively little about their part-time faculty and offer a paucity of resources to assist with their professional development.

Within each campus, there is typically a shared system of governance. As Richard Alfred (1998) notes, governance during the formative years of post–World War II community college development was little more than a president exercising her or his decisions with seemingly unbounded authority. However, as community colleges grew in size and complexity, many implemented college-wide governance structures that provided a systematic way for stakeholders to have input in decision making.

Common themes emerge when one looks at the concept of shared governance according to the Institute for Community College Development (2003, 3) at Cornell University:

- Collegial decision making
- Dialogue
- Discussion

➡ Mutual decision making
➡ Shared authority
➡ Control by groups of individuals working together
➡ Inclusion of all institutional stakeholders
➡ Responsibility for outcomes
➡ Responsibility shared by those affected by decisions
➡ Collaboration
➡ Complexity

Community colleges are generally governed by a board of trustees who are either elected or appointed. If the trustees are appointed, there will be variance as to who selects them. Some appointments, for example, might come from a governor's office; others may come from some local educational agency (LEA). According to a survey commissioned by the ACCT, prior leadership in the community, experience in business, and experience in education (in that order) were viewed as important in determining who would be chosen as a member of a board of trustees (ERIC Clearinghouse for Community Colleges 2002). Richard Richardson and Gerardo de los Santos (2001) find that twenty-three states have community colleges and technical institutes governed by a single statewide board and that eleven states have coordinating boards that focus on community colleges.

An increasing number of community colleges have foundations through which they raise funds for scholarships, building, and other purposes. Although a recent survey by the *Chronicle of Higher Education* reveals that community colleges are small players in the fund-raising world compared to Ivy League institutions such as Harvard, their importance is escalating, especially during times of tight public appropriations. These financial pressures have also exerted an influence on the changing role of the president, who increasingly adopts a fund-raising posture that is similar to what has customarily been found in the four-year sector.

### Accreditation

The United States has no federal ministry of education or other centralized authority exercising single national control over postsecondary education institutions in this country. The states assume varying degrees of control over education, but in general, institutions of higher education are permitted to operate with considerable independence and autonomy. As a consequence, U.S. educational institutions can vary widely in the character and quality of their programs.

In order to ensure a basic level of quality, the practice of accreditation arose in the United States as a means of conducting nongovernmental peer evaluation of educational institutions and programs. Private educational associations of regional or national scope have adopted criteria reflecting the qualities of a sound educational program and have developed procedures for evaluating institutions.

A regional accrediting association and possibly a statewide board of higher education (if such exists in a given state) usually accredit community colleges. In the United States, the U.S. Department of Education empowers six regional accreditation organizations to oversee the accreditation of educational institutions in the United States: the Middle States Commission on Higher Education; the New England Association of Schools and Colleges; the North Central Association of Colleges and Schools; the Northwest Association of Accredited Schools; the Southern Association of Colleges and Schools Commission on Colleges; and the Western Association of Schools and Colleges. Given that these regional accreditation organizations oversee both K–12 and higher education, each has a separate commission that oversees higher education.

## THE PROMISE OF HIGHER EDUCATION

### Community Colleges and Expanding
### Access to Higher Education

Access to higher education has expanded greatly in the United States during the post–World War II era. In 1944, the Servicemen's Readjustment Act (commonly known as the GI Bill) was enacted to provide tuition assistance to returning GIs. As a result, over 2 million people enrolled in higher education and 5 million enrolled in nondegree training programs (Forest and Kinser 2002). The great expanse of higher education that was ushered in as part of President Lyndon B. Johnson's Great Society programs followed, centering on the Higher Education Act of 1965, which signaled a dramatically new level of federal involvement in higher education. Amid the other Great Society programs at that time, the Higher Education Act greatly enhanced access to higher education by creating a number of financial assistance programs that are still, albeit in modified form, in existence today: equal opportunity grants; guaranteed student loans, and college work study programs (Dubrow 2002). These programs, which later fell under the jurisdiction of Title IV financial aid programs and were implemented as part of the act in the 1970s, have had a large role in facilitating growing access to higher education.

## Community Colleges and the Growth of Higher Education

The growth of educational opportunities in the twentieth century has taken on a universality that has extended to a wide range of modern societies. To a large extent, community colleges are a bellwether in changes that have occurred throughout all sectors of higher education. Numerous universities, such as Harvard University's Extension School, have emulated community college open admissions practices. Similarly, most baccalaureate and graduate institutions have continuing education divisions in which enrollment is open to all. Courses providing for the "practical" needs of business and industry, which community colleges have long offered, are now standard fare at most higher education institutions.

The tremendous growth of higher education in the United States during the last half of the twentieth century and the accompanying change to seeing college attendance as the norm for a growing segment of the population (eighteen- to twenty-two-year-olds) represent a remarkable development. It was fueled by post–World War II baby boomers' coming-of-age amid a post–World War II federal educational policy infrastructure that resulted in the notable expanse of higher education in the United States. As a result, a relatively homogeneous group of "youth" (Flacks 1971) emerged, essentially the aforementioned group of traditionally aged students. Amid post–World War II relative affluence and higher consumption, millions of such students came together in collegiate residential settings. This, in turn, provided the demographic foundation for the student movement of the 1960s.

The emergence and social construction of this occupationally idle group in a life stage that has been described as "prolonged adolescence," came about within the context of dramatic changes in the U.S. occupational structure during the post–World War II period. The changes were characterized by a precipitous decline in manufacturing jobs and an increase in service-sector jobs. In fact, it has been suggested that removing such a large group of adolescents from the workforce provided an economic buffer so that economic change and the conversion of a military economy to a peacetime and domestic post–World War II economy could proceed without the hindrance of millions of active job seekers.

Another development at this time was the increasing technological sophistication characterizing post–World War II production. This transfer of technology from military to domestic uses set the stage for the revolution in information technology that was to occur later in the twentieth century. The importance of university-based research and development for national defense was established during World War II when a new research partnership was forged between the federal government and higher education under the auspices of the Office of Scientific Research and Development (OSRD). Over eight hundred research contracts were signed between universities and the federal government during the war, and higher education emerged as the dominant site for governmental research after World War II. Whereas in 1940, 70 percent of federal research took place in government facilities, by 1944, 70 percent was performed at nongovernmental sites (Noble 1984, 10).

Scientific and technological ties between the federal government and academe were invigorated further when the Soviet Union launched *Sputnik I* in 1957. In response to this event, the National Defense Education Act of 1958 was enacted, providing funds for the expansion of science- and technology-based curricula in an attempt to combat what at that time was the alleged technology superiority of the Soviet Union. In tandem, the Defense Reorganization Act was passed creating a single federal office of Director of Defense Research and Engineering (DDR&E). This facilitated a formal organizational link between the Department of Defense and the academically based scientific community. DDR&E pushed for a strong military research budget that was of increasing benefit to university-based scientists. Similarly, the creation of the Advanced Research Projects Agency (ARPA), later known as the Defense Advanced Research Projects Agency (DARPA), cemented a closer connection between the federal government and academe regarding technology transfer from military to domestic uses (Dickson 1984, 119–120).

## CHALLENGES

### *Bifurcated Student Populations*

The typical undergraduate is no longer a student who enrolls full-time after completing high school and finishes his or her undergraduate education by the time he or she is twenty-two. Rather, the "nontraditional" undergraduate has become most common. As Susan Choy (2002, 25) reports:

> Today's undergraduate population is different than it was a generation ago. In addition to being 72 percent larger in 1999 than 1970 (with fall enrollment growing from 7.4 to 12.7 million), proportionately more students are enrolled part time (39 versus 28 percent) and at 2-year colleges (44 versus 31 percent) and women have replaced men as the majority (representing 56 percent of the total instead of 42 percent). There

are proportionately more older students on campus as well: 39 percent of all postsecondary students were 25 years or older in 1999, compared with 28 percent in 1970.

The "traditional" undergraduate—characterized here as one who earns a high school diploma, enrolls full time immediately after finishing high school, depends on parents for financial support, and either does not work during the school year or works part time—is the exception rather than the rule. In 1999–2000, just 27 percent of undergraduates met all of these criteria. Thus, 73 percent of all undergraduates were in some way "nontraditional."

At the same time, community colleges are concurrently serving a "traditional" age population, the members of what has been called the baby boom echo: a large number of college-age children of the baby boomers (Adelman 2003). As Clifford Adelman notes, this creeping demographic has resulted in a reversal of what many anticipated would occur in community colleges. As a result, community colleges are dealing with a number of distinct groups: the 25 percent of community college students who, according to Milliron's estimates, are reverse-transfer students (that is, students transferring from baccalaureate or doctoral institutions to community colleges) (Milliron 2002); the prototypical community college student who is twenty-eight years old and financially independent; and a growing number of eighteen-to-twenty-year-olds who are attending full-time.

As stated at the outset of this chapter, community colleges have long been known as havens for "nontraditional" students. The rise of the community college is an important part of the growth of higher education in the United States during the twentieth century. Although only 18 percent of Americans had some level of higher education in 1940, by 1967 this had increased to 25 percent, and by 1999, to 66 percent (ACE 2001, 1). Whereas enrollments in four-year colleges doubled between 1960 and 1990, community college enrollments quintupled during this period (Rosenbaum 2001). According to the U.S. Department of Education (Hoachlander, Sikora, and Horn 2003, 67), "The number of associate's degrees awarded between 1990–91 and 2000–01 increased by 20 percent, from 482,000 to 579,000. In contrast, the number of bachelor's degrees awarded increased more during the first half of the time period than the second half (15 vs. 4 percent), while the number of bachelor's degrees awarded increased by 6 to 7 percent in both 5-year periods."

Community colleges have become a major point of entry into higher education: 47 percent of first-time entrants into higher education credit-bearing programs begin their studies at a community college

(Vaughan 2000, 13). In states such as California, Florida, and Texas, the majority of public higher education enrollments are in community colleges. In California, for example, 65 percent of those who enroll in public higher education attend community college (National Center for Public Policy and Higher Education 2002, 10).

Unlike students enrolled in four-year colleges, the majority of community college students are enrolled part-time. In 1997, 63.3 percent of total community college enrollments were part-time, compared to 22.3 percent in four-year colleges (AACC 2000, 29). Compared to baccalaureate enrollees, community college students tend to be older and more ethnically and racially diverse (Coley 2000).

Students utilize community colleges in a variety of ways. As will be discussed throughout this book, it is a mistake to view community colleges simply as junior institutions to their baccalaureate brethren. Although one of the purposes of community colleges is to foster associate degree completion, with approximately 50 percent of matriculated students eventually transferring to a four-year institution, this is only one dimension of the community college. Those who criticize the community college for failing to uphold its mission focus almost exclusively on this one purpose, but it is inappropriate to simply use transfer rates as a measure of institutional success.

As stated by the U.S. Department of Education (Hoachlander, Sikora, and Horn 2003, 44):

> The transfer rates of community college students are related to their initial degree goals. About one-half (51 percent) of the students who intended to obtain a bachelor's degree transferred to a 4-year college, compared with about one-fourth (26 percent) of those who initially sought an associate's degree. Among students with an initial associate's or bachelor's degree goal, characteristics associated with high transfer rates include enrolling in a community college in the same year as high school graduation, always attending full-time, or having a parent with a bachelor's or higher degree. Students who began with a bachelor's degree goal were less likely to complete an associate's degree before transferring than transfer students who started with an associate's degree goal (19 v. 52 percent).

### *Community College Students as First-Generation Learners*

Another factor that constitutes an impediment to success for community college students is that many are the first in their families to engage in a higher education: 50 percent of community college students report that neither parent has any postsecondary training. This phenomenon leads to a scarcity of what has become known as cultural capital (Bourdieu and Passeron 1977) and social capital (Coleman 1990). Barbara Schneider (2002, 546) defines social capital as "the formation of networks through which norms and trust are created that advance a productive end, be that the intellectual and emotional well-being of children, civic engagement or economic prosperity." And Michael Apple (1993) notes that "the conception of cultural capital assumes that the fundamental role of educational institutions is the distribution of knowledge to students, some of whom are more *able* to acquire it because of cultural gifts that come *naturally* from their class or race or gender position."

Culturally, community college students are less likely to possess the repertoire of life skills and experiences that contribute to successful college study. They also lack the access to social networks that are often key for situating oneself in a career or educational path. Indeed, one of the challenges faced by community colleges is to instill a commitment toward learning among students who have often been the first in their families to attend college. Community colleges confront the formidable task of creating a culture that instills high levels of aspiration and success.

A related challenge facing community colleges is how to respond to students whose self-esteem as learners has often been lowered by their previous educational experience. Many of the less-than-positive episodes that have been described in works such as McGrath and Spear (1991) emanate from negative previous experiences. Related to this are the "at risk" factors community college students exhibit that have a negative impact on continuous enrollment. Applying Tinto's (1975) model of retention to community college students, it is evident that a number of characteristics typical of community college students—such as being less likely to have a parent who had enrolled in higher education or living in disadvantaged economic circumstances—inhibit integration into the college experience.

### International Students

Community colleges also serve as gateways for foreign nationals and are a magnet for international students who wish to study in the United States. With respect to international student enrollment, community colleges were the fastest growing sector of higher education between 1995 and 2000 (AACC 2002). This is particularly interesting, especially given the localized nature of community colleges. It also speaks to the alluring "promise" of educational opportunity in the United States and the importance of community colleges as U.S. higher education ambassadors to the world. Community colleges are viewed as desirable by foreign nations, for the reasons cited by the American Council on International Intercultural Education (ACIIE), an affiliate council of the American Association of Community Colleges.

During the 2001–2002 academic year, 582,996 foreign students enrolled in U.S. higher education institutions, up 6.4 percent from 547,867 in 2000–2001 (Chronicle of Higher Education International 2002). From 1988 to 1998, the number of international students at community colleges doubled (Lamkin 2000). Current constraints with the Student and Exchange Visitor Information System (SEVIS), however, threaten the viability and future vitality of international student enrollments. Under the terms of the USA Patriot Act passed in fall 2001, all foreign nationals who wish to study in the United States must have their credentials processed through the SEVIS system.

## THE BENEFITS OF THE COMMUNITY COLLEGE

### Community Colleges and Workforce Training

Community colleges are increasingly involved in workforce training initiatives (Dougherty and Bakia 2000), a dimension that has been replicated in other nations, such as Canada (Levin 2001; Organization for Economic Co-operation and Development [OECD] 2002) and the United Kingdom (Walford and Miller 1991; Whitty, Gewirtz, and Edwards 1993). Often this involvement takes the form of developing customized programs for the workforce needs of a local business or industry. Such arrangements may involve providing training in specific skills or technologies or ESL instruction for immigrant populations. In addition, many community colleges offer continuing education units (CEUs) that are required for maintaining licensure in a number of professions, professional development points that states are commonly requiring teachers to attain, and certifications in technology-oriented skills.

### Community Colleges as Cultural Institutions

Like other institutions of higher education, community colleges have a notable impact on the cultural and economic development of the areas in which they are situated. In many communities throughout the United States, community colleges serve as centers of cultural activities by providing a venue for theatrical and musical performances, for example. Many are intertwined with the civic life of the community in which they are located, providing low or no-cost meeting space for nonprofit organizations, and may in some fashion provide the social cohesion that many lament is missing from contemporary life in the United States (Putnam 2000; DeMetz 2004).

Millions come into contact with community colleges through noncredit programs. The offerings in these programs range from classes designed for cultural enrichment to those that provide a particular skill or competency. The AACC estimates that over 5 million people in a given year participate in noncredit programs at community colleges throughout the United States (AACC 2000).

### Economic Impact and Economic Return of a Community College Education

Community colleges have a substantial impact on the communities in which they are located, both as providers of employment and as producers of a skilled workforce (Maurrassee 2001; Center for Community Partnerships 2002). Recent studies show that their economic impact is vast. A review by CCbenefits Inc. of research on the economic and social benefits of New Jersey community colleges found the following:

- A student who completes an associate's degree will earn almost $400,000 more during her or his lifetime than a student with just a high school education.
- A student will earn more than $500 per year for every year that she or he works for every course completed at a New Jersey community college.
- "For every tax dollar invested in New Jersey community colleges, over $18 dollars in overall benefits are returned to the state" (New Jersey Council of County Colleges 2003).

Beyond their direct economic impact, community colleges indirectly generate numerous economic enhancements, a phenomenon that is referred to as the "multiplier effect." The Council for Higher Education in Newark (CHEN) defines this important concept in the following way (CHEN 2000):

> The multiplier adds two components to the direct effects. These are the indirect effect and the induced effect. The indirect effect traces the

direct spending related to institutional expenditures for goods and services to their suppliers where additional economic activity is generated.
The induced effect traces the spending of wage earners at the institutions and their suppliers, again generating new activities in a variety of
industries. The multiplier effect is expressed as the ratio between the
resulting total spending in the area's economy (direct, indirect, and induced) and the initial direct spending by the institutions. For example,
a multiplier of 2 means that for every dollar in direct spending, there is
an additional dollar generated in indirect and induced spending within
the impact area.

In Texas the multiplier effect is evident as community colleges account for over 350,000 jobs and an estimated 26.1 percent annual return
to students. The return rate to taxpayers is over 15 percent a year
(Christopherson and Robison 2002).

### *Community Colleges as Bastions of Democracy*

Although community colleges embody the principles of an egalitarian
civic culture, de facto they are marginal players in the pursuit of status
differentials. In fact, attending a community college is typically viewed
as a last-chance option for those who cannot gain admittance into a
more competitive institution. As open access institutions, community
colleges embody a unique egalitarian commitment to educating all.
Their inclusiveness reflects an all-embracing quality that symbolically
represents the ideals of freedom and unfettered social mobility. An important aspect of this role is that community colleges extend the
bedrock of citizenship even to the increasing number of foreign nationals who attend these institutions. Community colleges are faced with
the daunting task of reconciling the tension between access and excellence, although they are often the subject of great scorn when they attempt to do so.

As open access institutions that admit all who have completed a
high school degree and that provide college enrichment opportunities
to an increasing number of junior and senior high school students,
community colleges have been called the "people's colleges." They wel-
come those who have literally been shut out by a system of higher education whose admission practices are competitive and exclusionary.

Community colleges face the difficult task of balancing access
and excellence. Even though public community colleges are generally
open access institutions, they are under rigid scrutiny with respect to

educational outcomes. In a trend that is similar to the push for high-stakes testing in K–12, community colleges are being pressured to play a stronger gatekeeping role in selecting and sorting students with respect to academic proficiency. However, some observers are concerned that this will have a disproportionate impact on minorities and others who historically have been disenfranchised from higher education. The issue of access versus excellence will be discussed in Chapter 3.

The competitive structure of higher education replicates an inequitable structure of status differentials or prestige ratings that are attached to particular institutions. The rancor that surrounds the process of gaining admission into high-status higher education institutions, which is reflected in the tumult accompanying the annual release of the *U.S. News and World Report* college rankings, is symptomatic of the importance placed on gaining entry into prestigious institutions in order to maximize life chances.

To some extent, the inclusionary practices of community colleges are contrary to the market-based principles that currently underlie many social policy practices. Especially when it comes to educational reform, there is an increasing reliance on market-based mechanisms for bolstering quality and effectiveness. The widespread, albeit variant and highly controversial, practice of school choice is predicated on the belief that when forced to compete for student enrollments, schools will strive to excel in order to differentiate themselves from competitors.

Another way of understanding the role of community colleges as bastions of democracy is to understand their importance in relationship to citizenship. This means more than merely looking at the legal definition of a citizen, which focuses on the rights, privileges, and responsibilities of a native or naturalized citizen of the United States. Bryan Turner (1993, 5) discusses the set of social practices and mores that define members of a society that encompasses differentiated cultural and social institutions. Although social solidarity is based upon general and universal standards, a disparity between stratified markets and franchising political realms exists. Charles Lindblom (1977) describes this phenomenon as a historical tension between politics and markets in liberal democratic societies and notes that although all are guaranteed civic rights—such as the right to vote at the age of eighteen and an array of civil liberties—the impact of income differentials affects participation in the market. As documented by Edward Wolff (2002) and Bernadette Proctor and Joseph Dalaker (2002), these disparities continue to increase, as seen in the growing concentration of wealth and in the increasing percentage of the population living in poverty.

## THE "CRISIS IN EDUCATION" AND
## THE CONTEMPORARY IMPORTANCE
## OF COMMUNITY COLLEGES

In addition to their sheer numbers, dramatic growth, and expansive development during the last half of the twentieth century, the importance of community colleges can also be understood in the context of the growing knowledge economy. Throughout the last decades of the twentieth century, there was a mounting concern that higher education was not producing the human capital needed to fuel the human-resource needs of an emerging technologically intensive economy. This problem was largely attributed to the then-alleged poor quality of K–12 education, which was thought to have resulted from a diminishing of educational standards in the 1960s and 1970s. This so-called crisis in education became front-page news in the early 1980s as the U.S. economy continued to stagnate. In 1983 a number of highly publicized reports citing a crisis in the U.S. educational system were released, with the National Commission on Excellence in Education's *A Nation at Risk* (1983) receiving the greatest attention and typifying the genre. It was not just a simple curricular crisis that troubled the pundits; rather, they worried that the deplorable state of U.S. education impeded economic progress and threatened national security. A common theme that emerged from the plethora of reports released during this time was that education was partly to blame for U.S. economic failures: The schools were held responsible for a precipitous decline in U.S. productivity and for the U.S. loss of scientific and technological superiority to other nations. Many of these reports also suggested that schools should do a better job of discerning which students are the most technically or scientifically able in order to increase the number of scientists and engineers in the United States. The intensity of the concern over the poor quality of U.S. education was best captured by the National Commission on Excellence in Education in its now-infamous statement: "If an unfriendly foreign power had attempted to impose on America the mediocre educational performance that exists today, we might well have viewed it as an act of war" (National Commission on Excellence in Education 1983, 5).

Within higher education, the concern over quality was expressed in a number of ways. One stream of concern centered on what many argued was the looseness of curricular standards that grew out of the reforms of the 1960s and 1970s. Many critics argued that the overall permissiveness of these times resulted in such a nonprescriptive curriculum that "the basics" were no longer being covered.

Another dimension of this critique centered on the weakening of meritocratically based college admissions policies, which was an aspect of "excess capacity" on the part of many private higher education institutions and of the political demands of equal opportunity and affirmative action. Within higher education, this questioning of open access came in the form of a stringent critique of the open admissions policies implemented by CUNY (Traub 1994).

That workers would need to "[think] for a living" (Marshall and Tucker 1992) and the belief that knowledge would be "the new basis of wealth" (Thurow 1999) became the dominant prophecies reverberating throughout educational policy circles. In the hundreds of reports that were released in the 1980s and 1990s, the poor quality of education inhibiting economic development in the United States and throughout the world was a recurring theme. According to the National Center for Education and the Economy's Web site: "Knowledge—and the capacity to put knowledge to good use—is now the only dependable source of wealth all over the world."

It became commonplace to believe that increasing investment in human capital was the key input needed for economic prosperity. For example, in its sequel to the influential *Workforce 2000* (Johnston and Packer 1987), the Hudson Institute in *Workforce 2020* (Judy 1997) asserts that an upgraded educational system is urgently needed to maximize the promise of economic prosperity and upward social mobility in the twenty-first century. Similarly, the need for what has become known as "twenty-first century skills" was articulated in a report released in 1991 by U.S. Department of Labor, *What Work Requires of Schools: A SCANS Report for America 2000*. Appointed in 1990 by President George H. W. Bush as part of "America 2000," the Secretary's Commission on Achieving Necessary Skills (SCANS) articulates what is required from workers in this new economy: "Two conditions that arose in the last quarter of the 20th Century have changed the terms of our young people's entry into the world of work: the globalization of commerce and industry and the explosive growth of technology on the job" (U.S. Department of Labor 1991, viii).

The commission laments that schools are not organized to teach these skills. They assert that there are five foundational competencies that students need to learn in order to succeed in the contemporary workplace. However, whether such skills are actually required in a typical twenty-first-century workplace is a controversial matter. Organizations such as the Hudson Institute present a robustly optimistic portrayal of the new millennium workplace, as exemplified by the following passage from their report *Workforce 2020:* "The labor market of 2020 will demand highly educated workers who can create and apply sophisticated new technologies. . . . Dangerous, unpleasant, and monotonous workplaces will become much fewer in number, as the powerful trends favoring inventiveness strengthen in America" (Judy 1997, 121–122).

Analysts such as Stanley Aronowitz and William DiFazio (1994) are not as hopeful about the future of work in the United States. They assert that advances in technology have brought about substantial deskilling and a reduction in worker control over production processes. Similarly, others question whether there is such a great need for a highly educated workforce given the relative paucity of high-skilled jobs being created. The Bureau of Labor Statistics consistently shows that growth in service-sector jobs, which are typically low-skilled jobs, continues to dominate job creation. However, the evidence that a college degree is indispensable for high earnings potential is increasingly indisputable, as recently discussed by Arlene Dohm and Ian Wyatt (2002), who conclude that a college degree is crucial in gaining and maintaining a competitive edge in the world of work.

### Boosters and Detractors

The existing body of writing on community college is bifurcated with respect to supporters and detractors. On the one hand, there are countless stories about the empowerment that community colleges afford their learners. Recent studies report a high degree of satisfaction on the part of community college students with their credit-enrollment experiences. Analyzing students enrolled for credit in community colleges from 1999 to 2000, Kim VanDerLinden (2002) finds that approximately 75 percent of those enrolled in credit programs at community colleges state that community colleges made a major contribution to the learning and skills required for their jobs and similarly enhanced their academic proficiency. Likewise, Marlene Griffith and Ann Connor (1994) document the fact that community colleges give a voice to those who have been marginalized throughout their educational careers.

In contrast to such commendations of community colleges, there is a substantial body of research that questions their efficacy. For heuristic purposes, their criticisms can be classified as the following:

- Community colleges are an outgrowth of the various forms of tracking, segmentation, or stratification of educational opportunity in the United States.
- They restrict students' vocational opportunities to dead-end jobs.

- They have a "cooling-out" effect, displacing students' ambitions into areas with reduced aspirations and more limited life chances.
- They act as barriers to working-class ambitions and thus reproduce social inequality.
- They undermine entry into baccalaureate study (that is, they have poor transfer rates).
- There is only a loose coupling between community colleges and labor market needs.

Burton Clark's formulation of the "cooling-out" effect of community colleges (1960) remains the salient point in the literature criticizing the efficacy of community colleges. Clark essentially argues that the structural attributes of community colleges, albeit unseen and hidden, function to displace the ambitions of students into an arena of reduced aspirations and more limited life chances. Clark asserts that there is a discrepancy between a meritocratically based ideology that encourages student achievement and existing career opportunities. Although community colleges admit all applicants and foster the belief that opportunities do indeed exist, the reality is far different. For Clark, the primary feature of a community college's cooling-out trait is the redirection of students from transfer programs to terminal degree programs. When there has been explicit mention of community colleges, it has often been in the derisive context of this purported "cooling-out" effect (Burton 1960) and of their alleged reproduction of social inequality (Zwerdling 1976).

Kevin J. Dougherty's *Contradictory College: The Conflicting Origins, Impacts, and Futures of the Community College* (1994) stands as the seminal critical work. Dougherty argues that in comparison to students who begin their studies at four-year institutions, community college students are less likely to complete their baccalaureate degree. He asserts that transforming community colleges into baccalaureate institutions may be the only way of arresting this problem. Although Dougherty finds a number of admirable attributes associated with community colleges, such as their democratic embrace of open access, he is largely critical of their focus on vocational and technical education, which essentially operates as a "cooling-out" mechanism for the disproportionate number of minorities and working-class students enrolled in community colleges.

Dougherty also asserts that the community colleges' spirit of inclusion is, in part, overrated. He feels that community college students suffer from a competitive disadvantage with their baccalaureate counterparts when it comes to degree completion. Similarly, Elizabeth Monk-Turner

(1998) concludes that "community college entrance hurts most those it was supposedly established to serve" (Monk-Turner 1998, 94). In an earlier work, she found that students who initially entered higher education through a community college evidence lower occupational achievement than those whose career began in baccalaureate institutions. She offered the following reasons for this: (1) Community colleges provide an education inferior to that of four-year institutions. (2) A community college degree is less impressive to employers than a baccalaureate degree. (3) Those attending community colleges are more likely to choose low-status jobs due to a lack of confidence, encouragement, and social skills (Monk-Turner 1990). Both Dougherty and Monk-Turner suggest that students would be better served by four-year institutions' expanding and reaching out to the constituents currently served by community colleges than by community colleges' fine-tuning their transfer role.

Judith Eaton (1994) talks about the refocusing of the two-year college from its designation as a "junior" college to its designation as a "community" college. She asserts that in the process, there was a shift from a transfer function to an open access function, which in turn diluted the colleges' educational focus (1994, xi):

> Over time . . . the community college has drifted away from its higher education emphasis and, simultaneously, has redefined its commitment to access. Access remains pivotal in community college thinking, but commitment to it has become increasingly diffuse, undermining the community college role as the key entry point to higher education. What was initially intended as access to lower-division, college-level education that led to the baccalaureate degree became, instead, access to a range of educational and quasi-educational programs and services, many of which were not at the college level and were not accompanied by the baccalaureate as an educational goal. By allowing this to happen, the community college shifted from a crucial site of higher education opportunity to an ambiguous site of quasi-educational opportunity.

Eaton calls for a strengthening of the collegiate function of community colleges. "The collegiate function," she asserts, "places the community college firmly within higher education." She goes on to say: "Collegiate community colleges are neither extensions of high school nor one of the quasi-educational services offered by a community. The dominance of the collegiate function makes college-level studies the foundation of all institutional academic decision making. It is the core commitment that should set the agenda of the national leadership of community college enterprise" (3).

## UNDERSTANDING THE STUDENT
## EXPERIENCE IN COMMUNITY COLLEGES

Although the development of community colleges are an important part of the expansion of U.S. higher education in the twentieth century, the story of their ascendance is largely missing from existing histories of higher education. The classic histories of higher education, such as Frederick Rudolph's *American College and University* (1962) and Laurence R. Veysey's *Emergence of the American University* (1965), contain only small amounts of discussion about the "junior college," a term that was in fashion at that time. For the most part, historians have framed the story of the expansion of U.S. higher education primarily in terms of the "research university" (Geiger 1986); community colleges, if they are discussed at all, are treated as residual entities. Christopher Jencks and David Riesman, in their classic *The Academic Revolution* (1968), label community colleges the "anti-university colleges" and take a somewhat derisive tone in describing their existence and purpose.

It is critically important for researchers to understand how community college students socially construct their lives (Berger and Luckmann 1966) and the meaning they attach to these experiences. Although there is growing research literature on many organizational facets of community colleges, many of the analyses are devoid of appreciating the complex, internal structure of these institutions. Howard London's study *The Culture of a Community College* (1978) was the first important corrective to this omission. In what is commonly acknowledged as the first ethnographic study of the community college, London analyzes the rich texture of social interaction between teachers and students at a large, comprehensive urban community college offering a wide range of technical, vocational, and academic programs. Criticizing the restrictive methodological scope of Clark's study *The Open Door College* (1960), which, according to London, relied too heavily on the documentary analysis of administrative memorabilia, and Clark's reduction of the role of the community college to its "cooling-out" function within higher education (Clark 1960), London proclaims the importance of "thick descriptions" (Geertz 1977) of life in the community college in order to understand the nuances of institutional life.

One of London's most astute observations was that students were caught in a double-bind and faced contradictory imperatives. Students at City Community College, notes London, "created a perspective that diminished the possibility of success as defined by their middle-class, gate-keeping teachers. Indeed, the self-doubts of students, so intimately linked with social class, created a double bind: Suspecting their abilities to work with ideas led them to suspect the worth of working with ideas, yet mind and intelligence were held to be important indicators of worth and character" (1978, 27).

The contradiction expressed by London indicates the formidable task facing community colleges as they, in effect, seize the challenge of breaking with earlier educational practices found in K–12 school systems. Whereas students are typically selected and tracked early in their education, with the net effect of structurally limiting their educational opportunities, community colleges represent a noble attempt to reverse such practices. Community colleges literally open the doors to students who were left out.

Kathleen Shaw, James Valadez, and Robert Rhodes (1999) underscore how the "essence" of institutional life found within community colleges is far more complex than what appears at first glance. In their investigations (1999), they find the following paradox:

> Despite the "open-door" accessibility of these institutions, the question of whether community colleges enhance the social mobility of working-class and minority students remains an open one. In recent years, a spate of critical educational researchers has asserted that these colleges sort students into educational and career tracks that "cool out" the ambitions of working-class students. Yet current research by critical scholars has also uncovered community colleges whose cultures and educational practices are aimed at transforming students into active, empowered participants in the educational process. . . . The contradictory and often paradoxical nature of this research suggests that making generalizations about the community college sector as a whole is perhaps misguided.

In fact, it is the nuances of community colleges that many critics fail to appreciate. Citing the relatively low graduation rates and lack of eventual baccalaureate degree completion on the part of community college graduates, along with other indicators, some critics doubt their viability. By using graduation rates and other measures of baccalaureate institutions as indicators of "success," many pundits gloss over community colleges' unique characteristics. Such critics often do not appreciate the goals that community college students possess when they enter these institutions and the ways that community colleges fit into the life course of those who enroll.

The work of Clifford Adelman, senior policy analyst at the U.S. Department of Education, examines the nuances of being a community college student, and for that matter the changing patterns of college attendance in contemporary U.S. society. His monograph *The Way We Are:*

*The American Community College as American Thermometer* (1992) demonstrates that community college students typically attend a number of institutions and that, if their work is taken as a composite, they will demonstrate degree or program completion. He offers the following eloquent observation (1992, v–vi):

> The community college functioned in a variety of "occasional" roles in the lives of individuals. It accommodated their decisions to engage in learning on their own terms, and in their own time. Even if students were constrained by poor academic preparation or economic circumstances, they seemed to make of the community college what they wanted to make of it. They used the institution for a time, and then moved. Some came back. In some respect, these patterns are similar to the ways we use other normative institutions in our society, such as those of religion and the arts.

Adelman's work suggests that the meaning of "access" should be reconceptualized. One of his key observations, for example, is that community colleges should be thought of as civic institutions similar to museums and the like rather than as institutions whose primary goal is to foster transfer to baccalaureate institutions. As he points out, the educational pathways of community college students are hardly linear or predictable. In his analysis of data from the National Longitudinal Study of the High School Class of 1972 (NLS-72), Adelman notes that there is a lack of correlation between the aspirations of students and the realities of the job market. This observation was recently supported by Barbara Schneider and David Stevenson in *Ambitious Generation: America's Teenagers, Motivated but Directionless* (1999). To a large extent, this discrepancy between aspiration and reality reflects the larger disconnect and the loose coupling (Wcick 1995) between education and occupational opportunities. Many of the educational reforms introduced in the United States during the last decades of the twentieth century (for example, School to Work) were designed to mitigate such tendencies. It is interesting to note that community colleges were viewed as institutional antidotes to this problem.

One of the greatest criticisms raised against community colleges is their abysmal transfer rate. Choy (2002, 35) finds that "nontraditional students seeking an associate's degree were less likely than their traditional peers to earn the degree (27 versus 53 percent) and more likely to leave without the degree (47 versus 22 percent)."

Analyzing data from the 1990 Beginning Postsecondary Students Longitudinal Study (BPS), Ellen Bradburn and David Hurst (2001, xi) find that the transfer rate of community college students is higher than found in previous studies:

> BPS estimates of the percentage of beginning community college students whose expectations include a bachelor's degree or higher, as well as the percentage of students who transferred to a 4-year institution, are higher than estimates based on other data sets. [Kevin] Dougherty, for example, reviewed several studies and concluded that 30 to 40 percent of all community college entrants aspire to a bachelor's degree, while the present study found that 71 percent of community college students in BPS expect to complete a bachelor's degree or higher.

Bradburn and Hurst emphasize that the result one receives is in large part an artifact of how one measures or conceives an issue. Using what they call a "less-restrictive" definition of transfer yields a higher result (2001, 11):

> Including only students who have an academic major and are taking courses leading toward a bachelor's degree results in a high transfer rate (52 percent), but no more than about 1 in 10 community college students meets this definition, and it excludes 4 out of 5 transfer students. Restricting the pool to the 71 percent of students who expect to earn a bachelor's degree or higher yields a transfer rate of 36 percent, but fully 95 percent of all transfers have this expectation.

## EXPANDING THE MISSION
## OF COMMUNITY COLLEGES

Possibly one of the only factors that distinguishes community colleges from other segments of higher education is the restriction of their degree-granting authority to associate of arts and sciences degrees. However, the Florida Board of Education has recently given four community colleges permission to offer baccalaureate degrees (Armstrong 2002). Perhaps community colleges and their students pay a price for upsetting the normative hierarchy of status differentials. By suggesting that normative practices of doling out "scarce" rewards of privilege and prestige are merely a social construct of existing privilege, community college students and associated personnel are often scorned as second best. Taking such an audacious approach is fraught with complications. Through their open admissions policies, community colleges have provided many constituents with a "second chance" to succeed academically. Yet, as suggested by the title of

L. Steven Zwerling's epic 1976 work—*Second Best*—for some students this opportunity occurs against the backdrop of trying life circumstances within what some have depicted as less than ideal institutional settings. Community college students are more likely to work than their baccalaureate counterparts: 50 percent of all community college students work full time and 80 percent work part time. And given the diminishment of public funding for community colleges, it will be a challenge to acquire the resources necessary for remedying the competitive disadvantage that community college students face when entering higher education.

## CONCLUSION

Community colleges have provided millions with unbounded, lifelong educational opportunities. Through open admissions, they have garnered the reputation of being "the people's college" as they provide easy access to the tributaries of the "American Dream."

However, not all is rosy for America's community colleges. Low retention and graduation rates dampen public perceptions of their efficacy, while pundits lament their equivocation of academic values. The quest to procure both access and excellence will certainly be a major challenge as community colleges enter their second century of existence.

### *References*

Adelman, Clifford. 1992. *The Way We Are: The American Community College as American Thermometer.* Washington, DC: Office of Education Research and Improvement.

———. 2003. "A Growing Plurality: The Traditional Age Community College Dominant Student." *Community College Journal,* April/May.

Alfred, Richard L. 1998. *Shared Governance in Community Colleges.* Boulder, CO: Education Commission of the States.

American Association of Community Colleges (AACC). 1998. *Responding to the Challenges of Workforce and Economic Development: The Role of America's Community Colleges.* AACC White Paper.

———. 2000. *National Profile of Community Colleges: Trends and Statistics.* 3rd ed. Washington, DC: AACC.

———. 2002. Legislative Archive, Week of October 2, 2002. http://www.aacc.nche.edu/Content/NavigationMenu/GovernmentRelations/Legislative_Archive/Legislative_Archive.htm (accessed January 2, 2005).

———. 2003. "Summary Analysis: 2003 Community College Tuition Survey." http://www.aacc.nche.edu (accessed September 19, 2003).

American Association of Community Colleges and Association of Community College Trustees. 2000. *The Knowledge Net: Connecting Communities, Learners and Colleges.* Washington, DC: Community College Press.

American Council on Education (ACE). 2001. *A Brief Guide to U.S. Higher Education.* Washington, DC: ACE.

Annunziato, F. R. 1995. "Faculty Collective Bargaining at Exclusively Two-Year Colleges." *National Center for the Study of Collective Bargaining in Higher Education and the Professions Newsletter* 23 (April/May).

Apple, Michael W. 1993. *Official Knowledge: Democratic Education in a Conservative Age.* New York: Routledge.

Armstrong, J. David. 2002. *Chancellor's Newsletter,* Florida Community College System, May 28.

Aronowitz, Stanley, and William DiFazio. 1994. *The Jobless Future: Science, Technology, and the Dogma of Work.* Minneapolis: University of Minnesota Press.

Berger, Joseph B. 2002. "Truman Commission Report." In *Higher Education in the United States: An Encyclopedia,* ed. James Forest and Kevin Kinser. Santa Barbara, CA: ABC-CLIO.

Berger, Peter L., and Thomas Luckmann. 1966. *The Social Construction of Reality.* New York: Doubleday.

Bluestone, Barry, and Bennett Harrison. 1982. *The Deindustrialization of America: Plant Closings, Community Abandonment, and the Dismantling of Basic Industry.* New York: Basic Books.

Bourdieu, Pierre, and Jean-Claude Passeron. 1977. *Reproduction in Education, Society, and Culture.* London: Sage.

Bradburn, Ellen M., and David G. Hurst. 2001. *Community College Transfer Rates to 4-Year Institutions Using Alternative Definitions of Transfer.* NCES 2001-197. Project Officer: Samuel Peng. Washington, DC: U.S. Department of Education, National Center for Education Statistics.

Brint, Steven, and Jerome Karabel. 1989. *The Diverted Dream: Community Colleges and the Promise of Educational Opportunity in America, 1900–1985.* New York: Oxford University Press.

Callan, Patrick M., and Joni E. Finney. 2003. *Multiple Pathways and State Policy: Toward Education and Training beyond High School.* Boston: Jobs for the Future.

Carnegie Foundation for the Advancement of Teaching. 2000. *The Carnegie Classification of Institutions of Higher Education.* http://www.carnegiefoundation.org/index.htm (accessed September 19, 2003).

Carnevale, Anthony P. 2001. *Help Wanted . . . Credentials Required: Community Colleges in the Knowledge Economy.* Annapolis Junction, MD: Community College Press.

Center for Community Partnerships. 2002. *Universities and Community Schools.*

Philadelphia: Center for Community Partnerships, vol. 7, nos. 1–2 (Fall-Winter).

Choy, Susan P. 2002. "Nontraditional Undergraduates." In *The Condition of Education 2002*. Washington, DC: U.S. Department of Education.

Christopherson, Kjell A., and M. Henry Robison. 2002. *The Socioeconomic Benefits Generated by 50 Community College Districts in Texas*. Moscow, ID: CCbenefits.

Chronicle of Higher Education International. 2002. "Foreign Students by Place of Origin, 2001–2" (table). http://chronicle.com/stats/opendoors/2002/table7.htm (accessed December 24, 2004).

Clark, Burton. 1960. *The Open Door College*. New York: McGraw-Hill.

Cohen, Arthur M., and Florence B. Brawer. 1987. *The Collegiate Function of Community Colleges*. San Francisco: Jossey-Bass.

———. 2003. *The American Community College*. 4th ed. San Francisco: Jossey-Bass.

Colby, Anne, Thomas Ehrlich, Elizabeth Beaumont, and Jason Stephens. 2003. *Educating Citizens: Preparing America's Undergraduates for Lives of Moral and Civic Responsibility*. San Francisco: Jossey-Bass.

Coleman, James S. 1990. *Foundations of Social Theory*. Cambridge, MA: Belknap Press of Harvard University Press.

Coley, Richard J. 2000. *The American Community College Turns 100: A Look at Its Students, Programs, and Prospects*. Princeton: Educational Testing Services.

Commission on the Future of Community Colleges. 1988. *Building Communities: A Vision for a New Century*. Washington, DC: American Association of Community and Junior Colleges.

Community College Survey of Student Engagement. 2003. *Engaging Community Colleges: A First Look*. Austin: Community College Leadership Program, University of Texas at Austin.

Council for Higher Education in Newark. 2000. "Economic Impact Report." Newark, NJ.

DeMetz, Kaye. 2004. "Theater as Civic Leader." *Community College Journal of Research and Practice* 20, no. 2 (February).

Dickson, David. 1984. *The New Politics of Science*. New York: Pantheon Books.

Dohm, Arlene, and Ian Wyatt. 2002. "College at Work: Outlook and Earnings for College Graduates, 2000–2010." *Occupational Outlook Quarterly Online* 46, no. 3 (Fall). http://www.bls.gov/opub/ooq/ooqhome.htm (accessed January 31, 2003).

Dougherty, Kevin J. 1994. *The Contradictory College: The Conflicting Origins, Impacts, and Futures of the Community College*. Albany: State University of New York Press.

Dougherty, Kevin J., and Marianne F. Bakia. 2000. "Community Colleges and Contract Training: Content, Origins, and Impact." *Teachers College Record* 102, no. 1 (February).

Dubrow, Greg. 2002. "Higher Education Act." In *Higher Education in the United States: An Encyclopedia,* ed. James Forest and Kevin Kinser. Santa Barbara, CA: ABC-CLIO.

Eaton, Judith S. 1994. *Strengthening Collegiate Education in Community Colleges.* San Francisco: Jossey-Bass.

Education Commission of the States. 2000. *State Funding for Community Colleges: A 50-State Survey.* Denver, CO: Education Commission of the States.

ERIC Clearinghouse for Community Colleges. 2002. *Community College Trustees.* EdInfo 2002–07/. Los Angeles: University of California Graduate School of Education and Information Science.

Flacks, Richard. 1971. *Youth and Social Change.* Chicago: Markham.

Forest, James J. F., and Kevin Kinser. 2002. *Higher Education in the United States: An Encyclopedia.* Santa Barbara, CA: ABC-CLIO.

Garrett, Rick L. 1999. "Degrees of Centralization of Governance Structures in State Community College Systems." In *Fifty State Systems of Community Colleges: Mission, Governance, Funding, and Accountability,* ed. Terrance A. Tollefson, Rick L. Garrett, and William G. Ingram. Johnson City, TN: Overmountain Press.

Geertz, Clifford. 1977. *The Interpretation of Cultures.* New York: Basic Books.

Geiger, Roger L. 1986. *To Advance Knowledge: The Growth of American Research Universities, 1900–1940.* New York: Oxford University Press.

Griffith, Marlene, and Ann Connor. 1994. *Democracy's Open Door: The Community College in America's Future.* Portsmouth, NH: Boynton/Cook.

Hanks, J. D., and F. H. Williamson. 2002. "A House Divided: The Good, the Bad, and the Ugly." Unpublished manuscript.

Hoachlander, Gary, Anna C. Sikora, and Laura Horn. 2003. *Community College Students: Goals, Academic Preparation, and Outcomes.* NCES 2003-164. Project Officer: C. Dennis Carroll. Washington, DC: U.S. Department of Education, National Center for Education Statistics.

Institute for Community College Development. 2003. *Shared Governance in Community Colleges: Definition, History, Suggestions for Models and Implementation.* Ithaca, NY: SUNY and Cornell, January.

Jencks, Christopher, and David Riesman. 1968. *The Academic Revolution.* New York: Doubleday.

Johnston, William B., and Arnold E. Packer, with contributions by Matthew P. Jaffe et al. 1987. *WorkForce 2000: Work and Workers for the Twenty-First Century.* Indianapolis, IN: Hudson Institute.

Judy, Richard W. 1997. *WorkForce 2020: Work and Workers in the Twenty-First Century.* Indianapolis, IN: Hudson Institute.

Kerr, Clark. 1972. *The Uses of the University.* New York: Harper Torchbooks.

Lamkin, Anne. 2000. *International Students at Community Colleges.* Washington, DC: ERIC Clearinghouse, December.

Levin, John S. 2001. *Globalizing the Community College: Strategies for Change in the 21st Century.* New York: Palgrave Macmillan.

Levinson, David L. 1987. "High Technology's Impact on Higher Education Policy in Massachusetts." PhD diss., University of Massachusetts at Amherst.

———. 2003. "Introduction to Faculty Scholarship in Community Colleges." *Community College Journal of Research and Practice* 19, no. 7 (August).

———. 2004. "Introduction to Special Issue on Community Colleges as Civic Institutions." *Community College Journal of Research and Practice* 20, no. 2 (February).

Lindblom, Charles E. 1977. *Politics and Markets: The World's Political Economic Systems.* New York: Basic Books.

London, Howard. 1978. *The Culture of the Community College.* New York: Praeger.

Marshall, Ray, and Marc Tucker. 1992. *Thinking for a Living: Education and the Wealth of Nations.* New York: Basic Books.

Marshall, T. H. 1964. *Class, Citizenship, and Social Development.* New York: Doubleday.

Martin, Philip, and Elizabeth Midgley. 2003. *Immigration: Shaping and Reshaping America.* Washington, DC: Population Reference Bureau, vol. 58, no. 2.

Maurrassee, David J. 2001. *Beyond the Campus: How Colleges and Universities Form Partnerships with Their Communities.* New York: Taylor and Francis.

McGrath, Dennis, and Martin B. Spear. 1991. *The Academic Crisis of the Community College.* New York: State University of New York Press.

Milliron, Mark. 2002. "A Time for the Community College: 21st Century Dynamics, Trends, and Imperatives." In *Perspectives on Community Colleges: A Journey of Discovery,* ed. Norreen Thomas, with Albert L. Lorenzo and Mark David Milliron, contributing editors. Phoenix, AZ: Innovation Press.

Monk-Turner, Elizabeth. 1990. "The Occupational Achievement of Community and Four-Year College Entrants." *American Sociological Review* 55 (October): 719–725.

———. 1998. *Community College Education and Its Impact on Socioeconomic Status Attainment.* Lewiston, NY: Edwin Mellen.

National Center for Education and the Economy. N.d. http://www.ncee.org (accessed January 31, 2003).

National Center for Education Statistics (NCES). 2001. *Digest of Education Statistics.* Washington, DC: U.S. Department of Education.

National Center for Postsecondary Improvement. 2002. *Beyond Dead Reckoning: Research Priorities for Redirecting American Higher Education.* Palo Alto, CA: Stanford University Press.

National Center for Public Policy and Higher Education. 2002. "State Policy and Community College-Baccalaureate Transfer." San Jose, CA.

National Commission on Excellence in Education. 1983. *A Nation at Risk.* Washington, DC: U.S. Department of Education.

New Jersey Council of County Colleges. 2003. *New Study Identifies the Economic Benefits of New Jersey's Community Colleges.* Trenton, NJ, April 23.

Noble, David F. 1977. *America by Design: Science, Technology, and the Rise of Corporate Capitalism.* New York: Knopf.

———. 1984. *Forces of Production: A Social History.* New York: Knopf.

———. 2001. *Digital Diploma Mills: The Automation of Higher Education.* New York: Monthly Review Press.

O'Banion, Terry. 1997. *A Learning College for the 21st Century.* Phoenix, AZ: American Council on Education and Oryx.

———. 1999. *Launching a Learning-Centered College.* Mission Viejo, CA: League for Innovation in the Community College.

Organization for Economic Co-operation and Development (OECD). 2002. *Thematic Review on Adult Learning in Canada: Background Report.* Paris: OECD.

Parnell, Dale. 1985. *The Neglected Majority.* Washington, DC: Community College Press.

Parsad, Basmat, and Denise Glover. 2002. "Tenure Status of Postsecondary Instructional Faculty and Staff: 1992–98." Washington, DC: National Center for Educational Statistics.

Parsad, Basmat, and Laurie Lewis. 2003. *Remedial Education at Degree-Granting Postsecondary Institutions in Fall 2000.* NCES 2004-010. Project Officer: Bernard Greene. Washington, DC: U.S. Department of Education, National Center for Education Statistics.

Pedersen, Robert. 2000. "The Origins and Development of the Early Public Junior College: 1900–1940." PhD diss., Teachers College, Columbia University.

Peters, Thomas J, and Robert H. Waterman Jr. 1982. *In Search of Excellence: Lessons from America's Best-Run Companies.* New York: Harper and Row.

Powell, Walter W., and Paul DiMaggio, eds. 1994. *The New Institutionalism in Organizational Analysis.* Chicago: University of Chicago Press.

President's Commission on Higher Education. 1947. *Higher Education for American Democracy: A Report of the President's Commission on Higher Education.* New York: Harper and Brothers.

Proctor, Bernadette D., and Joseph Dalaker. 2002. *Poverty in the United States: 2001.* U.S. Census Bureau, Current Population Report P60-219. Washington, DC: Government Printing Office.

Putnam, Robert. D. 2000. *Bowling Alone: The Collapse and Revival of American Community.* New York: Simon and Schuster.

Reich, Robert B. 1991. *The Work of Nations: Preparing Ourselves for 21st-Century Capitalism.* New York: Knopf.

Richardson, Richard C., and Gerardo E. de los Santos. 2001. "Statewide Governance Structures and Two-Year Colleges." In *Educational Policy in the 21st Century,* vol. 2, *Community Colleges: Policy in the Future Context,* ed. Barbara K. Townsend and Susan B. Twombly. Westport, CT: Ablex.

Rosenbaum, James. 2001. *Beyond College for All: Career Paths for the Forgotten Half.* New York: Russell Sage Foundation.

Roueche, John E., Suanne D. Roueche, and Mark David Milliron. 1995. *Strangers in Their Own Land: Part-Time Faculty in America's Community College.* Washington, DC: Community College Press.

Rudolph, Frederick. 1962. *The American College and University.* New York: Vintage Books.

Schneider, Barbara. 2002. "Social Capital: A Ubiquitous Emerging Conception." In *Education and Sociology: An Encyclopedia,* ed. David L. Levinson, Peter W. Cookson Jr., and Alan Sadovnik. New York: RoutledgeFalmer.

Schneider, Barbara, and David Stevenson. 1999. *The Ambitious Generation: America's Teenagers, Motivated but Directionless.* New Haven, CT: Yale University Press.

Shaw, Kathleen, James R. Valadez, and Robert A. Rhodes. 1999. *Community Colleges as Cultural Texts: Qualitative Explorations of Organizational and Student Culture.* Albany: State University of New York Press.

Thurow, Lester. 1999. *Building Wealth: The New Rules for Individuals, Companies, and Nations.* New York: HarperCollins.

Tinto, Vincent. 1975. "Dropout From Higher Education: A Theoretical Synthesis of Recent Research." *Review of Educational Research* 45(1):89–125.

Tollefson, Terrance A., Rick L. Garrett, and William G. Ingram. 1999. *Fifty State Systems of Community Colleges: Mission, Governance, Funding, and Accountability.* Johnson City, TN: Overmountain Press.

Townsend, Barbara K., and Susan B. Twombly. 2001. *Community Colleges: Policy in the Future Context.* Westport, CT: Ablex.

Traub, James. 1994. *City on a Hill: Testing the American Dream at City College.* New York: Perseus.

Turner, Bryan S. 1993. "Contemporary Problems in the Theory of Citizenship." In *Citizenship and Social Theory,* ed. Bryan S. Turner. London: Sage.

Uhalde, Ray, Marlene Seltzer, Pamela Tate, and Rebecca Klein-Collins. 2003. *Toward a National Workforce Education and Training Policy.* Washington, DC: National Center for Education and the Economy.

U.S. Department of Labor. 1991. *What Work Requires of Schools: A SCANS Report for America 2000.* Secretary's Commission on Achieving Necessary Skills. Washington, DC: Government Printing Office.

VanDerLinden, Kim. 2002. *Credit Student Analysis: 1999 and 2000. Faces of the Future: A Portrait of America's Community College Students.* Washington, DC: American Association of Community Colleges.

Vaughan, George. 2000. *The Community College Story.* 2nd ed. Washington, DC: American Association of Community Colleges, Community College Press.

Veysey, Laurence R. 1965. *The Emergence of the American University.* Chicago: University of Chicago Press.

Walford, Geoffrey, and Henry Miller. 1991. *City Technical College.* London: Taylor and Francis.

Weick, Karl. 1995. *Sensemaking in Organizations.* Thousand Oaks, CA: Sage.

Whitty, Geoff, Sharon Gewirtz, and Tony Edwards. 1993. *Specialization and Choice in Urban Education: The City Technology College Experiment.* London: Routledge.

Wolff, Edward N. 2002. *Top Heavy: The Increasing Inequality of Wealth in America and What Can Be Done about It.* New York: New Press.

Zwerdling, L. Steven. 1976. *Second Best: The Crisis of the Community College.* New York: McGraw-Hill.

## Chapter Two

# ● **The Growth of Community Colleges in the Twentieth Century**

This chapter provides a timetable and interpretation of events that are important for understanding the rise of community colleges. Given that it takes a broad view of the sociohistorical factors that gave rise to community colleges, the chapter will discuss events pertaining to the history of primary and secondary schooling, demographic landmarks in the growth of the United States during the twentieth century, and other related phenomena. An interpretive essay follows this timetable, with references cited for readers who wish to pursue these issues in greater detail.

## CHRONOLOGY

**1791**

The Tenth Amendment to the U.S. Constitution is ratified, stating that "the powers not delegated to the United States by the Constitution, nor prohibited by it to the States, are reserved to the States respectively, or to the people." Since the Constitution does not give this responsibility to the federal government, this amendment signals the localized context for public schooling in the United States.

**1830–1860**

This is the era of the common school. A number of converging factors—rapid population growth, urbanization, and a dramatic increase in the number of immigrants coming to the United States—lead to the birth of the common school (an antecedent to what will later become known as the primary school). Although the movement toward common schools is somewhat different in every state, the creation of a centralized state apparatus for regulating public schools is a common goal.

**1848**

Massachusetts becomes the first state to develop a public education system.

**1862**

The first Morrill Act establishes a federalized system of land-grant universities, designed to expand access to higher education. The land-grant universities focus on agriculture and the mechanical arts.

**1880–1920**

This is the era of the progressive education movement. Closely associated with the work of John Dewey, this movement is centered on the acculturation through schooling of new immigrants coming to the United States, the application of "scientific" principles to the assessment of education, a focus on the individual needs of students, and the growing professionalization of teachers as educators.

**1890**

The second Morrill Act mandates that nonwhites have access to land-grant institutions, albeit in the form of what will come to be known as Historically Black Colleges and Universities (HBCUs).

**1901**

Joliet Community College is founded, the first community college in the nation.

**1910**

Phi Theta Kappa, the honor society for the two-year colleges, is formed. It begins under the name of Kappa Phi Omicron at Stephens College in Columbia, Missouri, in 1910. In 1918 the name Phi Theta Kappa is chosen, and it is recognized as the official honor society of the two-year college in 1929.

**1914**

The Smith-Lever Act creates cooperative extensions at land-grant colleges. This field-based approach to education will be incorporated into cooperative education programs at colleges and universities.

## 1917

Congress passes the Smith-Hughes Act, which promotes vocational education in the states by appropriating funds to hire teachers in applied fields such as agriculture and the trades.

## 1918

By this year, all states have mandated compulsory schooling.

## 1920–1921

The American Association of Junior Colleges is founded. "Junior" is dropped from its title in 1992.

## 1944

The Servicemen's Readjustment Act, commonly known as the GI Bill, is passed. Under this act, the federal government subsidizes tuition, fees, books and other educational materials, and living expenses for veterans returning from World War II. Over 8 million veterans receive educational benefits during the next seven years.

## 1947

The Truman Commission presents its report, *Higher Education for American Democracy.* The report emphasizes the importance of providing to all Americans a "general education" that underscores civic responsibility. The commission suggests that such an education can be provided by a network of low-cost community colleges throughout the nation.

## 1958

Congress passes the National Defense Education Act, which provides low-interest loans to college students and loan forgiveness to those who enter teaching as a profession.

## 1960s

This decade sees the largest growth in community colleges during a specific decade. During this period, 487 new community colleges are created, for a total of 909 by the end of the decade.

**1965**

The Higher Education Reauthorization Act is passed. This land-mark act, passed as part of President Lyndon B. Johnson's Great Society programs, provides for dramatically expanded access to higher education. Of the seven titles in the original act, the most important are Title I (strengthens community service and contin-uing education programs), Title II (improves teacher recruitment and teacher education programs), Title III (authorizes financial assistance to select groups of institutions, such as tribal colleges and HBCUs), Title IV (creates student financial aid programs), and Title V (supports institutional development to institutions serving Hispanic students).

**1968**

The League for Innovation in the Community College is founded. It becomes the premier organization advocating the use of tech-nology for enhancing pedagogy at community colleges.

**1972**

The Higher Education Act of 1965 is reauthorized (the first of seven times that this has occurred). The Basic Educational Op-portunity Grant (BEOG) program is created, which provides fi-nancial aid directly to students rather than to institutions. This will later become the Pell grant program. Title IX, outlawing gen-der discrimination, is also part of this reauthorization; Title IX will eventually have a significant impact on collegiate athletic programs.

**1983**

The National Commission on Excellence in Education releases *A Nation at Risk,* which asserts that U.S. schools are in a deplorable state, putting the nation's future "at risk."

**1984**

The Carol. D. Perkins Vocational and Applied Technology Educa-tion Act is passed, a federal initiative that provides operational and research support for "best practices" in vocational educa-tion. The act focuses on developing learning competencies needed for successful employment in technical areas.

**1994**

> The School-to-Work Opportunities Act is passed to fund the creation of local partnerships between government, business, labor, education, and community-based organizations in an attempt to strengthen the connection between schooling and employment.

**1998**

> The Amendment to the Higher Education Act of 1965 is passed, adding a number of provisions to the 1965 act, largely in areas related to student codes of conduct. A particularly controversial provision concerns the denial of federal financial aid to any student convicted of possession of an illicit drug.

## THE DEVELOPMENT OF COMMUNITY COLLEGES IN THE UNITED STATES: AN INTERPRETIVE ESSAY

Community colleges are a twentieth-century phenomenon: Although none existed at the turn of the century, there were close to 1,200 by the year 2000. Community colleges originated and developed during a period of significant population growth and demographic, social, and economic change in the United States. The scope of these changes can be seen in Table 2.1.

Taking a broad sweep of twentieth-century developments that had an impact on the growth of community colleges, the following emerge:

- A dramatic growth in industrial production vaulted the nation into international economic dominance. Whereas manufacturing was the primary driving force in the economy at the beginning of the twentieth century, service industries were dominant by its end.
- Technological innovations, initially tied to mechanizing the labor process and militaristic applications for wartime, became increasingly dispersed throughout the economy. By the century's end, information technology had transformed virtually all aspects of the workplace and constituted a baseline currency for the global economy. This "technical revolution" created a plethora of specialized, high-skilled jobs that fueled a need for workforce training, which community colleges were willing and able to provide expeditiously.

*Table 2.1*

**A Century of Dramatic Change, 1900–2000**

|  | *1900* | *2000* |
| --- | --- | --- |
| U.S. population (in millions) | 76 | 281 |
| Percent of population in West | 5.7 | 22.5 |
| Percent of population in Northeast | 27.6 | 19 |
| Percent of population foreign-born[a] | 14 | 11 |
| Percent metropolitan | 28 | 80 |
| Median age | 22.9 | 35.3 |
| Percent nonwhite | 12.5 | 25 |
| Percent in farming | 33 | 2.5 |
| Percent high school grads | 6.4 | 72.4[b] |
| Percent living in suburbs | n/a | 50 |

*Source:* Data for this table were compiled from the following sources: Hobbs, Frank, and Nicole Stoops. 2002. *Demographic Trends in the 20th Century.* U.S. Census Bureau, Census 2000, Special Reports, Series CENSR-4. Washington, DC: Government Printing Office; Kent, Mary M., and Mark Mather. 2002. "What Drives U.S. Population Growth?" *Population Bureau* 57, no. 4 (December); Lavin, David E., and David Hyllegard. 1996. *Changing the Odds: Open Admissions and the Life Changes of the Disadvantaged.* New Haven, CT: Yale University Press; Schmidly, Diane. 2001. *Profile of the Foreign-Born Population in the United States: 2000.* U.S. Census Bureau, Current Population Reports, Special Studies No. P23-206, December. Washington, DC: Government Printing Office; and U.S. Bureau of the Census. 2001. *100 Years of Change: Share of the U.S. Population by Region.* Washington, DC: Government Printing Office.

*Notes:* [a]The percentage of foreign-born U.S. residents dipped to a little over 5 percent of the population in 1970 and has risen steadily during the past thirty years to 11 percent.

[b]Figure is for 1990.

- The emergence of multinational corporations gradually displaced the economic determinacy of nation-states, and a global infrastructure was produced that has altered patterns of domestic job growth. The current wave of international outsourcing of jobs by such U.S.-based corporations as Dell Computers is just one contemporary dimension of this practice.
- A bureaucratized organizational response to the massive number of immigrants entering the United States initially resulted in an array of educational practices that replicated a factory/industrial

model in which management (administration) and labor (teachers) are segmented as discrete functions and tasks and in which students are dealt with en masse through the application of standardized instruction.

- ➤ Increasing sociocultural tensions emerged between individual and social concepts of achievement. As I will discuss later, this conflict is endemic to advanced liberal democratic societies. Within education, this conflict was manifested in the vacillation of liberal democratic educational policy between individual and societal determinants of educational attainment and between local and federal control of schooling. Within state policy regarding the structure and organization of community colleges, this conflict has taken a variety of disparate forms. Whereas some states group community colleges into centralized districts, others allow for relative autonomy among community colleges. In some states, such as West Virginia and Pennsylvania, community colleges are considered branches of the state university system; in others, such as Connecticut, community colleges constitute one of three higher educational sectors (the others in Connecticut being the Connecticut State Universities and the University of Connecticut).

- ➤ Professionalization and codification of expertise— which characterize various domains of specialized knowledge, including schooling and educational administration—grew. This was accompanied by a progressive education movement that simultaneously focused on student-centered instruction in a supportive learning environment and on the implementation of large-scale, bureaucratic administrative procedures to educate a growing number of students. Curriculum differentiation became a dominant way of managing the educational demands placed on schools. This duality and differentiation came to be a harbinger for community colleges in that the progressive education movement encased the creation of community colleges, which are dominated by the tension of standardization versus individualized instruction, concern over the family and other external inputs, and the student-centered pedagogy à la Dewey. There was increasing market segmentation in higher education as the sector moved from a selective to massive motif, which reflected the rise of academic specialization and professions, growing stratification of the populace, and the extension of adolescence.

•◦ Schooling became increasingly important in the United States for acculturating, training, and educating a diversified population whose cognitive skills were in constant need of upgrading and expansion as the nation moved from a manufacturing to a knowledge-based economy. Schools became ever more central to the fortification of the nation's social fabric, as seen through the emerging importance of schools for acculturation, citizenship, and occupational training. Perceptions of "school quality" became an important measurement of the desirability of particular residential communities, and schooling came to represent the "symbolic promise" of upward mobility.

## CONCEPTUALIZING HISTORICAL CHANGE

It is useful to consider the emergence and growth of community colleges as being overdetermined by a composite of factors previously identified. The concept of overdetermination is defined as follows (Cullenberg 1999: 18–19):

> Overdetermination is a theory of existence that states that nothing exists in and of itself, prior to and independent from everything else, and therefore all aspects of a society exist only as the result of the constitution (mutual determination) of all of a society's other aspects. . . . This theory of causality is clearly not the dominant notion of causality today, which instead is one where a billiard ball metaphor of mechanistic causality applies, where some things come first and others follow. It is not a theory where you can single out a prime mover(s) and argue that "X" is the cause of "Y." . . . The emphasis is on qualitative analysis, by which I mean non-reductive differences and a refusal to characterize events by formally comparable metrics.

By taking into account a myriad of determinants in a way that does not reduce them to linear causative factors, we can appreciate the complex constellation of social changes that brought community colleges into being. This analytical approach has been advantageously used by educational historians when discussing the rise of schooling in the United States. In explaining the development of public schooling in the United States during the antebellum era, the educational historian Carl Kaestle (1983, 64) states: "There is no simple causality between urbanization, population expansion, and educational reform in the U.S. from 1830–1860; rather, one needs to consider inter-related changes in economic, political, cultural and demographic trends in the U.S."

## REVIEW OF MODELS FOR EXPLAINING
## THE DEVELOPMENT OF COMMUNITY COLLEGES

Founded in 1901, Joliet Junior College is commonly acknowledged to be the first community college. To a large extent, community colleges originated as lower extensions of colleges or universities and as higher extensions of secondary schools. They represented a way for localities to assert community-based development. Community colleges are rooted in the populist context of the Progressive Era in the United States.

A number of schemata have been developed to explain the development of community colleges during the twentieth century. James Ratcliff's model (1994) places the growth of community colleges within larger tenets of educational history. D. Tillery and W. Deegan (1985) take a more linear perspective in analyzing the creation of community colleges in the context of five generations of change; their model is somewhat modified by Harold Geller (2001), who suggests a sixth generation. The basic tenets of each model will be reviewed, and then, borrowing from them and other factors in U.S. educational history, I will develop an interpretation that draws upon a number of salient features.

Judith Eaton (1994) talks about four different models of community colleges that were advocated by leaders of community colleges between 1900 and 1920: the junior college, that is, the lower division of a college of liberal arts or a university; normal schools accredited for two years of college work; public high schools that were extended to include the first two years of college work; and small private colleges that limited their college work to two years.

Tillery and Deegan (1985) describe five generations of the U.S. community college: (1) from 1900 to 1930, the extension of the secondary school; (2) from 1930 to 1950, the junior college generation; (3) from 1950 to 1970, the community college generation; (4) from 1970 to 1985, the comprehensive community college generation; (5) from 1985 to the present, a period to which they do not assign a name. Geller (2001) suggests that a sixth generation should be added to Tillery and Deegan's typology: the learning community college, modeled after the work of Terry O'Banion (1999).

In Ratcliff's schema, the development of the community colleges may be seen as a response to seven historical streams in educational history:

- Local community boosterism
- The rise of the research university

- ❖ The restructuring and expansion of the public educational system
- ❖ The professionalization of teacher education
- ❖ The vocational education movement
- ❖ The rise of adult, continuing and community education
- ❖ Open access to higher education

Ratcliff's categories are useful for exploring the unresolved tensions inherent within each of these epochs. Categorical parameters and oppositions that are endemic to educational policy today will be introduced. These tensions and analytical conflicts explain some of the irreconcilable pressures that community colleges face today.

It is also instructive to examine the forces behind the growth of community colleges in the context of a polarity between local and federal control of education. It is important to understand the localized tradition of community colleges in order to understand their contemporary stature. As Cohen and Brawer (2001) note, community colleges in the United States began as community schools. Many had their origins in existing secondary school systems within the localized educational tradition in the United States. Historians of elementary and secondary education, such as Lawrence Cremin (1988) and Carl Kaestle (1983), see the localized development of common schools as one product of the U.S. Constitution's restriction of federal power to specific areas, including public education. Moreover, many analysts feel this localized tradition is what has defined the community college, whose programs are usually fast-tracked in response to the needs of (local) business and industry.

In elucidating the origins of community colleges, it is important to recognize that at the beginning of the twentieth century they were largely evolving from secondary schools, which at the time were new to the educational scene and were only beginning to test their boundaries (Jencks and Riesman 1968; Pedersen 2000), and some of which were vocational and technical in nature (ECS 2000). This contrasts with what Robert Pedersen (2000) identifies as two common misinterpretations concerning the social forces spurring the growth of community colleges: One celebrates the transformational role of the community college, while the other lauds the community college for its anti-elitist role in society. Although community colleges have historically been viewed as the antithesis to the rigid admissions standards found in higher education institutions at that time, Pedersen suggests that the evidence does not support the contention that the junior colleges reduced selectivity. In fact, he finds that the junior colleges in existence at that time often had

*Table 2.2*
**The Growth of Community Colleges in the Twentieth Century**

| Years | Number of community colleges added |
|---|:---:|
| 1901–1910 | 25 |
| 1911–1920 | 49 |
| 1921–1930 | 106 |
| 1931–1940 | 58 |
| 1941–1950 | 92 |
| 1951–1960 | 82 |
| 1961–1970 | 497 |
| 1971–1980 | 149 |
| 1981–1990 | 48 |
| 1991–2000 | 49 |

*Source:* American Association of Community Colleges. 2004. "Community College Growth by Decade." http://www.aacc.nch.edu (accessed December 28, 2004).

admissions standards that were actually higher than those of existing baccalaureate institutions.

## FACTORS INFLUENCING COMMUNITY COLLEGE DEVELOPMENT

### *Population Change and Immigration*

During the twentieth century, the population of the United States more than tripled as successive waves of immigrants transformed the nation's racial and ethnic composition and dramatically changed the proportionate country of origin of the populace. These demographic changes are important because they are intertwined with educational policy developments during that time and have much to do with changes that are currently being experienced by community colleges and generally within higher education.

Between 1900 and 1990, the overall population in the United States grew from 76,212,168 to 248,709,873, and the percent of the population living in urban areas rose from 36.6 percent to 75.2 percent (U.S. Bureau of the Census 1995, Urban and Rural Population: 1900–1990). Immigration played a major role in the demographic transformation of the United States during the twentieth century. Throughout the past century and continuing into the twenty-first century, a recurrent theme in U.S. history has been the need to assimilate large waves of immigrants, in terms of both acculturation and workforce training. As groups of immigrants came to the United States in the late 1800s and early 1900s, schools became an important agent of assimilation. Between 1890 and 1910, 12 million immigrants entered the United States, creating a number of tensions for the new republic. Many argued for an expanded role of the state in providing an array of social services designed to acculturate these groups, who were largely of eastern European origin. Illustrative of this was the work of Jane Addams and the social welfare reforms that she advocated (Lasch 1965).

Changes in the nationality of immigrants have occurred since the late 1800s, successively transforming the U.S. mosaic. The shift in national origins can be seen by comparing the homelands of the immigrants who entered during 1882 and 1907, two peak immigration years. Of those arriving in 1882, 87 percent came from northern and western Europe, and 13 percent came from southern and eastern Europe. Only 19 percent of immigrants arriving in 1907 were from northern and western Europe, while 81 percent were from southern and eastern Europe. The immigrants who arrived in 1907 also included the first large numbers of Jewish and Eastern Orthodox Christian immigrants (Martin and Midgley 2003, 15).

### *Schooling for Acculturation and Assimilation*

As the United States became an immigrant nation, the importance of education for acculturation and assimilation became paramount. The intent was to acculturate all Americans into a common set of cultural practices, and an Anglo-conformist model (Gordon 1964)—that is, one based on the practices of the original largely English-derived colonists—dominated. These concerns were in part the impetus for the expansion of common schools and, as is illustrated in the case of Massachusetts, a reason for a growing number of statewide departments of education. Common schools, asserts David Nasaw (1979, 4), "were charged with re-forming the moral character of the children of failed artisans and farmers from both sides of the Atlantic; the expanded high schools at the turn of the century with preparing their poor, working-class, and immigrant adolescents for future lives in city and factory." The creation of the common school represented an early U.S. attempt to instill a sense of civil society through education (Kaestle 1983).

As the population became more diverse, the importance of creating a citizenry that encompassed unity, discipline, and social order prevailed (Kaestle 1983, 77). Awareness also grew of the applied importance of education and of the positive role it could play in the development of the nation. Horace Mann, the first secretary of the Massachusetts Board of Education and recognized as the founder of public education, advocated a strengthened system of public education in the face of "growing sectarian, ethnic and partisan diversity and the unveiling of more distant cultures" (Messerli 1972, 340). Heralding the common school as "the greatest discovery ever made by man" (Massachusetts Department of Education 1937, 63), Mann asserted that

> our common schools are a system of unsurpassable grandeur and efficiency. Their influences reach, with more or less directness and intensity, all the children belonging to the State, children who are soon to be the State. They act upon these children at the most impressionable period of their existence, impairing qualities of mind and heart, which will be magnified by diffusion, and deepened by time, until they will be evolved into national character, into weal or woe, into renown or ignominy, and, at least, will stamp their ineffaceable seal upon our history. (Quoted in Filler 1965, 86)

One of the challenges facing the United States at this juncture was how to create a common culture among the nation's growing ethnic diversity. Arthur M. Schlesinger Jr. (1992) and others have expressed concern that the diffuse nature of contemporary ethnic politics threatens social cohesion in the United States. To frame this in another way: How could the nation create a civic culture from a nation made up of such diversity? Schools have been cited as an important resource for uniting what many have traditionally viewed as a fragmented mosaic of ethnic politics. Especially problematic for the creation of civic culture was how to balance the emerging focus on the individual while at the same time cultivating a universalistic cultural orientation.

That the United States is an immigrant nation has great importance for community colleges, for they have become important receiving posts for newcomers. Not only has immigration transformed the student composition of community colleges—resulting in community colleges having increasingly diverse student populations and thereby acting as a vanguard of similar changes for higher education in general—but community colleges have become increasingly important sites for ESL training. This expansive mission of community colleges has propelled them onto center stage with respect to some of the most pressing issues of our times. The effects of these changes run the gamut from the ethnic and racial transformation of the U.S. population to the need to provide meaningful upwardly mobile career pathways for an increasingly diverse workforce, and these changes thus have a significant impact on community colleges.

## THE DEVELOPMENT OF COMMUNITY COLLEGES AND THE PROFESSIONALIZATION OF HIGHER EDUCATION DURING THE TWENTIETH CENTURY

A litany of factors must be taken into account in order to explain how and why community colleges grew so dramatically in the twentieth century. On one level, internal developments within higher education and the community college sector were important. William Rainey Harper, the president of the University of Chicago at the turn of the twentieth century, called for the creation of a new educational sector to address the educational needs of students who had advanced beyond secondary school but were not yet ready for the rigors of what would essentially be identified as graduate instruction today. And as the century progressed, community college professionals formed a number of professional organizations to advance their cause, such as the American Association of Junior Colleges (founded in 1920, which evolved and in 1992 renamed itself the American Association of Community Colleges [AACC]), the League for Innovation in the Community College (founded in 1968 by a small number of "vanguard" community colleges), and the Association of Community College Trustees (ACCT) founded in 1972.

Some states, such as California, Florida, and Texas, considered the creation of strong community college systems paramount for an emerging post–World War II public higher education system. It was common for students to enroll in these two-year colleges before transferring to baccalaureate institutions.

The professionalization of community college leaders, as has been the case in other sectors and occupational groups, played an important role in the growth of this higher education sector. Through the codification of a body of knowledge whose province and control is delimited by a select group whose legitimization is attained through a specific set of credentials, professionals exercise considerable control and domination in a given field (Abbott 1988; Larson 1987). Achieving this legitimacy involves going through a socialization and educational process that involves mastery of a particular knowledge field that has been circumscribed by the profession itself.

Community college administration became such a focus of professional knowledge. In constituting "administration" as a discrete body of knowledge, a number of community college leadership programs were created espousing this new field of study. Rather than focusing on specific, narrowly constructed, discipline-based knowledge, this body of literature embraced a managerial conception of knowledge and later a focus on pedagogy (Callahan 1962). The managerial side had to do with leading large-scale bureaucratic organizations, whose leaders are often caught in a balancing act among local boards of trustees, state educational officials, collective bargaining agents, and so on.

As community colleges have grown in size and scope, managerial concerns have become paramount. Community college leaders have been taken with various forms of responsive organizational management, as inspired by works such as Thomas Peters's and Robert Waterman's *In Search of Excellence* (1982), which calls for greater grassroots involvement in decision making by those on the front lines. Similar concerns have led colleges to implement such management theories as Total Quality Management (TQM), the Constant Quality Initiatives Network (CQIN), and the pursuit of Baldrige Criteria for high-performing organizations.

The concept of a "learning college," as promulgated by Terry O'Banion, founding CEO of the League for Innovation, is a cogent and poignant organizational model for community colleges that places a focus on how institutions can optimally respond to the needs of diverse learners. Similarly, a "science" of how best to incorporate developmental education has been developed by organizations such as the National Association of Developmental Education, and teaching methodologies as highlighted by the National Institute of Staff and Organizational Development. Research, as carried out by the National Center for Education Statistics and AACC, has also helped to identify best practices. In addition, the role of the community college in addressing workforce and community needs became paramount, increasing the importance of the two-year college throughout the later part of the twentieth century.

A number of community college leadership programs have emerged, with the one at the University of Texas at Austin being the best known. Recently Walden University announced a new online leadership program, directed by Terry O'Banion. Numerous community college leaders serve as faculty in this program. Strong leadership by community college presidents continues to be a critical component in the growth of the community college, and in many ways it has been the "transformative

leadership" of the community college president that has created an ambitious path for the future (Roueche, Baker, and Rose 1989).

　　Another important aspect of community college development is
the pronounced regional differences in how states embrace the community college. In states such as California, Texas, and Florida, strong
community college systems have been a mainstay of the public higher
education systems. In those states, it is often the norm for students to
begin their first two years of study at the community college and then
transfer to a baccalaureate institution for degree completion. However,
in states such as Massachusetts, where the private higher education sector has historically flourished while the public higher education sector
languished, community colleges were seemingly an afterthought. They
came into being relatively late and account for a small percentage of
college enrollments in Massachusetts.

### *Institutionalism*

An important part of this discussion is the *institutionalization* of community colleges. The creation of discrete entities called "community colleges" rested on the development of new organizational structures. In
understanding the process by which societies create such entities, it is
useful to apply the insights of what has come to be called the "new institutionalism in organizational theory." Organizational theory, whose
roots are found in the writings of the classical sociologist Max Weber on
bureaucracy, looks at organizations as emanating from the need to ra-
tionally organize a set of complex "inputs" or processes in order to attain some desirable "output." The development of bureaucracies, which
Weber argued were endemic to the development of capitalism in the
nineteenth and twentieth centuries, shared a number of common features, such as a discernible structure of hierarchy and authority, a division of labor manifested in the array of discrete roles that people assumed in the enterprise, a set of clearly codified rules and regulations
that govern actions and behaviors, a process of selectivity and recruitment that is based on how well individuals stack up to a set of technical
qualifications and abilities, and a *raison d'être* based on the ability to deliver goods and services expeditiously.

　　Since Weber put forth this theory in the late nineteenth century,
there have been a number of modifications. One of the most promising
for understanding the development of community colleges is a body of
theory known as the "new institutionalism in organizational theory"
(Powell and DiMaggio 1991). This body of research is extremely applica-
ble to the contemporary organizational scene, which harnesses the use

of technology to individualize what were the "massive" processes of bureaucracy as conceived during an era of mass production. Central for our purposes is how this paradigm focuses on the transformative power of institutions, whose cognitive appeal rests upon their legitimacy as organizations. In the case of community colleges, the key issue here is that these two-year institutions were increasingly viewed as the optimal site for delivering the first two years of baccalaureate-level education and for providing open access to students who may have hitherto been excluded from higher education.

Steven Brint and Jerome Karabel (1989) argue that the vocational focus of community colleges became their mark of differentiation from other higher education sectors. According to them, community college leaders consciously turned in this direction, resulting in the devaluing in community colleges of a liberal arts education and the transfer function. Between 1890 and 1920, Brint and Karabel suggest, there was a transformation of the education system from a "relatively undifferentiated organization" to an "orderly and highly stratified educational system that remains with us today." As they note: "The creation of 'ladders of ascent' through education thus gave new life to the American ideology of equality of opportunity at the very moment when fundamental changes in the economy threatened to destroy it" (Brint and Karabel 1989, 5).

### Politics versus Markets

An important development during the antebellum period was the emergence of the United States as an economic power in the context of the nation's struggling to define what has become known as the "new federalism." The act of balancing the countervailing tendencies of political versus market-based decisions has been a defining dimension of the new republic since its inception (Lindblom 1977).

In discussing the origins of the U.S. high school, the educational historian David Labaree touches on this point, asserting that "the American public high school is the product of a continuing struggle between politics and markets. . . . the high school was founded to produce citizens for the new republic but quickly became a vehicle for individual status attainment. The intrusion of the market transformed the purposes and practices of the high school, shifting the balance from republican virtue to capitalist commerce" (1988, 1). The architects of the U.S. Constitution took a decidedly antistatist position when the nation was created, making the new nation unlike the European powers of the time. Although Americans have typically embraced a localized or at times "free market" perspective with regard to the taming of social problems (Katznelson and Weir 1985), the relatively early creation of public schools in the United States was an exception to this market-driven tendency. As Ira Katznelson and Margaret Weir (1985, 28) note:

> In the United States the commitment to state schooling and to high primary school enrollments came much earlier than in other major Western societies. Most of the major industrialized countries achieved almost universal school attendance by World War I, and all others achieved it just after World War II. This goal had been achieved, at least for white American children, in large measure by mid-century and in full by the end of the nineteenth century.

This early endorsement of public schools is at least in part related to the centrality of schooling for citizenship, as Michael Katz (1968) demonstrates in his aptly titled book *The Irony of Early School Reform.* The centrality of public education for citizenship constituted an important theme for the creation of public schools, especially in the context of a new republic that was increasingly populated, during the antebellum period, by foreign nationals.

Another way of understanding the tension between market and politics is to examine the theoretical construct of what is meant by liberalism, in particular the liberal democratic state that is a primary part of the U.S. cultural and historical tradition. The antinomies, tensions, and contradictions within this formulation may have a lot to do with the conflicts that have arisen concerning the role of the community college in U.S. society, conflicts that some see as reflecting the seemingly irreconcilable differences that are part of contemporary, capitalistic liberal democracy.

This conundrum of liberalism versus democracy is characterized in the words of political sociologist Alan Wolfe as the "predicament of liberal democracy." As Wolfe (1977, 3) states, "liberalism refers to self-interests and free market, whose tenets are encapsulated in the philosophy of Hobbes. . . . democracy is anti-capitalistic in that it stands for participation and equality as represented in the work of Rousseau." He goes on to note the following paradox: "The predicament of liberal democracy is that liberalism denies the logic of democracy and democracy denies the logic of liberalism, but neither can exist without the other" (7). Patricia Broadfoot (1996, 222) amplifies upon this, saying: "This Tocquevillean dilemma, this tension between liberalism and democracy, between the democratic demand for leveling and the continuing existence of inequalities, tends to generate expectations and needs which the educational system is necessarily unable to meet."

This conundrum is in part due to the conflicting mandates that are placed upon the liberal, democratic capitalist state. James O'Connor (1973, 6) points to the need of the capitalist state "to fulfill two basic and often contradictory functions—*accumulation* and *legitimation.*" Gosta Esping-Anderson (1985, 165) observes that the incompatibility of these tenets "rests on the realization that a combined commitment to universalism, entitlements, and equality is not feasible within existing state-economy relations." In essence, the problem is how to provide for *social* needs when the focus centers on the *individual.*

The emergence of a democratic, liberal nation-state brought with it a number of vexing ideological problems, especially when it came to the classic tension between individual and societal needs. These tensions and contradictions help us understand the constraints facing the comprehensive community college today. It is an important cultural tenet in the United States that achievement and upward mobility are possible for all, based on meritocratic principles. However, as captured in Michael Young's brilliant 1958 satire, *The Rise of the Meritocracy 1870–2033,* there is a dark side to a totally meritocratic-based society. Technical measures of ability such as I.Q. tests, for example, often ignore other factors that contribute to success. Moreover, a total meritocracy has the danger of ushering in a closed circle of elites who control entry into the pathways of success. And the standards of meritocratic assessment, beyond being a "scientific" and allegedly fully objective way of measuring proficiency, are themselves social constructs laden with a specific constellation of values that are often presented as "objective."

## TENSIONS SURROUNDING LOCAL VERSUS FEDERAL CONTROL

A defining feature of U.S. educational policy has been the vicissitudes surrounding national and local determinants of control. As the Tenth Amendment to the U.S. Constitution states: "The powers not delegated to the United States by the Constitution, nor prohibited by it to the States, are reserved to the States respectively, or to the people." The Constitution does not give this responsibility to the federal government, hence the development and oversight of public schools is left to the states. This "reserve power clause" is critical for understanding the devolution of educational policy in the United States. Marshall, Mitchell,

and Wirt (1989) assert that each state's unique political culture consti-
tutes a subculture that will texture educational policy. Salomone (1986, 2) underscores the fact that education in the United States departs from the European model of heavy centralized control.

> Our decentralized system of public schooling is quite distinct from the highly centralized systems of western Europe. From its inception, American education has been a diffuse enterprise driven by a strong political culture of local control. The framers of the United States Constitution, in their efforts to prevent the tyranny of the majority and to preserve the pluralistic spirit of the fledgling nation, reserved certain matters to the states. Implicit among these was education. The states subsequently incorporated educational provisions in their own constitutions and enacted compulsory education laws. And so education was raised above a public benefit to the level of a guaranteed state right. The states further created local school districts and delegated to them the responsibility to manage the daily operation of the schools. Along with that function came the power to raise educational revenue through taxation.

Although this principle forms the bedrock of this nation's social and political policies, it has also created an uneven landscape with respect to the provision of education because property taxes remain the major revenue stream for funding primary and secondary public education. As a result, there is a strong correlation between a community's affluence and the level of its educational spending. This has led to a number of legal challenges to what many contend is an inequitable structure of finance. The Abbott case in New Jersey is one of the better-known challenges to inequitable school financing. In *Abbott v. Burke,* the New Jersey Supreme Court mandated equitable "standards-based" education and educational funding for suburban and urban schoolchildren.

Although this localized tradition is an important aspect of U.S. educational policy, its implementation has not been positive for everyone. The concept of states' rights has legitimated many of the most regressive, even outright racist, educational policies. For example, then Alabama governor George Wallace blocked black students' access to the University of Alabama under the banner of heralding "states' rights" in the 1950s and 1960s. As William Bowen and Derek Bok (1998) note, the exclusion of black Americans from higher education brought with it much toil and misery, as exemplified by phenomenally high rates of poverty: Prior to World War II, approximately 90 percent of black Americans lived in rural poverty in the South. The recently enacted No Child Left Behind Act (NCLB) is legislation on the other side of the local versus federal divide: It is a federal act that prescribes strict definitions of student performance to school districts throughout the nation. Although this act has been met with much disdain because of its inflexible definition of what is a substandard school, the importance of NCLB is the symbolic meaning of such sweeping federal involvement during a time of "free-market" responses to the social problems.

Although education in the United States has historically been a localized affair, there have been episodic periods of federal engagement. For example, although the development of the common school during the antebellum period is viewed by many as the quintessential form of local control, shortly after the Civil War the federal government created the U.S. Department of Education to assist with the gathering of pertinent information on a national level. Creation of the U.S. Department of Education in 1867, moreover, provided a formal organizational mechanism for the government to collect "such statistics and facts as shall show the condition and progress of education in the several states and territories" and to disseminate information concerning "the organization and management of schools and school systems, and methods of teaching, as shall aid the people of the United States in the establishment and maintenance of efficient school systems, and otherwise promote the cause of education throughout the country" (Kursh 1965, 11–12).

The Morrill Acts of 1862 and 1890 created a pronounced federal role in securing conditions necessary for localized educational development. In many respects, the creation of land-grant colleges and the Smith-Lever Act of 1914, which created cooperative, field-based educational programs at universities, represented the beginnings of what Clark Kerr (1972) termed the "multiversity."

The Morrill Act of 1862 propelled higher education in an applied direction. It provided funding for a land-grant college in each state and cemented a utilitarian vision within the structure of purpose of higher education in the United States. As Roger Geiger (1986, 5–6) states: "By putting federal money behind the cause of agricultural and mechanical education, the Morrill act galvanized tendencies in American higher education that were by the Civil War still largely inchoate." In addition, he notes that "more indirectly, the idea of utility was connected with the gradual spread of the elective system, which allowed students to choose the courses that best fit their own future needs."

The Morrill Acts of 1862 and 1890 established land-grant colleges and marked the first time that the federal government got involved in an applied curriculum—agricultural and then mechanical arts—at the college level. It is also important that the acts created a partnership between the federal government, state governments, and locally controlled (albeit sometimes private) educational institutions (Ferleger and Lazonick, 1994). These acts provided federal seed money to localities for the purpose of creating higher education institutions that would provide agricultural and mechanical training and scientific advances needed by the new republic (Lucas 1994). According to the text of the Morrill Act of 1862 (also known as the Land-Grant College Act of 1862), land in every state "equal to thirty thousand acres for each senator and representative in Congress to which the States are respectively entitled by the apportionment under the census of eighteen hundred and sixty" was provided for the purpose of creating "Colleges for the Benefit of Agriculture and Mechanical Arts." The Morrill Act of 1890 provided further support by offering each state funds for college operations, beginning with $15,000 in the first year, with annual increases of $1,000 for the ensuing ten years.

There is significant variance among community colleges with respect to local versus central control. Similarly, the financing of community colleges varies tremendously among the states, with about 50 percent of the states having a centralized structure and the remainder a decentralized one. The issue of local versus federal control applies to the financing of community colleges in the following manner: Community colleges are typically viewed as localized institutions, with many receiving substantial fiscal support from local counties and municipalities. At the same time, they rely on federal support, largely through financial programs such as Pell grants which constituted $7.2 billion in federal aid to students in 1991, going to 3.8 million students. For community college students, Pell grants are by far the dominant form of student aid received and constitute by far the largest relative percentage of any form of financial aid (Choy and Berker 2003). Although community colleges are often considered to be "local" institutions, their existence would not be possible without the substantial federal aid being given to community college students.

### The Ideological "Promise" of Schooling for Upward Mobility

Analysts who have surveyed the U.S. scene have commented on the perhaps naïve optimism that Americans place on schools (Boli 1989; Fuller and Rubinson 1992). As Boli (1989, 49) states: "The recurring effort to improve the school despite the massive evidence that reforms generally do not change the schools very much or make them more effective in achieving their goals reveals the enormous faith in schooling that characterizes modern society."

The perception of schools as a positive aspect of state formation in the United States is in contrast to the antipathy expressed in many western European countries toward public schooling (Katznelson and Weir 1985). Americans have historically displayed a very positive attitude toward schooling. Unlike among their western European counterparts, among Americans the creation of schools was welcomed and was not viewed as the imposition of state control (Katznelson and Weir 1985; Wrigley 1982). In Europe the development of public schools was often seen as an act of state imposition and therefore met with resistance. The belief and ideology in the United States that schools are important agents for upward social mobility contrasts sharply with many transcontinental nation-states whose "selection and sorting" mechanisms are rather fixed and determined for children at an early age.

Extending this belief and ideology to higher education, it is clear that enrollment in community colleges symbolically represented a pathway toward fulfillment of the "American Dream," and the symbolism is even more powerful because this is a venue where access is provided to all, often at a cost far below the "market costs" for a college education.

Schools play an important role in the selection and sorting mechanism that underlies our liberal democratic state. Sociologists of education have observed that schools are stuck with the unenviable task of creating and implementing a process that essentially selects students for the relatively scarce resource of upwardly mobile work in the United States. Schools function not only as the organizational vehicles but also as the legitimating agents of this process.

### *Immigration, Acculturation, and Citizenship*

The symbolic construction of citizenship within the context of conflicting cultural tenets is problematic, yet it has been a central feature of public schooling in the United States. Recent studies of the origins of mass schooling in Western societies assert that the expansion of public education is explained not by the economic gains brought about by an increasingly schooled populace (Fuller and Rubinson, 1992) but by the symbolic promise and "ceremonial construction" that schools offer. John Boli (1989, 50) asserts that mass schooling "is a ritual ceremony, not a rationalized technical enterprise. . . . schooling is the major initiation ceremony, or rite of passage, of modern society." Schooling has become an essential enterprise for the construction of citizenship in liberal democracies (Boli 1989, 50): "The compulsory character of mass schooling thus derives from its role in ritually preparing individuals and citizens of the national polity. . . . Children must go to school, but nothing else is required of them to participate in economic, political, and religious life; there are no polity-wide examinations to evaluate the competence of individuals with respect to starting a business, voting, or joining a church. In the modern model, one must go to school to become a citizen."

### *Bureaucratization, Professionalization, and Control*

A proactive, interventionist spirit infuses the community college movement. An important aspect of this spirit was the question of whether "one best system" (Tyack 1974) could be created within the context of a heavily localized environment, for the "idea of community/local schools became anathema to many during the twentieth century." Horace Mann, the first secretary of the Massachusetts Board of Education, "believed that schooling would lay the foundation for the responsible exercise of citizenship in a free society, but only a particular kind of schooling: publicly supported, publicly controlled, and open to all" (Cremin 1980, 137).

According to Mann, an activist state was a prerequisite for the creation of a binding moral order in public schools. The creation of a public school system in Massachusetts by the appointment of a Board of Education by Governor Edward Everett in 1837 was an important symbolic act. Although the board was given little formal power, it represented the nation's first systematic attempt to involve the polity in the regulation of common schools, which at that time numbered 3,000 in Massachusetts (Cremin 1980, 155). Discussing what prompted the early rise of public education in Massachusetts, Katz (1968, 43) states: "Faced with the decline of the family and the disintegration of society, Massachusetts schoolmen proclaimed that the state must assert itself and emphasize its character as a parent who should guard its family of children."

Importantly, there is a significant cultural component to the founding of common schools. Increased enrollment in elementary schools, according to Kaestle (1983, 29), reflected "the value placed on an educated citizenship in a Protestant republic . . . and . . . the value placed on discipline in a volatile society whose leaders were attempting to reconcile political liberty with mobility, ethnic diversity, and expansive capitalism." Alexis de Tocqueville considered the availability of public education in New England an important safeguard for the maintenance of democracy (Tocqueville 1966, 303).

Another side of the dialectic surrounding the advent of schooling for social mobility and its democratic moments concerns the movement toward centralized control at the behest of professional educators. The emergence of professions during this era was important for education as a growing cadre of "experts" came to control the destiny of public schools. As David Tyack (1974, 14) notes, educational reformers during the Progressive Era left an imprint on education, stressing "consolidation, bureaucratization, and professionalization of rural education." It is also significant that the creation of numerous discipline-based associations occurred during this era.

In fact, it was the "emancipatory" focus on what could be done to spur individual achievement that was the hallmark of educational reform during the Progressive Era. One of the features of progressive education is its focus on the individual and on the scientific management of schools in order to tailor them to meet the needs of the individual student. During the Progressive Era, the curriculum became increasingly segmented, testing became commonplace, and the nation witnessed the rise of vocational education.

One issue that shaped higher education at the onset of the twentieth century and continues today is curriculum differentiation. To what extent should the curriculum differ with respect to a student's vocation? The educational historian Lawrence Cremin observes that the process of centralization was uneven, for localism still exerted an important influence: "The development of state systems must be seen in a nineteenth-century context of localism: neither the ideology nor the technology of political control at the state level had been developed to the point where it was seen as a replacement for political control at the district, town, or county level" (Cremin 1980, 174).

The bureaucratization of schools was a way for professionals to wrest control from laypeople. "Incipient bureaucracy" was the organizational model of schools that was adopted in the mid-nineteenth century (Katz 1987, 49). Incipient bureaucracy represented an attack on "democratic localism," arguing that this decentralized structure of schools was inefficient. Such an institutional structure was viewed as a surrogate for families "in crisis." Moreover, public schools in the mid-nineteenth century "equated cultural diversity with immorality and deviance" (Katz 1987, 17).

The adoption of an incipient bureaucratic model for schools reflected a faith in institutions: "Proponents of bureaucracy argued that the heightened importance of education in urban society required a vast increase in the proportion of community resources devoted to schooling and the attendance of all children" (Katz 1987, 51). And furthermore, "community control of schools became anathema to many of the educational reformers of 1900. . . . As advocates of consolidation, bureaucratization, and professionalization of rural education, school leaders in the twentieth century have given the one-room school a bad press" (Tyack 1974, 14).

## THE EMERGENCE OF THE RESEARCH UNIVERSITY AND HIGHER EDUCATION SEGMENTATION

The organization of universities into departmental units was something that William Rainey Harper championed. As Geiger (1986, 38) notes: "The American structure of higher education depended for its intellectual vigor on both decentralized competition and scientific concentration." Although U.S. education appeared to be open, internal segmentation became an important feature. Raymond Callahan (1962) called this segmentation the emergence of a "cult of efficiency," which represented the application to education of the workplace organization principles advocated by Frederick Taylor.

During the Progressive Era, higher education in the United States grew in importance and stature. The industrialization of the nation and the creation of corporate behemoths and benefactors were beneficial to universities during this period. Philanthropists of the day, such as John D. Rockefeller, through the Rockefeller Foundation, and Andrew Carnegie, through the Carnegie Foundation for the Advancement of Teaching (Lagemann 1983), became important shapers of higher education. According to Geiger (1986, 45), "after 1900 both focused their giving increasingly on higher education and advancement of knowledge." This focus steered U.S. higher education toward curricula differentiation and segmentation, with "Carnegie Units" becoming the standard for parceling out units of curriculum instruction.

As the research university developed during the first twenty years of the twentieth century, substantial concern was expressed that U.S. universities were primarily teaching institutions, unlike the research-based European universities. "American students entered the university with far less preparation than their European counterparts and were consequently far more dependent upon their mentors for basic instruction" (Geiger 1986). In many ways this situation reflected the "loose coupling" among elements of U.S. education, which many viewed as a detriment, growing out of the decentralized traditions of the nation's polity. Geiger (1986, 68) goes on to say that "a recurrent dream of American university builders was to jettison a major portion of this teaching burden in order to orient the universities more definitively toward research." Hence, enter the community college.

The rise of the research university ushered in an era of status differentials and segmentation in higher education. Influenced by the progressive education movement, which was at its zenith during that time (Cremin 1988), William Rainey Harper proposed that the university extend into the community, a function he envisioned being performed by two-year colleges. Harper also encouraged the creation of a correspondence school in 1892, which Columbia University did. In addition, he argued for the creation of extension divisions that would operate on a for-profit basis (Bok 2003, 81–82).


## CONCLUSION

A number of factors overdetermined the emergence of community colleges in the United States during the twentieth century. In part, community colleges grew out of a burgeoning K–12 educational system that provided both a skilled labor force for the nation's growing economy and a mechanism for assimilating the large number of immigrants coming to the United States. Given the historical antinomies of local versus centralized control of educational policy in the United States, it is no wonder that there is great variance in the form and structure of community college systems throughout the nation. Similarly, the states vary with respect to how community colleges are linked to other sectors of public higher education. It will be interesting to see how these tensions are played out in the twenty-first century.

### *References*

Abbott, Andrew. 1988. *The System of Professions: An Essay on the Division of Expert Labor.* Chicago: University of Chicago Press.

Alba, Richard, and Victor Nee. 1997. "Rethinking Assimilation Theory for a New Era of Immigration." In "Immigrant Adaptation and Native-Born Responses in the Making of Americans," special issue, *International Migration Review* 31, no. 4 (Winter).

American Association of Community Colleges (AACC). N.d. "Community College Growth by Decade." http://www.aacc.nche.edu/Content/NavigationMenu/AboutCommunityColleges/HistoricalInformation/CC-Growth/CCGrowth.htm (accessed March 6, 2004).

Bok, Derek. 2003. *Universities in the Marketplace: The Commercialization of Higher Education.* Princeton: Princeton University Press.

Boli, John. 1989. *New Citizens for a New Society: The Institutional Origins of Mass Schooling in Sweden.* Oxford: Pergamon.

Bowen, William G., and Derek Bok. 1998. *The Shape of the River: Long-Term Consequences of Considering Race in College and University Admissions.* Princeton: Princeton University Press.

Brint, Steven G., and Jerome B. Karabel. 1989. *The Diverted Dream.* New York: Oxford University Press.

Broadfoot, Patricia M. 1996. *Education, Assessment, and Society.* Maidenhead, Berkshire, U.K.: Open University Press.

Callahan, Raymond E. 1962. *Education and the Cult of Efficiency.* Chicago: University of Chicago Press.

Choy, Susan P., and Ali M. Berker. 2003. *How Families of Low and Middle Income Undergraduates Pay for College: Full-Time Dependent Students in 1999–2000.* NCES 2003–162. Project Officer: C. Dennis Carroll. Washington, DC: U.S. Department of Education, National Center for Education Statistics.

Cohen, Arthur, and Florence Brawer. 2001. *The American Community College.* 3rd ed. San Francisco: Jossey-Bass.

Cremin, Lawrence A. 1980. *American Education: The National Experience, 1783–1876.* New York: Harper and Row.

———. 1988. *American Education: The Metropolitan Experience, 1876–1980.* New York: Harper and Row.

Cullenberg, Stephen. 1999. "Overdetermination, Totality, and Institutions: A Genealogy of a Marxist Institutionalist." *Journal of Economic Issues* 33, no. 4 (December).

Eaton, Judith S. 1994. *Strengthening Collegiate Education in Community Colleges.* San Francisco: Jossey-Bass.

Esping-Anderson, Gosta. 1985. *Politics against Markets: The Social Democratic Road to Power.* Princeton: Princeton University Press.

Ferleger, Louis, and William Lazonick. 1994. "Higher Education for an Innovative Economy: Land-Grant Colleges and the Managerial Revolution in America." In *Business and Economic History* 23, no. 1 (Fall): 116–128.

Filler, Louis. 1965. *Horace Mann on the Crisis in Education.* Yellow Springs, OH: Antioch Press.

Fuller, Bruce, and Richard Rubinson. 1992. *The Political Construction of Education: The State, School Expansion, and Economic Change.* Westport, CT: Praeger.

Garrett, Rick L. 1999. "Degrees of Centralization of Governance Structures in State Community College Systems." In *Fifty State Systems of Community Colleges: Mission, Governance, Funding, and Accountability,* ed. Terrence A. Tollefson, Rick L. Garrett, and William G. Ingram. Johnson City, TN: Overmountain Press.

Geiger, Roger L. 1986. *To Advance Knowledge: The Growth of American Research Universities, 1900–1940.* New York: Oxford University Press.

Geller, Harold A. 2001. *A Brief History of Community Colleges and a Personal View of Some Issues.* Fairfax, VA: George Mason University.

Gordon, Milton. 1964. *Assimilation in American Life.* New York: Oxford University Press.

Hobbs, Frank, and Nicole Stoops. 2002. *Demographic Trends in the 20th Century.* U.S. Census Bureau, Census 2000, Special Reports, Series CENSR-4. Washington, DC: Government Printing Office.

Jencks, Christopher, and David Riesman. 1968. *The Academic Revolution.* New York: Doubleday.

Kaestle, Carl. 1983. *Pillars of the Republic: Common Schools and American Society, 1780–1860.* New York: Hill and Wang.

Katz, Michael. 1968. *The Irony of Early School Reform.* Cambridge, MA: Harvard University Press.

———. 1987. *Reconstructing American Education.* Cambridge, MA: Harvard University Press.

Katznelson, Ira, and Margaret Weir. 1985. *Schooling for All: Class, Race, and the Decline of the Democratic Ideal.* New York: Basic Books.

Kent, Mary M., and Mark Mather. 2002. "What Drives U.S. Population Growth?" *Population Bureau* 57, no. 4 (December).

Kerr, Clark. 1972. *The Uses of the University.* New York: Harper Torchbooks.

Kett, Joseph F. 1994. *The Pursuit of Knowledge under Difficulties: From Self-Improvement to Adult Education in America, 1750–1990.* Stanford, CA: Stanford University Press.

Kursh, Harry. 1965. *The United States Office of Education: A Century of Service.* Philadelphia: Chilton.

Labaree, David F. 1988. *The Making of an American High School: The Credentials Market and the Central High School of Philadelphia, 1838–1939.* New Haven, CT: Yale University Press.

Lagemann, Ellen Condliffe. 1983. *Private Power for the Public Good: A History of the Carnegie Foundation for the Advancement of Teaching.* Middletown, CT: Wesleyan University Press.

Larson, Magalli Safatti. 1987. *The Rise of Professionalism: A Sociological Analysis.* Berkeley and Los Angeles: University of California Press.

Lasch, Christopher, ed. 1965. *The Social Thought of Jane Addams.* Indianapolis, IN: Bobbs-Merrill.

Lavin, David E., and David Hyllegard. 1996. *Changing the Odds: Open Admissions and the Life Changes of the Disadvantaged.* New Haven, CT: Yale University Press.

Lindblom, Charles E. 1977. *Politics and Markets.* New York: Basic Books.

Lucas, Christopher J. 1994. *American Higher Education: A History.* New York: St. Martin's Griffin.

Marshall, Catherine, Douglas Mitchell, and Frederick Wirt. 1989. *Culture and Education Policy in the American States.* New York: Falmer Press.

Marshall, T. H. 1965. *Class, Citizenship, and Social Development.* New York: Anchor Books.

Martin, Philip, and Elizabeth Midgley. 2003. *Immigration: Shaping and Reshaping America.* Washington, DC: Population Reference Bureau, vol. 58, no. 2.

Massachusetts Department of Education. 1937. *Horace Mann Centennial 1837–1937.* Boston: Massachusetts Department of Education.

Messerli, Jonathan. 1972. *Horace Mann: A Biography.* New York: Knopf.

Nasaw, David. 1979. *Schooled to Order: A History of Public Schooling in the United States.* New York: Oxford University Press.

O'Banion, Terry. 1999. *Launching a Learning-Centered College.* Mission Viejo, CA: League for Innovation in the Community College.

O'Connor, James. 1973. *The Fiscal Crisis in the State.* New York: St. Martin's.

Pedersen, Robert P. 2000. "The Origins and Development of the Early Public Junior College: 1900–1940." PhD diss., Columbia University.

Peters, Thomas, and Robert Waterman. 1982. *In Search of Excellence: Lessons from America's Best-Run Companies.* New York: HarperCollins.

Powell, Walter, and Paul DiMaggio. 1991. *The New Institutionalism in Organizational Analysis.* Chicago: University of Chicago Press.

Ratcliff, James, ed. 1994. *Community Colleges.* 3rd ed. ASHE Reader Series. Lexington, MA: Ginn Press.

Roueche, John E., George A. Baker III, and Robert R. Rose. 1989. *Shared Vision: Transformational Leadership in American Community Colleges.* Washington, DC: Community College Press.

Salomone, Rosemary C. 1986. *Equal Education under Law: Legal Rights and Federal Policy in the Post-Brown Era.* New York: St. Martin's.

Schlesinger, Arthur M. Jr. 1992. *The Disuniting of America: Reflections on a Multicultural Society.* New York: Norton.

Schmidly, Diane. 2001. *Profile of the Foreign-Born Population in the United States: 2000.* U.S. Census Bureau, Current Population Reports, Special Studies No. P23–206, December. Washington, DC: Government Printing Office.

Tillery, Dale, and William Deegan. 1985. "The Evolution of Two-Year Colleges through Four Generations." In *Renewing the American Community College: Priorities and Strategies for Effective Leadership,* ed. William Deegan and Dale Tillery. San Francisco: Jossey-Bass.

Tocqueville, Alexis de. 1838. *Democracy in America.* New York: Library of America, 1966.

Tollefson, Terrence A., Rick L. Garrett, and William G. Ingram. 1999. *Fifty State Systems of Community Colleges: Mission, Governance, Funding, and Accountability.* Johnson City, TN: Overmountain Press.

Tyack, David B. 1974. *The One Best System: A History of American Urban Education.* Cambridge, MA: Harvard University Press.

U.S. Bureau of the Census. 1995. *Urban and Rural Population: 1900 to 1990.* Washington, DC: Government Printing Office.

——. 2001. *100 Years of Change: Share of the U.S. Population by Region.* Washington, DC: Government Printing Office.

Wolfe, Alan. 1977. *The Limits of Legitimacy: Political Contradictions of Contemporary Capitalism.* New York: Free Press.

Wrigley, Julia. 1982. *Class Politics and Public Schools: Chicago 1900–1950.* New Brunswick, NJ: Rutgers University Press.

Young, Michael. 1958. *The Rise of the Meritocracy, 1870–2033.* London: Thames and Hudson.

*Chapter Three*

# ⊷ Community Colleges and Access versus Excellence

Unbridled access to educational opportunities has long been a hallmark of the American creed. At the outset of the new republic, public officials were adamant about extending public schooling to all. Massachusetts took the lead in implementing a system of public education, as discussed in Chapter 2. Open, albeit mandatory, access to elementary schools was guaranteed through implementation of compulsory schooling in the United States by 1918. Community colleges represent an extension of this principle to a higher level.

Unlike tertiary education in most advanced industrial societies, higher education in the United States is open to all. However, in an era when selectivity is often equated with excellence, how can community colleges offer educational quality in such an open environment?

Gauging the predominance of this issue throughout the history of education in the United States, it is clear that restricted access has not been tantamount to excellence. Educational reformers during the antebellum era were quick to point out the shortcomings of public education, a criticism that continued with great verve throughout the nineteenth and twentieth centuries. As David Tyack and Larry Cuban show in *Tinkering Toward Utopia: A Century of Public School Reform* (1995), there has been an unyielding effort to reform education from the outside-in. This effort has been characterized by a plethora of attempts to legislate changes in educational policy, on the assumption that somehow these changes will trickle into the pedagogical practices found within classrooms. On a similar theme, Richard Elmore (2003, 23) notes the historic disconnect between reforms in educational policy and what actually occurs in the classroom:

> Education policy in the U.S. has arguably not been much about education, at least the sort of education that occurs among teachers and students in classrooms. It has, however, been a great deal about policy, the kind of high-level political discourse that generates controversy and electoral credit for public officials. The great political and social struggles

around education in the twentieth century have been about issues like
the expansion of access to schooling (e.g., mandatory attendance), the
institutional forms of schooling (the comprehensive high school, vocational education, what to do about the middle grades), and inequalities
of opportunity among different types of children (financing inequities,
compensatory education, desegregation, special education). While these
struggles have been significant in their own right and have changed
much about the institutional structure, role of access, and social conditions of schooling in the United States, they have done little directly or
intentionally about what teachers and students experience on a daily
basis in classrooms. Indeed, the major theme of education policy seems,
until recently, to have been the disconnect between policy and practice.

David Berliner and Bruce Biddle (1995) suggest that many external at-
tacks on educational quality represent a political agenda, manufacturing an alleged "crisis" to serve the political interests of powerful constituents.

Issues of access versus excellence for community colleges similarly cannot be separated from the political context in which they arise.
During times when state treasuries have been somewhat flush and
higher education was in an expansionary mode, in part due to macro-
structural developments—such as the ending of World War II and the
need to accommodate millions of students who enrolled under the provisions of the GI Bill—the focus was on expanding access. Similarly,
when a policy of open admissions was implemented in the City University of New York (CUNY) in 1970, during a time of much social upheaval
and in the aftermath of the Great Society programs of the 1960s, the
focus shifted to how to accommodate a dramatic increase in the number of learners. This is not to suggest that concerns over quality were
abandoned; rather, at this time issues of capacity were more critical.

With respect to the issue of access, higher education in the
United States has certainly been more restrictive than elementary
schooling. The private institutions that dominated the U.S. higher education scene in the late nineteenth and early twentieth centuries—such
as Harvard, Yale, and Princeton—restricted admission to the economically privileged. Although the Morrill Acts of 1862 and 1890 provided the
basis for public land-grant institutions, college attendance was still a
rarity in the United States in the early twentieth century.

It is largely through selective admissions processes that higher
education institutions have attempted to maintain excellence—the
more restrictive the better, in terms of the prestige and status of the institution. Samuel Kipp, Derek Price, and Jill Wohlford (2002) report that

"unequal opportunity" to enroll in higher education continues to persist throughout the United States. They find a number of disparities in higher education in the fifty states, and they report (2002, 6) that

> the percentage of admissible institutions varies widely from state to state; the percentage of affordable institutions also varies widely from state to state; affordability more often requires borrowing for low-income dependent students than for median-income dependent students; far fewer institutions are accessible to both dependent and independent low-income students than to their median-income counterparts; except for many public and two-year institutions, most colleges and universities are generally not accessible to low-income independent students to attend full time even with borrowing; and among accessible institutions, even median-income independent students generally must borrow to make them affordable.

Community colleges, however, typically admit all who apply. Given their abandonment of the almost sacrosanct quality-assurance process of restricting admission, how is it possible for community colleges to claim and attain excellence?

Access to higher education in the United States has expanded steadily throughout the twentieth century. The maturation of public higher education, especially since World War II, has provided millions with unprecedented opportunities for entry into higher education. However, similar to issues raised in assessing quality in K–12 schooling, concerns about quality in higher education are pervasive and have resulted in a number of responses designed to enhance accountability, such as focus on assessing learning outcomes. As discussed previously, one of the difficulties involved in assessing the effectiveness of community colleges is the inadequacy of the performance measures that are used for baccalaureate institutions. To subject a community college to the same standards of effectiveness as those typically used at an exclusive residential educational institution that caters to a relatively homogeneous full-time population of eighteen-to-twenty-two-year-olds would be inappropriate.

This chapter looks at the conundrum of access versus excellence for community colleges. Faced with an increasingly diverse array of constituents, community colleges are engaged in providing a plethora of learning support services ranging from developmental learning and ESL courses to honors programs and Institutes for Learning in Retirement.

Often needing to be "all things to all people," community colleges are finding it difficult to provide these services in the context of diminishing fiscal support. The chapter concludes with a depiction of the struggles CUNY has faced as it has attempted to provide open admission during the past quarter of a century while maintaining high academic standards.

## ACCESS VERSUS EXCELLENCE: THE CONUNDRUM OF DEMOCRATIC LIBERALISM

As discussed in Chapter 2, the contradictions between liberalism and democracy are a defining feature of contemporary liberal democracies. Many of the great social problems of the day revolve around the conflict between individual or market responses and social or collective responses. The individualistic tenets of liberalism are an important ideological component of the way meritocracy is structured in capitalist societies. The sociologist Michael Lewis describes this explanatory tendency as the "individual as central sensibility thesis" (Lewis 1993, 8), in which attainment or success is viewed on an atomistic level, as an attribute of individuals. Rooted in part within the Puritanical/Calvinistic ethos of the new republic, this construct results in ascribing social dysfunction and disarray to individual agency. As suggested by the notion of "blaming the victim"—a concept that William Ryan (1976) used to describe the way many social welfare policies are structured in the United States—the social roots or political reasons for social dysfunction and disarray are glossed over and never seen. Rather, everything is reduced to an individual level. Instead of addressing the structural roots of inequality—such as an inequitable distribution of wealth or the movement of jobs to countries where labor costs are lower—this mode of explanation holds the individual "at fault," or responsible. As a result, policy focus of programs inspired by this explanatory tendency is on changing individual behavior or actions.

The focus on individuals, especially with respect to market-based acquisitive activity, is at the root of a number of popular contemporary education reform efforts. School choice as an educational reform strategy is one example of such an approach. The intent is that "market competition" will foster a variety of choices and enrollment will be guided by what is most appealing in a given educational market basket. This theory is predicated on the belief that consumers will choose the "best product" and that institutions that do not effectively compete will wither away unless they improve their output—in this case the quality of education offered to students. The mantra governing such strategies for educational improvement is, to paraphrase an East Coast clothier's ads, that an informed consumer is the best customer. The theory is that educational consumers will select the most appealing alternative, thereby taking business away from an inferior competitor. School vouchers are similar in that they give an individual a choice of where to expend a modicum of funds. Such approaches are what C. Wright Mills laments in the "sociological imagination" when he bemoans Americans' inability to see the larger social context surrounding their successes and failures (Mills 1960).

Schools are the primary institutional site within liberal democra cies for playing out a number of larger sociocultural tensions. The sociologist John Boli discusses how schools act in a promissory fashion when it comes to brokering an array of conflicts. According to Boli (1989), the relentless, albeit unsuccessful, attempts at educational reform reflect the cultural importance of schools and the unwavering faith placed on their ability to resolve many of these conundrums. Schools, asserts Boli, attempt to perpetuate what he identifies as four dominant values of Western society: universality, egalitarianism, standardization, and individualism. At times various conflicting and contradictory aspects of these values becomes manifest in schools. For example, although treating every student as a unique learner is an important aspect of effective educational processes, the organizational need to standardize curriculum and instruction often smothers such efforts. Similarly, tailoring instructional programs to specific learners, which is often done by grouping students of comparable potential academic ability—a practice referred to as ability grouping or tracking, which will be discussed later in this chapter—undermines universality.

Despite repeated attempts to reform schools, there is little evidence that such efforts make a difference. Boli states that "the recurring effort to improve the school despite the massive evidence that reforms generally do not change the schools very much or make them more effective in achieving their goals reveals the enormous faith in schooling that characterizes modern society, a faith that is shared by both functionalist defenders of schooling and 'radical' theorists." He concludes that mass schooling "is a ritual ceremony, not a rationalized technical enterprise" and asserts that schooling should be viewed not as an organizational vehicle for transmitting knowledge but as a "major initiation ceremony, or rite of passage, of modern society" (Boli 1989, 49).

### The Promise of Equality and Persistence of Inequality

Certainly one of the most important aspects of schools is the "promise" that is made that achievement will be based on merit. In many ways the hallmarks of liberal democracy—with its focus on the individual whose achievements are unfettered by the limitations imposed by external social structures—are captured in schools. The founding of the nation was predicated upon a belief that there should be equality for all. As the Declaration of Independence states, "We hold these truths to be self-evident, that all men are created equal, that they are endowed by their Creator with certain unalienable Rights, that among these are life, liberty and the pursuit of happiness. That to secure these rights, governments are instituted among men, deriving their just powers from the consent of the governed."

Although all have the right to "life, liberty and the pursuit of happiness," there is no guarantee that the outcome will be equitable. Recent studies of the distribution of wealth in the United States demonstrate that prosperity is skewed in favor of the relatively small percentage of the population that owns and controls marketable assets. According to the U.S. Bureau of the Census, "The distribution of wealth in the United States has a large positive skew, with relatively few households holding a large proportion of the wealth" (U.S. Bureau of the Census 2003, 2). Similarly, the poverty rate, which had declined steadily following the implementation of a number of social welfare programs—food stamps, social security supplemental income, and the indexing of social security benefits to increases in the cost of living and rate of inflation—has steadily risen since the late 1990s.

Although all are guaranteed access to public schools, there is no requirement that these schools be fiscally equitable. Local community assets and revenues constitute an important vehicle for financing education. On average, a school district receives 50 percent of its appropriations from the state, 43 percent from local revenues, and 7 percent from the federal government. The pursuit of equity in school funding focuses on strategies for closing the gap between local districts' abilities to contribute revenues to their schools. Since local funds are commonly based at least in part on property taxes, less-wealthy communities are not able to raise as much money for schools as wealthier districts, leaving their children at a considerable disadvantage. The higher the share of funding that states provide for education, and the more states target that money, the better the chances for increasing equity in the system (Hatch 2003, 32, 35).

This disparity in local funding has led to a string of lawsuits, in which most rulings have upheld the state's responsibility to secure equitable funding. One of the most significant is the *Abbott v. Burke* (1990) case in New Jersey, in which the court ordered the commissioner of education to provide the following for what were to become designated as

Abbott school districts: educational programs that are comparable to those offered in suburban schools, including early childhood education programs and state-of-the-art facilities; reduction in class sizes; and implementation of state-mandated educational outcomes (Education Law Center 1990). Similar concerns have been expressed over inequities in early childhood learning and the impact of these inequities on future achievement. The centrality of the importance of a firm educational foundation for all is underscored by Valerie E. Lee and David T. Burkham in their *Inequality from the Starting Gate: Social Background Differences in Achievement as Children Begin School* (2002). In their analysis of the U.S. Department of Education's Early Childhood Longitudinal Study, Kindergarten Cohort, Lee and Burkham found that by the time children begin kindergarten, those who are disadvantaged are substantially behind their advantaged peers in developmental and cognitive skills. They emphatically state that this is not due to genetic or biological reasons. Rather, the delays are a product of disadvantaged social and familial circumstances, including a lack of exposure to books and to cultural and educational experiences. The authors state, "Socioeconomic status—SES—is quite strongly related to cognitive skills. Of the many categories of factors considered—including race/ethnicity, family educational expectations, access to quality child care, home reading, computer use, and television habits—SES accounts for more of the unique variation in cognitive scores than any other factor by far. Entering race/ethnic differences are substantially explained by these other factors; SES differences are reduced but remain sizeable" (Lee and Burkham 2002, 2).

Another related issue concerns the persistence and reappearance of segregated schools. Gary Orfield and the Harvard Desegregation Project (Frankenberg, Lee, and Orfield 2003) found that schools are resegregating after what appeared to be years of racially balanced schools. Analyzing the NCES Common Core of Data for 2000–2001, the authors found a disturbing reversal in desegregation patterns within the nation's schools. As the nonwhite school population has increased, there has been a growing segmentation by race.

Sociologists of education have long studied how schools, often in an unmitigated fashion, reproduce social inequality. The tracking of students from an early age is a primary mechanism for reproducing inequality. Defenders of tracking assert that it is based upon some meritocratic standard and that forming a homogeneous group of learners makes the job of the teacher easier. Some have asserted that tracking is tantamount to a self-fulfilling prophecy in which those in the lower tracks are doomed to a lack of achievement due to the reduced expectations that their teachers have of them. Furthermore, they assert, it ultimately pigeonholes students assigned to the lower tracks—assignments that are strongly associated with the socioeconomic status of the student: Studies repeatedly confirm that those assigned to the lowest track are disproportionately poor and nonwhite (Oakes 1985).

## THE COMPLEXITY OF MEASURING COMMUNITY COLLEGE EFFECTIVENESS

In community colleges, two of the most prevalent measures of effectiveness are retention and graduation rates. Both measures are problematic in that students enter community colleges with a disparate set of objectives. Any meaningful measure must begin with an understanding of why students initially enter a community college, and measures of success must be appropriately benchmarked. According to the NCES, "Students who start their postsecondary education at community colleges have diverse degree goals. About one-fourth of the students who began at a public 2 year institution at some time during the 1995–96 academic year said that they intend to transfer to a 4 year institution and complete a bachelor's degree, and about one-half said that they were working on an associate's degree" (U.S. Department of Education 2003, 44). Approximately one-half of those who intend to transfer to a baccalaureate institution complete their goal, compared to one-quarter of those who initially intended just to complete an associate's degree.

Another study found that over 71 percent of those who enter a community college intend to obtain a baccalaureate degree (Bradburn and Hurst 2001), a figure that is higher than found in the research reported by the NCES in Hoachlander, Sikora, and Horn 2003 or in Kevin Dougherty's (1994) studies of transfer rates. It also found a 33 percent transfer rate, which is higher than the "22 percent found by the Transfer Assembly Project" (Cohen and Sanchez 1997). However, as the report's authors note, they are less restrictive with respect to the population they are studying. Their study included those taking remedial courses regardless of the number of credits.

A number of outcome measures have been developed to ascertain the effectiveness of community colleges. Richard Alfred, Peter Ewell, James Hudgins, and Kay McClenney (1999) suggest that a comprehensive composite evaluation of community colleges would include measurement of the following parameters:

1. Student goal attainment
2. Persistence
3. Degree completion rates
4. Placement rate in the workforce
5. Employer assessment of students
6. Licensure/certification pass rates
7. Client assessment of programs and services
8. Demonstration of critical literacy skills
9. Demonstration of citizenship skills
10. Number and rate who transfer
11. Performance after transfer
12. Success in subsequent, related course work
13. Participation rate in service area
14. Responsiveness to community needs

Although these are laudable measures, it is rare to find an institution that incorporates all of them into a multidimensional performance indicator.

### The Dilemma Facing Community Colleges

Judith Eaton (1994, 72–73) speaks eloquently to the conundrum faced by community colleges regarding the maintenance of academic excellence while embracing open access:

> Over and over, since 1900, one question has remained unanswered for these institutions: how can any educational institution marry the inclusionary principle of opportunity with the exclusionary principle of excellence? Selective four-year institutions and universities are not confronted with this dilemma. They do not make extensive inclusionary claims that lead to open-door admissions. Elementary and secondary education also avoid this dilemma. They are precluded by law from making exclusionary claims. Indeed, as [Jerome] Karabel suggests, access and achievement may not be realizable in a single institution. . . . To date, the community college enterprise has enshrined the dilemma, not resolved it.

The mantle of excellence has been at the heart of recent efforts to reform education, which often involve setting exemplary educational benchmarks that are to be achieved. In Goals 2000, for example, the following benchmarks were articulated:

1. By the year 2000, all children will start school ready to learn.
2. By the year 2000, the high school graduation rate will increase to at least 90 percent.
3. By the year 2000, American students will leave grades 4, 8, and 12 having demonstrated competency in challenging subject matter, including English, mathematics, science, history, and geography, and every school in America will ensure that all students learn to use their minds well, so they may be prepared for responsible citizenship, further learning, and productive employment in our modern society.
4. By the year 2000, U.S. students will be first in the world in mathematics and science achievement.
5. By the year 2000, every adult American will be literate and will possess the skills necessary to compete in a global economy and exercise the rights and responsibilities of citizenship.
6. By the year 2000, every school in America will be free of drugs and violence and will offer a disciplined environment conducive to learning. (*Education Week,* quoted in Sadovnik, Cookson, Semel, and Levinson 2002, 228)

Although Goals 2000 certainly provided laudable goals for K-12, they were not achieved. The United States continues to languish in worldwide comparisons of science and mathematics achievement (Kleiner and Farris 2002). Passage of the No Child Left Behind Act in 2001 was an attempt to bolster accountability standards for U.S. primary and secondary education by tying federal appropriations to school performance (U.S. Department of Education 2001). The jury is out, however, as to the effectiveness of this legislation given that, at the time this book was being written, the legislation was causing much consternation among legislators and the public regarding its implementation.

### *Accountability and High-Stakes Testing*

There has been an increasing concern over educational quality, leading many to look for ways to hold schools more accountable for student performance. The advocacy of various benchmarks whose attainment is ascertained by the administering of high-stakes testing has become a core principle in K–12 education reform. In addition to concerns about what is actually being measured by these tests and about whether or not these initiatives have simply transformed pedagogy into a process of "teaching to the test," a major issue has been whether these tests do indeed accurately measure achievement of the benchmarks.

The American Educational Research Association (2000) expresses concern regarding the deleterious consequences of high-stakes testing when there is no concomitant allocation of appropriate resources:

> If high-stakes testing programs are implemented in circumstances where educational resources are inadequate or where tests lack sufficient reliability and validity for their intended purposes, there is potential for serious harm. Policy makers and the public may be misled by spurious test score increases unrelated to any fundamental educational improvements; students may be placed at increased risk of educational failure and dropping out; teachers may be blamed or punished for inequitable resources over which they have no control; and curriculum and instruction may be severely distorted if high test scores per se, rather than learning, become the overriding goal of classroom instruction.

Within K–12 education a vociferous debate is raging concerning the relationship between educational expenditures and quality. Typically this debate has taken the form of assessing whether class size has an impact upon educational achievement. Eric Hanusek (2002) argues that simply throwing money at the problem of school failures—for example, as seen in bolstering "inputs" by investing in reducing class size—has not improved academic success. Rather, it would be more advantageous to invest in improving teacher quality and in taking measures to attract competent professionals, such as by increasing the pay of teachers, rather than simply attending to the largely symbolic issue of class size (which, as Hanusek points out, has decreased in recent years). However, this does not negate the need for funding equity, which has been at the heart of reforms such as those of the previously discussed Abbott school district in New Jersey.

Access versus excellence is also an issue of concern to international organizations such as the Organization for Economic Co-operation and Development (OECD) as seen in its 2002 edition of *Education Policy Analysis* (which discusses the K–12 level). In reviewing the results of surveys undertaken by OECD under its Program for International Student Assessment (PISA), it states (OECD 2004: 174–178):

> Achieving an equitable distribution of learning outcomes without losing high performance standards represents a significant challenge. Analyses at the national level have often been discouraging: . . .

schools appear to make little difference in overcoming the effects of disadvantaged home backgrounds. Indeed, it has sometimes been argued that if school systems become more inclusive—for example, by increasing the proportion of young people who complete secondary school—then quality is bound to suffer. The international evidence from PISA is more encouraging. . . . the comparisons of the relationships between student performance and the various aspects of socioeconomic background . . . show that some countries simultaneously demonstrate high average quality and relatively high equality of outcomes among students from different socioeconomic backgrounds.

As in K–12 education, part of the challenge for community colleges is to obtain sufficient funding so that they are able to foster both access and excellence.

In many states, community colleges are on the front line when it comes to cutbacks. This is especially problematic because maintaining high standards while remaining accessible is a costly endeavor. The high costs of supplemental instructional support and the labor-intensive nature of effective developmental education create an enhanced fiscal burden for these institutions. In addition, their allocations are often less than those of their four-year public counterparts to start with, and the pay scales for community college faculty and staff are less than those of the personnel at four-year colleges. However, the promise of excellence for all is both the bane and attraction of community colleges.

### Measuring Success

Fostering student success is a daunting challenge as many students who enter community colleges arrive with a number of academic developmental needs. Providing the supplemental instructional supports that these students require is costly. At the same time, community colleges operate under conditions that engender close scrutiny of their efforts. Particularly during times of fiscal austerity, community colleges are increasingly held accountable for producing demonstrable outcomes that indicate student success.

Unfortunately, many of the indices used to measure student success do not correspond to the reasons many students enter community colleges. For example, although graduation and completion rates are typically used to assess institutional success, these are not appropriate benchmarks for students whose purpose for entering a community college may be simply to complete a few courses or to transfer without an associate's degree to a baccalaureate institution. As the NCES states (Hoachlander, Sikora, and Horn 2003, iii): "Because community colleges serve students with a wide range of goals and academic preparation, holding community colleges accountable only for student attainment may understate their effectiveness in meeting a variety of objectives."

The aspirations of students entering community colleges are similar to those of students entering baccalaureate institutions. In an analysis of data from three longitudinal studies, it can be seen that approximately 90 percent of all students who enroll in community colleges aspire to achieve "a formal credential or transfer to a 4-year institution." Data show that "about 63 percent of students intending to obtain a formal credential had either done so or had attended a four year degree institution" (Hoachlander, Sikora, and Horn 2003, vi). This NCES study reports that "when success is defined as any degree attainment or 4-year transfer, about one-half (51 percent) of all community college students (BPS) and nearly two-thirds (63 percent) of more traditional students (NELS) had achieved successful outcomes" (Hoachlander, Sikora, and Horn 2003).

The Community College Survey of Student Engagement (CCSSE) has emerged as an important tool for assessing the effectiveness of community colleges (http://www.ccsse.org). This instrument is an outgrowth of the National Survey of Student Engagement (NSSE), which has been in existence since 2000 as part of a composite of measures that have been used to assess engagement at baccalaureate institutions (http://www.indiana.edu/~nsse). The assumption behind these measures is that the more effective an institution is at engaging a student in curricular and cocurricular activities, the greater the likelihood that that student will persist throughout a particular course of study and graduate. Given that some aspects of life at baccalaureate institutions—such as an on-campus residential experience—are not typically part of a community college student's experience, a number of modifications have been made when applying this survey to the student experience at community colleges. It should also be noted that unlike the data from the engagement survey used for baccalaureate institutions, data from the community college survey can be reported out at an institutional level, though CCSSE does provide a disclaimer regarding the value of comparing institution to institution.

In 2002, when the CCSSE was administered to a national, albeit self-selected, sample of community colleges, a number of challenges were identified.

Because of the multiple reasons students have for attending community colleges and the different levels of engagement desired, students' interpretations of success vary, which makes it difficult to assess the meaning of engagement. For example, someone attending a community college to take a single course will have a very different experience and expectation of engagement from those of someone who is enrolled on a full-time basis. Two-thirds of community college students attend part-time; the opposite is true at four-year institutions. States Kay McClenney (2003): "'Capture time'—the time a college has to engage students—is limited, so what colleges do to make the most of that time is critical." Academic preparedness varies greatly from student to student, with developmental needs being paramount for a majority of learners. Furthermore, for many students it is an economic struggle to attend a community college: Over 40 percent of students who were initially surveyed identified ability to pay as a factor.

In administering the survey for the second time in 2003, CCSSE developed the following five benchmarks for assessing the effectiveness of community colleges: active and collaborative learning, student effort, academic challenge, student-faculty interaction, and support for learners. According to this survey, there is episodic evidence that shows student engagement in these areas. Although there appears to be significant work in these areas, community colleges continue to face a challenge to provide a level of engagement that enhances student learning (Community College Survey of Student Engagement 2003).

Many of the questions that make up the student engagement surveys are based on what has become a classic for assessing pedagogical effectiveness in higher education institutions—Arthur Chickering's and Zelda Gamson's seven principles of effective learning (Chickering and Gamson 1991). These principles are

- *Communication:* Communication between students and professors is encouraged. Encouragement and enthusiasm on the part of faculty is directly related to student motivation and involvement. It may be, in fact, the most important factor in a student's ability to overcome difficult times, to succeed at challenging academic endeavors, and to maintain engagement in the learning process. When students know several faculty members well and are confident in their commitment to good teaching and academic success, students' belief in themselves and their learning is enhanced. This, in turn, allows each student to assess his or her own values and personal or professional goals.

◆ *Encouragement:* Students' involvement in learning increases when they are encouraged to work collaboratively with others, to share ideas and responsibilities when working on research projects, and to present findings in class. When students have the opportunity to interact intellectually, to be creative and original in their thinking, and to support or debate the perspectives of others, higher-level thinking occurs, making the learning process an exciting, engaging endeavor.

◆ *Relevance of course work:* It is crucial that students relate course content to their own lives if learning is to be relevant and meaningful. When students are not personally engaged in the academic process and merely listen to lectures, memorize information, and then repeat it back to the professor on an exam, true learning has not been realized. By talking about what one is learning, writing about it, and applying content to one's life, ownership of the learning process occurs.

◆ *Student evaluation:* Student evaluation, done in a supportive, encouraging way, is crucial. When beginning a new course, it is helpful for students to assess what it is they know and what it is they desire to know in the content area. Thus, learning can become focused. Students benefit from suggestions by their professors relating to the improvement of their performance. In this way, students have role models and will eventually become empowered to assess their own learning.

◆ *Organizational skills:* Time management and organizational skills are critical to academic success and, often, must be taught. Learning to use one's time effectively, especially when working on long-term assignments or projects, can be challenging for many. The clarity with which an institution defines "time expectations" can lead to successful performance for students, faculty, administrators, and other professional staff.

◆ *High expectations:* When educators believe in a student, the message that he or she is capable of successful academic achievement is conveyed. High expectations, across the board, should be an aspect of all academics' educational philosophy. A mentor's expectation of a strong performance often becomes a self-fulfilling prophecy. In turn, an institution should hold high expectations for all of its players, from support staff to top-level administrative officials.

◆ *Respect for individual learning styles:* An awareness of and respect for individual learning styles, interests, and talents is essential. A teacher needs to understand the learning process and the implications of multiple intelligences. All students should be presented with the opportunity to learn in the way they learn best and the opportunity to then build upon their successes to venture into more challenging areas.

As noted throughout this volume, an important dimension concerning whether a student has a "successful" experience is the expectations that he or she brings to the experience. In her study of reasons for noncompletion of a degree, Ellen Bradburn (2002, 1) states:

> Not all students plan to complete a degree when they enter college. Among all beginning postsecondary students in 1995–96, the expectations and objectives of students who began at public 2-year institutions differed from those of students who began at 4-year institutions. Even among students who began at public 2-year institutions, educational expectations were relatively high (i.e., higher than could be accomplished at a 2-year institution): 33 percent eventually expected to complete a bachelor's degree, and another 29 percent expected to complete an advanced degree, i.e., a degree beyond the bachelor's. But students who began at public 2-year institutions were less likely than students who began at 4-year institutions (59 percent at both public and private not-for-profit 4-year institutions) to expect to complete an advanced degree. They were also more likely to expect that their eventual educational attainment would be less than a bachelor's degree (16 percent vs. 1–2 percent of those who began at 4-year institutions). Finally, students who began at community colleges expressed a range of reasons for enrolling at such an institution: 38 percent indicated that they chose that institution to prepare for transfer to a 4-year college or university; 22 percent chose the institution to gain job skills; and another 16 percent enrolled for personal enrichment.

### *Assessing Outcomes*

As are other sectors in higher education, community colleges are under pressure to demonstrate positive student learning outcomes. "Outcomes assessment," as it is commonly called, is also the result of a general concern about accountability in higher education, and regional accrediting organizations increasingly demand that the institutions they accredit demonstrate effectiveness in this area. For example, the Middle States Commission on Higher Education recently revised their assessment criteria so that student learning outcomes are at the center of their new standards of excellence (Middle States Commission on Higher Education 2002).

The focus on outcomes assessments stems from the previously discussed need to discern quality. The AAHE's nine "Principles of Good Practice for Assessing Student Learning Outcomes" is one of the best summaries available (American Association of Higher Education n.d.). Summarizing the AAHE's nine principles and the work of others, such as Jeffrey Seybert (2002) and Peter Dlugos (2003), we can identify the following key components of what constitutes effective assessment:

- ⬦ In order for an institution to effectively assess student learning, it must, in its mission statement, contextualize student learning in such a way that accomplishments are viewed in terms of whether or not the goals and values of the institution are successfully transmitted to the learner. Assessment is an instrumental process that helps an institution evaluate how well it is performing its mission; it is not an end in itself. An institution must also determine what aspects of its operation it wishes to assess.

- ⬦ Learning is a multifaceted process that requires an array of institutional supports. Students need to be guided in understanding and reflecting on how they learn. For example, a student's preferred style of learning should be assessed. As Howard Gardner asserts (1993), there are varying learning styles, all of which are effective; which is effective for a particular learner depends on that learner's proclivities. It is important for an institution to assist a student in identifying his or her learning style and to make faculty aware so that they can appropriately vary their pedagogy to respond to the diverse learning styles of students in a given class.

- ⬦ Assessments of student learning and institutional effectiveness must be triangulated. This means that a sole, exclusive method of assessment is not appropriate; assessment methods should vary. For example, a professor should assess student learning in a multidimensional fashion. This might include assessing a portfolio of a student's work, his or her performance on an objective examination, the quality of the student's involvement in a group project, his or her classroom participation, and other aspects of learning.

- ⬦ Assessments of student learning should be done over time, and an institution should perform a baseline assessment when a student enters the institution. Baseline measures should consist of an array of performance measures, such as

- performance on reading, writing, and mathematics proficiency tests;
- a video tape of incoming oral communication skills, an evaluation process that is practiced by Alverno College in Milwaukee, Wisconsin (http://www.alverno.edu);
- a transcription of life experiences, perhaps by using the Secretary's Commission on Achieving Necessary Skills (SCANS) assessment, based on the 1991 report issued by the U.S. Department of Labor, *What Work Requires of Schools* (http://wdr.doleta.gov/SCANS/whatwork/whatwork.html) as developed by Johns Hopkins University (http://www.scans.jhu.edu/NS/HTML/Index.htm);
- an assessment of prior learning using one or a combination of several measures pioneered by a number of institutions, such as the Community College of Vermont (http://www.ccv.edu), the College of Public and Community Service (CPCS) at the University of Massachusetts at Boston (http://www.cpcs.umb.edu), and Cambridge College (http://www.cambridgecollege.edu).

Most important, assessment needs to be a continuous process; it cannot be done in an episodic, shotgun approach.

- There must be clear, discernible goals in order to make assessment meaningful. Clarifying such goals starts with having students identify the reasons for their enrollment. As discussed earlier, students enroll in community colleges for a number of reasons, and assessing success means assessing the realization of specific goals, not measuring standard though at times irrelevant criteria, such as whether a student graduates if that was not the original intent. On an institutional level, there must be a clear set of goals that need to be attained. These goals would emanate from the college's mission statement and would be reflected in its strategic plan, whose elements would be assessed accordingly.
- Assessment, like accreditation, can be a community-building process in which participants participate in dialogues and discover common purposes as they engage in campus-wide conversations. All constituents must be actively involved in assessment activities. Faculty must take a central role in this process, but in addition, learning support services—such as supplemental instruction, tutoring, counseling, and library services—must

get involved in the process. Furthermore, auxiliary operations—ranging from the bursar and building and grounds to a college's foundation and development—should be involved in assessment. The need for institutions to assess all dimensions of their operations—from student learning to energy consumption—is increasingly prescribed by accrediting agencies, such as the Middle States Commission on Higher Education. In addition, the evidentiary base that is attained through assessment can be infused back into institutional decision making.

•➤ Information and data generated by assessment activities should then be routed back to the institution for improvement purposes. Jeanne Ballantine's (2002, 599–604) open system approach is a useful construct for understanding how this process works. In Ballantine's schema, a number of inputs are fed into a feedback loop, which are then conditioned by a number of socio-environmental factors. As a continuous, dynamic process, an open systems approach promotes an understanding of how the results of systemic evaluation can be incorporated into an organization's decision-making processes.

Alverno College, in Milwaukee, Wisconsin, has become a national leader in developing outcomes across the curriculum. In addition to completing requirements in a major field of study, students at Alverno College must demonstrate proficiency in the following eight abilities: communication, analysis, problem solving, valuing in decision making, social interaction, developing a global perspective, effective citizenship, and aesthetic engagement (Alverno College n.d.). Alverno College has received a McArthur Genius Grant for these efforts, and through the Alverno Institute it disseminates its work throughout the nation and world.

### *Meritocracy*

The belief that student advancement in an educational system is based on objective measures of achievement and attainments is the primary source for believing in the legitimacy of a meritocratic system. Jürgen Habermas (1975) contends that there is a legitimation "crisis" in the Western world, largely because the technical, rational standards that constitute a functioning meritocracy are no longer present. With respect to competitive higher education admission practices, this crisis is exemplified in the phenomenon of "legacy" admissions (in which family members of alumni are admitted to selective universities without meeting the admission standards imposed on other applicants) and in the process of constructing applications for admission that are often the product of external entities—at times professionals hired by affluent families—to craft the ideal entrance essay (Steinberg 2002).

Meritocracy assumes some system of differentials based on a scarcity of rewards. The idea of proficiency testing is predicated on the belief that there are relatively few advantageous slots and that it is society's task to select and sort. Merit is viewed as the basis of social selection in the United States. It is assumed that people earn their social positions through some "objective" assessment of aptitude, whether through a performance appraisal or through demonstrated achievement; that is, it is assumed that a person's social position is deserved. "Rule by merit," which is the etymological meaning of the word "meritocracy," is thought to prevail as an organizing ideology for the distribution of relatively scarce societal rewards (Hoffer 2002).

Community college admission practices essentially undermine the process of selection based upon competition for scarce opportunity. They call into question the very idea of using achievement as a way of regulating access. Left to its own devices, selection simply on the basis of merit runs the risk of reproducing a select, definitive set of social participants. This "danger" is the subject of Michael Young's infamous novel *The Rise of the Meritocracy, 1870–2033* (1958), in which he discusses the tyrannical potential of "pure" meritocratic systems. What occurs, suggests Young, is that the "meritocratic" group essentially reproduces itself by constructing selection mechanisms that favor the very attributes that members of the group possess. The relatively uniform social composition of the meritocratic group is then essentially reproduced from generation to generation.

Studies of educational attainment continue to demonstrate the centrality of wealth and affluence in predicting academic achievement. Even though social background does not measure ability, it does afford access to various exclusive social and cultural capital networks. Sociologists of education have introduced two conceptual frameworks to explain this determinacy: social capital and cultural capital.

The concept of social capital is based on the writings of the late sociologist James Coleman. Social capital, like economic capital, can be viewed as an asset that can be utilized to achieve a desirable end. Barbara Schneider (2002) points to the following defining characteristics of social capital:

➡ It is embedded within the social relationships of people and is created through these ties.

➡ It makes possible the achievement of desirable ends through access to a particular field of social networks.

➡ It operates in the context of social systems and both facilitates and constrains actions.

➡ It can be "produced" via families, religious organizations, and schools, often in a way that allows participants to transcend deleterious social circumstances.

Community colleges can provide the social capital, the lack of which can impede a student's success. Given that many community college students are first-generation college students, they do not have familiarity with college life. Lacking any effective role models, they need support and nurturing to succeed. Especially important for fostering student success at community colleges is an investment in supplemental instructional support—such as tutoring services, study skills, and an in depth orientation toward college life.

The concept of cultural capital is most closely associated with the work of the French sociologist Pierre Bourdieu, who coined the term. One way of conceptualizing cultural capital is to think of it as the repertoire of skills available to help navigate everyday life. Often associated with a "high-brow" style of living, cultural capital can be viewed as the ability to discern the nuances of social interactions in a way that masters the often unsaid, taken-for-granted assumptions that guide social interaction. For example, effective interviewing for a job requires the applicant to master such behaviors as maintaining appropriate eye contact, using socially acceptable linguistic expressions, and exhibiting positive body language. As with all aspects of culture, cultural capital is something that is learned or acquired. Like social capital, this domain of knowledge is often an abyss for the first-generation college student. It can be taught through a college's career and placement services, in an orientation-to-student-life course, or through other institutional mechanisms. Just as is true of social capital, the acquisition of cultural capital is key for student achievement.

Sociological studies of what determines educational success continue to find that social background and material wealth are the most important predictors of scholastic achievement. Similarly, critics of standardized testing assert that many of the objective assessment exams that students take (such as the Scholastic Aptitude Test [SAT]) measure social background rather than true proficiency (Medina and Neill 1990; Crouse and Trusheim 1988).

Community college students are typically poorer than their counterparts at baccalaureate institutions. As community college tuitions rise in the context of further state cutbacks, the ability of students to continue attending is jeopardized. In recent discussions about the reauthorization of the Higher Education Amendment Act, there is mounting concern that cutbacks in federal financial aid will most heavily affect community college students. Throughout higher education, an increasing financial burden is being placed on those who can least afford it. "Needs-blind" admission practices wane, and a student's ability to pay becomes a litmus test in competitive admissions practices.

### Market-Based Reforms

The ascendance of market-based principles in shaping the delivery of educational services has become an emerging paradigm for K–12 reform. John Chubb's and Terry Moe's *Politics, Markets, and America's Schools* (1990) is the classic work proposing the application of market principles to education. In this work, Chubb and Moe assert that the root of education's problems is the monopoly that public educational systems have had over schooling. As monopolies, schools have little incentive to respond to calls for reform that are externally generated. Chubb and Moe argue that the only way to improve schools is through the creation of alternative institutions that are market-responsive.

Many school choice programs have been modeled in accordance with this theory. Their basic operating philosophy is that through competition, educational institutions will be forced to improve and to be responsive to the customer in order to sustain sufficient enrollments. Recently this principle has been extended to the many private, for-profit entities that have become involved in the "business" of education. Among the most famous have been the Edison Schools, whose flamboyant founder, Chris Whittle, secured the services of Benno Schmidt, former president of Yale, to popularize their proposed school structures to a nationwide audience. Although the first few years of the Edison Schools' existence were tenuous, they have been more successful of late and have received a number of contracts to create and operate primary and secondary schools. Edison Schools expect to serve over 250,000 students in twenty states by the end of the 2004–2005 academic year (Edison Schools 2004).

Because of their open access practices, community colleges appear challenge the organizational principles that are commonly used to assure quality within social institutions. The idea that excellence can be achieved without competitive pressures contradicts the market-based principles that organize social life and structure educational policies. Within education, the issues of school vouchers and school choice are poignant illustrations of just how important and pervasive competitiveness is as an organizing principle in current strategies for educational reform. For example, the reauthorization in 2001 of the Elementary and Secondary Education Act (ESEA), commonly referred to as the No Child Left Behind Act (NCLB), offers academic options for parents whose children attend failing schools. Under NCLB, children who attend schools that are identified as needing improvement or failing to meet state standards will have the opportunity to transfer to a better public school. Parents will be given the option to choose a different school within their school district, with transportation to that school provided. If a child attends a failing school—one that has failed to meet state standards for three of the preceding four years—supplemental educational services must be provided. Providers must meet state guidelines and offer services that will enhance the students' opportunities to meet academic standards. In addition to helping ensure that a child has access to a high-quality education, the aforementioned choice and academic support requirements serve as an incentive for low-performing schools to improve to avoid the risk of losing students. Losing students is associated with the loss of a portion of the district's annual budget and, often, state funds. In addition, if a school does not demonstrate yearly progress, it will be placed under a "corrective action plan," and if it continues to fail, the state may eventually initiate a restructuring plan (National Education Association 2002).

The governing principles of market competition are often being applied to educational institutions, as evidenced by this aspect of the No Child Left Behind Act. To some extent, the growth of for-profit institutions constitutes a competitive challenge to publicly funded community colleges. However, because of the high cost associated with attending these institutions, whether they truly pose a competitive challenge remains to be seen.

## THE AFFORDABILITY OF HIGHER EDUCATION

According to the U.S. Department of Education (Horn, Wei, and Baker 2002), increases in the availability of financial aid offset the increases in tuition that occurred for full-time community college students between the 1992–1993 school year and the 1999–2000 school year. This was not the case for part-time students, whose financial aid eligibility is limited. Pell grants, which have been the primary federal mechanism for providing financial aid for higher education, are woefully inadequate to meet the need for funding, states the National Association of State Student

Grant and Aid Programs (NASSGSP 2004) The correction of this inadequacy is an important aspect of the AACC's testimony in support of the
reauthorization of the Higher Education Act, under which financial aid
programs come. AACC calls for the doubling of Pell grants and for the
implementation of other criteria besides graduation rates, which place
community colleges at a disadvantage when it comes to institutional
performance assessment. It states: "Over the next decade, college enrollment is expected to increase by 14%, of which 80% will be minorities,
and of these minorities, one-fifth will live below the poverty line. It is imperative that Congress continue to invest in providing aid to students
and families with need, to ensure both access to college and economic
prosperity" (AACC 2004).

## CHALLENGES OF ATTAINING
## AND MAINTAINING EXCELLENCE

One of the challenges facing community colleges is the maintenance of
a high-quality instructional workforce. Full-time community college
faculty have heavy teaching loads, typically fifteen contact hours a semester, which is far greater than the six-credit or nine-hour norm at selective higher education institutions. Thus, the average full-time community college instructor has far less time than her or his four-year
counterparts to engage in research and professional development.

However, in response to this concern, community college advocates suggest that they have a competitive advantage by being "teaching" institutions. By focusing on instruction, often in classes far smaller
than the norm found in a four-year institution, many assert that community colleges provide a better classroom product. Because teaching
occurs in relatively small class settings and because the instruction is
provided by the full-time instructors—in contrast to the stereotypical
graduate-student teaching assistant instructing introductory-level
courses at prestigious research institutions—community colleges may
offer more individualized and personalized instruction. However, W.
Norton Grubb's study of teaching in community colleges raises doubts
about the validity of this prophecy. In their study of community college
teaching, Grubb and his associates (1999) find that many of the faculty
they observed did not import "best practices" of community college instruction into the classroom. They conclude that "many community colleges are not, contrary to rhetoric, teaching institutions, because they
do not use their institutional policies and resources to improve the qual-

ity of instruction" (Grubb, Worthen, Byrd, Webb, Badway, Case, Goto, and Villeneuve 1999, 281). They attribute these problems to the organizational structure of community colleges, which often do little to provide collective faculty development for instructors. The technical nature of much of the curriculum often renders it devoid of interactive group learning. In addition, there is a tension between the prescriptive nature of much of the curriculum and the effectiveness of constructivist learning, which can involve an impromptu stance on the part of the instructor in order to respond to the nuances of such learning.

Honors programs provide community colleges with a claim to excellence. Approximately 25 percent of all community colleges offer honors programs (Outcalt 1999). They also provide a notable savings for students, many of whom attained impressive academic credentials as high school students but decided it would be financially prudent to first enroll in an honors program at a community college and then transfer to an Ivy League university (Winter 2002). However, this is not to say that community college honors programs do not have their critics. Some observers suggest that honors programs at community colleges emulate tracking, whose negative aspects have been experienced by many community college students. In addition, some suggest that to segment students via an honors program engenders invidious comparisons among students, comparisons that undermine the open-access ethos of community colleges.

Another area in which community colleges provide excellence and high-quality education is in supplying the skilled labor needed for a competitive economy. The importance of a well-educated workforce for U.S. economic vitality was underscored by the spate of reports released in the early 1980s that pointed to the sorry condition of education in the United States. Perhaps the most infamous pronouncement was that of the National Commission on Excellence in Education in its *A Nation at Risk*. The commission stated (1983, 5):

> Our Nation is at risk. Our once unchallenged preeminence in commerce, industry, science, and technological innovation is being overtaken by competitors throughout the world. This report is concerned with only one of the many causes and dimensions of the problem, but it is the one that undergirds American prosperity, security, and civility. We report to the American people that while we can take justifiable pride in what our schools and colleges have historically accomplished and contributed to the United States and the well-being of its people, the educational foundations of our society are presently being eroded by a rising

tide of mediocrity that threatens our very future as a Nation and a people. What was unimaginable a generation ago has begun to occur—others are matching and surpassing our educational attainments.

If an unfriendly foreign power had attempted to impose on America the mediocre educational performance that exists today, we might well have viewed it as an act of war. As it stands, we have allowed this to happen to ourselves. We have even squandered the gains in student achievement made in the wake of the Sputnik challenge. Moreover, we have dismantled essential support systems which helped make those gains possible. We have, in effect, been committing an act of unthinking, unilateral educational disarmament.

A vocal chorus of pundits believe that the United States continues to suffer from a lack of a technologically sophisticated workforce. Although there has been a considerable downturn in information technology companies, there are surveys that continue to demonstrate deficiencies in workers' skills in this area and, hence, a need to look elsewhere for skilled workers. Robert Reich (1991) and others have pointed to the rise of "symbolic analysts" and their importance in producing wealth and economic productivity. More recently, Richard Florida (2002), in his book on the "creative class," demonstrates the significance of this highly skilled cadre, calling them the "movers and shakers" behind economic growth and development.

In addition, there is substantial concern that many U.S. workers lack the "soft skills" required for successful employment. Many analysts point to the importance of collaborative work, communicative competency, and general problem-solving ability and numeric literacy as key ingredients for economic prosperity and worker productivity.

### Learning Communities and Peer Mentoring

The formation of learning communities provides an effective way to create cohorts of students who by virtue of being in a shared learning environment form a support structure. Often such cohort groups occur in programs—such as nursing and allied health—in which students progress in lockstep through a curriculum whose requirements are uniform and highly prescriptive. Besides providing a peer-support structure, learning communities allow instructors to team together so that they obtain a composite picture of student abilities across a number of subject areas. This also allows faculty to create an assessment of student learning that is far more comprehensive and integrative than is possible when evaluation is done in discrete and at times disjointed courses.

Community colleges have pioneered the learning community movement. LaGuardia Community College, which is part of CUNY, is a recognized national leader in this movement. Perhaps LaGuardia's greatest achievement is the creation of learning communities in the context of a student body whose diversity is unparalleled. The ability to form peer-learning networks that use cultural differences as a way of strengthening learning within a classroom setting is particularly powerful at LaGuardia and other institutions whose students are extremely diverse. Students representing nationalities whose native countries are in political conflict come together to form a supportive peer-learning network.

The Maricopa Community Colleges in Phoenix, Arizona, the largest community college district in the nation, made up of ten colleges that enroll over 270,000 students, have developed a number of different models of learning communities (International Education Services 2004). These models include:

- *Linked or paired courses.* This is the simplest form of the learning community, in which two courses are paired. Coregistration is encouraged, but not mandatory. Each course is taught separately, but there may be some joint assignments, projects, and discussions.
- *Freshman Interest Groups (FIGs).* In this model, a cohort of freshmen enroll as a small group (about thirty-five students) in three in-place, topically related courses. No faculty coplanning is expected, although faculty may participate in an orientation event for students in a FIG.
- *Coordinated Studies Program.* This is considered the most "seamless" of all the ILC models. This model is characterized by a multidisciplinary program of study involving a cohort of students and faculty drawn from different disciplines. Faculty plan and participate in all parts of the program. Courses are integrated into a "block" around a central theme (Sullivan 2001).

### The Learning College

The concept of a learning college is useful for understanding how a higher education institution can be organized so as to center its mission, goals, and organizational structure on learning. Terry O'Banion, former CEO and president of the League for Innovation in the Community College and acknowledged as the founder of the learning college movement, articulates the following core organizing principles for the learning college (O'Banion 1997, 47–61):

➥ The learning college creates substantial change in individual learners. Its focus is on the learning pathway that an individual student assumes and centers an institution's resources on the goal of achieving this end.

➥ The learning college engages learners in the learning process as full partners who must assume primary responsibility for their own choices. A learning college creates self-reflective students who with proper guidance direct themselves as they set forth on specific academic and career pathways. A premium is placed upon "self-assessment," which, in part, can only come about if the student receives constructive feedback and criticism from mentors. Teachers take on the role of being learning coaches who guide students along particular pathways.

➥ The learning college creates and offers as many options for learning as possible. As is certainly the case for comprehensive community colleges, students have a wide choice of degree and certificate programs in which they can enroll. For example, Bergen Community College in Paramus, New Jersey, an institution with approximately 14,000 credit students, offers students over eighty credit and certificate programs from which to choose. An important feature of this aspect of a learning college is that students attain a common core of knowledge—typically in the format of general education requirements—that allows them to transfer internally among programs.

➥ The learning college assists learners in forming and participating in collaborative learning activities. As I emphasized in the previous section, learning communities are the method par excellence for promoting collaborative learning. However, collaborative learning can also occur within a single-course setting in which the instructor creates group activities for students and when there is true participatory learning.

➥ The learning college defines the roles of learning facilitators in response to the needs of the learners. The metaphor of teacher as coach is important here, for the key is to facilitate learning, not spoon-feed information. In order for this instructional strategy to succeed, students must be self-motivated learners who have some sense of the academic direction they wish to follow and know what they want to achieve.

➥ The learning college and its learning facilitators succeed only when improved and expanded learning can be documented for learners. Here the focus is on discernible outcomes that can be demonstrated in an evidentiary fashion. This can be done through a variety of methods that should be transparent to an evaluator.

### Service Learning

Another pedagogical innovation designed to engage students as active learners, thereby tapping into their applied talents, is what is known as service learning. There has been a movement throughout higher education to add a service-learning component to much of the curriculum. The Campus Compact, whose headquarters are housed at Brown University in Providence, Rhode Island, is the primary organization that promotes this endeavor nationwide. Service learning allows students to integrate classroom learning with comparable "real-world" experiences. Similar principles can be seen in such national programs as Ameri-Corps.

### Supplemental Instruction

Community colleges typically provide an array of supplemental supports for student learning. These are considered central in order to assure success for students who have deficiencies in basic skills, need additional assistance in mastering the content of a particular course, or need to acquire study skills. Tutoring services, language laboratories, and teaching of research and organizational skills are just some of what can be provided to assist student learning. In addition, community colleges generally offer an array of student support services such as academic and career counseling, health services, and a wide range of cocurricular activities.

## ONLINE LEARNING

Learning anytime and anyplace is a central mantra of online learning. Online learning allows students to study from the comfort of their home or office. As reported by the Sloan Consortium (Bourne and Moore 2003), the most effective online learning is that which students perceive as personalized and engaging.

The number of community colleges offering online instruction has steadily increased. At present, 90 percent of public community colleges offer online learning, the highest percentage of any higher education segment in the United States (Waits and Lewis 2003). Besides offering courses that are fully online, community colleges are also engaged in enhancing existing courses through technology, whether it be through hybrid courses (courses offered via an array of instructional modalities, most often as a combination of in-class didactic and distance learning, typically alternating class sessions between the two) or Web-enhanced courses (in which an instructor makes heavy use of a companion Web site where students engage in online chats, access supplemental course materials, and in general extend the classroom beyond the traditional brick-and-mortar context).

An interesting example of online learning is Western Governors University, a competency-based initiative started by nineteen state governors in 1998. Accredited by four regional associations, this is a totally virtual initiative. The University of Phoenix, acknowledged as the largest university in the world, is the sine qua non of distance learning. They have branded their mode of learning "FlexNet Internet Classes" and emphasize its flexibility, a boon to students who may be juggling family, work, and school. One may "attend" class from home, from work, or while traveling. A degree may be earned within two to three years, and commuting to class is not necessary. The student is required, however, to attend one class on campus to meet the instructor and classmates and for several weeks he or she will study with a "Learning Team" via the Internet. For the final workshop, the student returns to the campus for presentations, the final exam, and the instructor's summary (University of Phoenix n.d.).

An exemplary statewide online community college initiative is the New Jersey Virtual Community College (http://www.njvccc.cc.nj.us). This initiative is a consortium among the nineteen community colleges in New Jersey, where there is a standardized tuition and fee structure and where students can take courses from any campus. Not only does this increase the educational options for students throughout New Jersey and equalize the educational playing field, but it also increases cost-effectiveness by providing a wide variety of choices while avoiding program duplication.

One of the challenges facing online education is the high attrition rate that often occurs in online courses: On average, 50 percent of those who enroll in an online class do not complete it. Part of this attrition may stem from an expectation by students that online courses require less effort on their part, which has been shown not to be the case. Another factor is the effectiveness of the instructor: Teaching an online course requires a pedagogical approach that differs from in-class instruction. Acknowledging the importance of training online instructors, a number of institutions have created training programs for online teaching. At Bergen Community College, Judith Davis, head of the English Department, created an online teacher training program called TOPP, the Online Professor's Program.

In addition to proficiency with the technology required to place courses online, another important dimension of online learning concerns the pedagogical skills required in an online environment. Because discussion in online courses occurs in an asynchronous, cybernetic fashion, such courses require the instructor to utilize deft mediation skills to maintain threaded discussions among classmates. Besides responding to points raised by class members, an instructor must also pose questions and raise issues that engender community-wide deliberation. Online courses also place extra demands on students: They must be able to pace themselves and to a large extent they must be independent, self-motivated learners. Assessment of online learning goes beyond the simple true/false, multiple choice test format unless assessment is done in a traditional, didactic fashion, which essentially defeats the 24/7, anytime, anyplace intent of online learning. Some providers of online learning, such as the University of Phoenix, occasionally bring classmates together to provide a face-to-face component to their courses.

In addition to online courses, colleges are providing a number of Internet-based services for online learning, many of which are required by regional accrediting agencies when colleges are able to offer entire degree programs online. These services include online registration, online advisement, online tutoring, online reference services, and other amenities that are provided to anytime and anyplace learners.

### The Digital Divide

Of mounting concern has been the access to technology that is afforded to students. Alfredo G. de los Santos Jr., Gerardo E. de los Santos, and Mark Milliron (de los Santos, de los Santos, and Milliron 2003) have written extensively about this issue. They note the discrepancy that exists between white and nonwhite Americans, a gap that will grow larger as minority enrollment in community colleges grows in proportion to white community college enrollment. In their writing, they note that there is an observable gap between high- and low-income residents when it comes to ownership and access to information technology. Although there has been some gain in low-income access and use of information technology (Kleiner and Farris 2002), a significant difference persists. NCES notes that schools in impoverished areas had noticeably fewer classrooms connected to the Internet than did schools in higher-income districts, 79 percent compared to 90 percent. Similarly, there were fewer computers per student capita in impoverished schools than in more affluent schools (Kleiner and Farris 2002).

There are a number of ways community colleges can bridge the digital divide. As a baseline measure, they should assess the computer literacy of incoming students. Although many traditional-age students have been exposed to information technology, their fluency varies. Community colleges should also develop a strategic plan for deploying information technology and instructional technology. An important ingredient for assuring success is faculty commitment and belief in the need to bridge the digital divide. It is common to have members of an instructional staff who are neither familiar nor comfortable with technology, although the number of such instructors is diminishing. Similarly, to deploy information technology throughout an institution's administrative infrastructure—such as moving to Web-based registration and e-commerce—often requires a learning curve for constituents who are accustomed to paper-based transactions.

Another way community colleges bridge the technological divide is to offer industry certifications in information technology (IT) training. As discussed by Clifford Adelman (2000), there is a "parallel universe" of certifications that have arisen in the context of the information economy, a universe that constitutes another, albeit somewhat hidden and often unappreciated, domain of professional certification outside of traditional degree-granting institutions. What is important is that entry into IT often involves the attainment not of a specific degree but, rather, of certifications. Through programs such as the Cisco Systems' academic offerings and other certification programs—for example, those developed by Microsoft and Oracle—certifications can be attained in a variety of settings, such as proprietary schools and public, comprehensive community colleges. In essence, Adelman suggests that this rise in certifications constitutes an "information technology guild," which has largely escaped the attention of established higher education institutions.

The League for Innovation in the Community College is the premier national community college organization engendering a close connection between the IT industry and community colleges. Featuring many IT corporate sponsors, such as Microsoft, Gateway Computers, Hewlett-Packard (HP), and Cisco Systems, the League for Innovation in the Community College has taken an aggressive stance in making IT part and parcel of a community college's operation, constituting an operational dimension that should become ubiquitous as community colleges become increasingly savvy with respect to incorporating IT into all aspects of their daily operations.

## THE CITY UNIVERSITY OF NEW YORK:
## BALANCING ACCESS AND EQUITY

CUNY is the largest city-based public university system in the nation. Composed of nineteen colleges serving over 400,000 students annually, CUNY is also the oldest urban system of higher education, with roots extending back to 1847 with the creation of City College. New York City is one of the most ethnically diverse cities in the world, with perhaps the largest immigrant population. Approximately 38 percent of its current population is foreign-born, equaling the percent of foreign-born in New York City during 1910 (Moss, Townsend, and Tobier 1997). Its 2000 population of 8,008,278, as enumerated by the U.S. Bureau of the Census, was its highest in history and reflects the number of immigrants settling in the city.

Throughout its existence, CUNY has been at the center of what amounts to a morality play over what should be the mission of highly subsidized, and at one time free, higher education. In many ways it represents a parable of the tensions of equity versus excellence that have been played out in U.S. higher education during the past hundred years. Its history also represents the centrality of education for assimilation and acculturation into the structure of opportunity and advancement in the United States. However, it also illustrates the fact that the construction of any structure of opportunity is a highly politicized process that is not immune from larger political and sociohistorical tensions of a given epoch.

CUNY represents a laudable attempt to provide a free college education to populations who were disenfranchised from the then-existing channels for attaining a higher education. The call for an integrated system of higher education in New York came on the heels of World War II. Prior to World War II, the City College and other municipal colleges in New York City originally catered largely to European Jewish immigrants (Gorelick 1981). In the 1940s, the GI Bill and the changing demographics of New York City's population placed new demands on the city for expanded public higher education opportunities. Sandra Roff, Anthony Cucchiara, and Barbara Dunlop (2000) provide a good chronology of these changes, which included a relatively late embrace of community colleges.

Known as the "Harvard University for the poor," which in part reflected its competitive admissions practices, in 1970 CUNY adopted an unprecedented policy of open admissions, guaranteeing all high school graduates in New York admission into one of its colleges. With open admissions came a great expansion of developmental education—

something that also occurred at its four-year colleges, which some suggest led to the devaluing of a CUNY degree (Traub 1994)—and fiscal strain as the city suffered a financial crisis in the 1970s, best epitomized in the October 30, 1975, *New York Daily News* headline "Ford to City: Drop Dead."

One of the most detailed analyses of open admissions is that offered by David E. Lavin and David Hyllegard in *Changing the Odds: Open Admissions and the Life Chances of the Disadvantaged* (1996). Lavin and Hyllegard consider in depth CUNY's open admission experiment and how it fared. Its implementation began in September 1970 as a way of increasing access to higher education for the population of a city whose demographics were not reflected in CUNY's student body. At that time, even community colleges were selective, requiring an overall 75 average on a high school transcript. Also important, and problematic, was the need to orchestrate CUNY institutions with the changing economic structure of New York City and to a large extent of the nation at large: a decline in traditional manufacturing, an increase in service-sector employment, and so on.

An important aspect of open admissions was the guarantee that a student from New York would be accepted into some branch of the university and the guarantee that those who graduated from one of the community colleges would be admitted into a four-year branch. However, as Lavin and Hyllegard note (1996, 17), this grand experiment was doomed to be seen as a failure, even if it succeeded in opening access to higher education: "In the way [this] public debate was framed, CUNY had launched a no-win policy: if many of the new students graduated, standards had gone down the drain. If they flunked out, open admissions had failed because it could not eradicate the effects of severe disadvantages that students brought with them to college."

In evaluating the success of this experiment, Lavin and Hyllegard (1996, 200–201) note the difficulties involved in overcoming the myriad causes of "disadvantage," which range from labor market issues to social capital disadvantage. They find little support for allegations that open admissions diluted the academic quality of CUNY. They assert that some of the generational or cultural conflicts might have been masked as deficiencies in academic standards, but this was not the case (207). They conclude their work by noting that the city's fiscal crisis meant CUNY could no longer be a tuition-fee institution and resulted in the end of open admissions as originally conceived (209). In many ways, the ending of the CUNY open admissions experiment was part of the erosion of accessibility into higher education that occurred in the 1970s and 1980s. Also missing in analyses of open admissions by critics was the positive economic impact that it had, increasing wage earnings for groups who, without their newly received (and first-generational) college education, would not have been able to do as well as they did.

Thomas Bailey and Elliot Weininger (2002) state that the percent of foreign-born students in the system rose from just under 30 percent in 1990 to just over 40 percent by 1999. By 1997, 48 percent of those in the CUNY entering class were foreign-born, greater than the percentage of foreign-born students found in the 2000 census for New York City. This dramatic increase in the immigrant population entering CUNY constitutes the most pronounced finding, with foreign-born students equally distributed between two- and four-year colleges. Lavin and Hylleyard (1996) find that although open admissions did enhance the life chances of the working poor, it also served to segment the system into a hierarchy of four-year and community colleges.

At present, CUNY requires all students to complete its proficiency exam once they complete sixty credits. This was implemented in part in response to a highly critical report written by Benno Schmidt, in *The City University of New York: An Institution Adrift* (1999), and initiatives designed to bolster academic proficiency have been credited for the upsurge of CUNY.

## DEVELOPMENTAL EDUCATION

Practically all public community colleges offer some form of remedial education, and increasingly, community colleges have become the primary site for remedial education in higher education. There has been a growing trend toward segregating remedial education within two-year colleges and reducing the presence of remedial courses at baccalaureate institutions. NCES (1996, 11) reports that a "greater percentage of public 2 year than of other types of institutions indicated that remedial enrollments had increased; public and private 4-year institutions reported decreases in remedial enrollments more often than did 2-year institutions."

Those enrolled in remedial courses generally exhibit a successful outcome. NCES (1996, 13) reports: "About three-quarters of the students enrolled in remedial reading, writing or mathematics courses pass or successfully complete those courses. The percentage of students passing remedial reading and writing courses was lower in public 2-year than in other types of institutions, and for remedial mathematics it was lower in public 2-year and 4-year than in private 2-year and 4-year."

Increasingly, community colleges have become the primary site of remediation in higher education. This can be seen in the case of

CUNY after the period of open admissions. Whereas in 1972 both four-year institutions and community colleges offered developmental education, such courses have increasingly become the province of community colleges.

Similarly, many states are moving in the direction of isolating remediation within community colleges. Although to some people this fortifies the image of community colleges as dumping grounds for the educationally challenged, other observers suggest that community colleges can embrace this role in a creative work that spurs baccalaureate completion.

A number of developmental education strategies that researchers have identified as "best practices" can be distilled from studies (McCabe 2000; McCabe and Day 1998; Roueche and Roueche 1999; Workforce Strategy Center 2003). Most successful developmental education practices integrate developmental students with other learners rather than isolating them. Practices that range from peer mentoring, the formation of learning communities, and the ability to venture into credit-bearing classes while taking remedial courses are identified as being the most effective.

The Workforce Strategy Center (2003) suggests that basic skills are best taught within a meaningful context for the learner. It is also important to utilize an instructional staff who has expertise in developmental learning. Also the key is to provide students with a multitude of services that provide supplemental support, such as tutoring services.


## CONCLUSION

Measuring the efficacy of community colleges is a complex task. Students enter these institutions for disparate reasons. Of those students working for credit, some are interested in just taking a course or two whereas others wish to complete an associate's degree and then transfer to a baccalaureate institution. Other students enroll in an array of noncredit courses for reasons that range from a desire to attain certification in an information technology–related skill to simple recreational purposes.

Like other educational sectors, community colleges have been challenged by regional accreditation agencies to provide evidence of student learning and institutional effectiveness. The Community College Survey of Student Engagement (CCSSE) is one of the more promising assessments in that it offers a rubric of measures that predict the efficacy of pedagogical strategies and cocurricular offerings.

CUNY's experience with the trials and tribulations of open admissions provides an interesting case study of the nuances involved in adopting such a policy. And the controversy that ensues over whether this has been a successful or failed strategy perhaps reflects the irreconcilable tension between access and excellence.

### References

Adelman, Clifford. 2000. "A Parallel Universe." *Change* 32, no. 3 (May/June).

Alfred, Richard L., Peter Ewell, James Hudgins, and Kay McClenney. 1999. *Core Indicators of Effectiveness for Community Colleges: Toward High Performance*. 2nd ed. Washington, DC: Community College Press.

Alverno College. N.d. "Alverno's Eight Abilities." http://www.alverno.edu/about_alverno/ability.html (accessed November 7, 2004).

American Association of Community Colleges (AACC). 2004. "Position on Reauthorization of the Higher Education Act." http://www.aacc.nch.edu (accessed January 1, 2005).

American Association of Higher Education. N.d. http://www.aahe.org/assessment/principl.htm (accessed December 23, 2004).

American Educational Research Association. 2000. "AERA Position Statements. High Stakes Testing in Pre K–12 Education." http://www.aera.net/policyandprograms/ (accessed January 4, 2005).

Astin, Alexander, Trudy W. Banta, K. Patricia Cross, Elaine El Khawas, Peter T. Ewell, Pat Hutchings, Theodore J. Marchese, et al. "Principles of Good Practice for Assessing Student Learning." http://www.aahe.org/assessment/principl.htm (accessed March 22, 2004).

Bailey, Thomas, and Elliot Weininger. 2002. *Performance, Graduation, and Transfer of Immigrants and Natives in City University of New York Community Colleges*. New York: Community College Research Center, Teachers College, Columbia University.

Ballantine, Jeanne. 2002. "Open Systems Approach." In *Education and Sociology: An Encyclopedia*, ed. David L. Levinson, Peter W. Cookson Jr., and Alan R. Sadovnik. New York: RoutledgeFalmer.

Banta, Trudy W. 2002. "Student Competence as the Basis for Designing Curricula, Instruction, and Assessment." *Assessment Update* 14, no. 1 (January/February).

Berliner, David C., and Bruce Biddle. 1995. *The Manufactured Crisis: Myths, Fraud, and the Attack on America's Public Schools*. Boulder, CO: Perseus.

Boli, John. 1989. *New Citizens for a New Society: The Institutional Origins of Mass Schooling in Sweden*. New York: Pergamon.

Bourne, John, and Janet C. Moore. 2003. *Elements of Quality Online Education: Practice and Direction*. Needham, MA: Sloan Center for Online Education at Olin and Babson Colleges.

Bradburn, Ellen. 2002. *Short-Term Enrollment in Postsecondary Education: Student Background and Institutional Differences in Reasons for Early Departure, 1996–98.* Washington, DC: National Center for Educational Statistics.

Bradburn, Ellen M., and David G. Hurst. 2001. *Community College Transfer Rates to 4-year Institutions Using Alternate Definitions of Transfer.* NCES 2001–197. Project Officer: Samuel Peng. Washington, DC: U.S. Department of Education, National Center for Education Statistics.

Chickering, Arthur W., and Zelda F. Gamson. 1991. "Applying the Seven Principles for Good Practice in Undergraduate Education." In *New Directions for Teaching and Learning,* ed. Arthur W. Chickering and Zelda F. Gamson. San Francisco: Jossey-Bass.

Chubb, John E., and Terry M. Moe. 1990. *Politics, Markets, and America's Schools.* Washington, DC: Brookings Institution.

Cohen, A. M., and J. R. Sanchez. 1997. *The Transfer Rate: A Model of Consistency.* ERIC ED409952. Los Angeles: Center for the Study of Community Colleges.

Cole, Jonathan R. 2003. "The Patriot Act on Campus: Defending the University Post 9–11." *Boston Review,* Summer.

Community College Survey of Student Engagement (CCSSE). 2003. *Engaging Community Colleges: National Benchmarks of Quality.* Austin: Community College Leadership Program, University of Texas.

Crouse, James, and Dale Trusheim. 1988. *The Case against the SAT.* Chicago: University of Chicago Press.

Datnow, Amanda, and Robert Cooper. 2002. "Tracking." In *Education and Sociology: An Encyclopedia,* ed. David L. Levinson, Peter W. Cookson Jr., and Alan R. Sadovnik. New York: RoutledgeFalmer.

de los Santos, Gerardo E., Alfredo G. de los Santos Jr., and Mark David Milliron, eds. 2003. *Digital Divide to Digital Democracy.* Tempe, AZ: League for Innovation in the Community College.

Dlugos, Peter. 2003. "Using Critical Thinking to Assess the Ineffable." *Community College Journal of Research and Practice* 27, no. 7 (August).

Dougherty, Kevin J. 1994. *The Contradictory College: The Conflicting Origins, Impacts, and Futures of the Community College.* Albany: State University of New York Press.

Eaton, Judith S. 1994. *Strengthening Collegiate Education in Community Colleges.* San Francisco: Jossey-Bass.

Edison Schools. 2004. "Edison Schools to Serve More than 250,000 students in 2004–2005." *Edison Schools News.* http://www.edisonschools.com.news (accessed December 30, 2004).

Education Law Center. 1990. *Abbott v. Burke II.* Newark, NJ. http://www.edlawcenter.org (accessed December 30, 2004).

Elmore, Richard. 2003. "Change and Improvement in Educational Reform." In *A Nation Reformed? American Education 20 Years after a Nation at Risk,* ed. David Gordon and David T. Gordon. Cambridge, MA: Harvard University Press.

Florida, Richard. 2002. *The Rise of the Creative Class and How It's Transforming Work, Leisure, Community, and Everyday Life.* New York: Basic Books.

Frankenberg, Erica, Chungmei Lee, and Gary Orfield. 2003. *A Multiracial Society with Segregated Schools: Are We Losing the Dream?"* Cambridge, MA: Civil Rights Project, Harvard University.

Gardner, Howard E. 1993. *Multiple Intelligences: The Theory and Practice.* New York: Basic Books.

Gorelick, Sherry. 1981. *City College and the Jewish Poor: Education in New York, 1880–1924.* New Brunswick, NJ: Rutgers University Press.

Grubb, W. Norton, Helena Worthen, Barbara Byrd, Elnora Webb, Norena Badway, Chester Case, Stanford Goto, and Jennifer Curry Villeneuve. 1999. *Honored but Invisible: An Inside Look at Teaching in Community Colleges.* New York: Routledge.

Habermas, Jürgen. 1975. *Legitimation Crisis.* Boston: Beacon Press.

Hanushek, Eric A. 2002. "Evidence, Politics, and the Class Size Debate." In *The Class Size Debate,* ed. Lawrence Mishel and Richard Rothstein. Washington, DC: Economic Policy Institute.

Hatch, Thomas. 2003. "The 'Long Haul' or 'Boom or Bust': Gauging the Future of Reform in Turbulent Times." *Education Week* 23, no. 2: 32, 35.

Hoachlander, Gary, Ana C. Sikora, and Laura Horn. 2003. *Community College Students: Goals, Academic Preparation, and Outcomes.* NCES 2003–164. Project Officer: C. Dennis Carroll. Washington, DC: U.S. Department of Education, National Center for Education Statistics.

Hoffer, Tom. 2002. "Meritocracy." In *Education and Sociology: An Encyclopedia,* ed. David L. Levinson, Peter W. Cookson Jr., and Alan R. Sadovnik. New York: RoutledgeFalmer.

Horn, Laura, Christine Chang Wei, and Al Baker. 2002. *What Students Pay for College: Changes in the Net Price of College Between 1992–1993 and 1999–2000.* NCES 2002–174. Project Officer: Dennis Carroll. Washington, DC: U.S. Department of Education, National Center for Education Statistics.

International Education Services. 2004. "Maricopa Community Colleges." http://www.maricopa.edu/international (accessed January 5, 2005).

Kipp, Samuel M. III, Derek V. Price, and Jill K. Wohlford. 2002. *Unequal Opportunity: Disparities in College Access among the 50 States.* Indianapolis, IN: Lumina Foundation for Education.

Kleiner, Anne, and Elizabeth Farris. 2002. *Internet Access in U.S. Public Schools and Classrooms: 1994–2001.* NCES 2002–018. Project Officer: Bernard

Greene. Washington, DC: U.S. Department of Education, National Center for Education Statistics.

Lavin, David E., and David Hyllegard. 1996. *Changing the Odds: Open Admissions and the Life Chances of the Disadvantaged.* New Haven, CT: Yale University Press.

Lee, Valerie E., and David T. Burkham. 2002. *Inequality from the Starting Gate: Social Background Differences in Achievement as Children Begin School.* Washington, DC: Economic Policy Institute.

Lewis, Michael. 1993. *The Culture of Inequality.* 2nd ed. Amherst, MA: University of Massachusetts Press.

McCabe, Robert H. 2000. *No One to Waste: A Report to Public Decision-Makers and Community College Leaders.* Washington, DC: Community College Press.

McCabe, Robert, and Phillip R. Day Jr. 1998. *Developmental Education: A 21st Century Social and Economic Imperative.* Mission Viejo, CA: League for Innovation in the Community College.

McClenney, Kay. 2003. "Engaging Community Colleges: A First Look." *Community College Survey of Student Engagement (CCSSE) Highlights* 2, no. 7 (May).

Medina, Noe, and Monty Neill. 1990. *Fallout from the Testing Explosion: How 100 Million Standardized Exams Undermine Equity and Excellence in America's Public Schools.* Cambridge, MA: Fairtest.

Messerli, Jonathan. 1972. *Horace Mann: A Biography.* New York: Knopf.

Middle States Commission on Higher Education. 2002. *Characteristics of Excellence in Higher Education: Eligibility Requirements and Standards for Accreditation.* Philadelphia: Middle States Commission on Higher Education.

Mills, C. Wright. 1960. *The Sociological Imagination.* Oxford: Oxford University Press.

Moss, Mitchell, Anthony Townsend, and Emmanuel Tobier. 1997. *Immigration Is Transforming New York City.* New York: New York University, Taub Urban Research Center.

National Association of State Student Grant and Aid Programs (NASSGSP). 2004. *Thirty-Fourth Annual Survey Report on State-Sponsored Student Financial Aid.* http://www.nassgap.org (accessed January 1, 2005).

National Center for Education Statistics (NCES). 1996. *Remedial Education at Higher Education Institutions in Fall 1995.* Washington, DC: U.S. Department of Education, October.

National Commission on Excellence in Education. 1983. *A Nation at Risk.* Washington, DC: U.S. Department of Education.

National Education Association. 2002. *Elementary Secondary Education Act: A Toolkit.* Washington, DC: National Education Association.

Oakes, Jeannie. 1985. *Keeping Track: How Schools Structure Inequality.* New Haven, CT: Yale University Press.

O'Banion, Terry. 1997. *Creating More Learning Center Community Colleges.* Tempe, AZ: League for Innovation in the Community College.

Organization for Economic Co-operation and Development (OECD). 2004. *Learning for Tomorrow's World: First Results from PISA 2003.* Paris: OECD.

Outcalt, Charles. 1999. *Community College Honors Programs.* Los Angeles: ERIC Clearinghouse for Community Colleges, University of California at Los Angeles.

Parsad, Basmat, and Laurie Lewis. 2003. *Remedial Education at Degree-Granting Postsecondary Institutions in Fall 2000.* NCES 2004-010. Project Officer: Bernard Greene. Washington, DC: U.S. Department of Education, National Center for Education Statistics.

Ratcliff, James, ed. *Community Colleges.* 3rd ed. ASHE Reader Series. Lexington, MA: Ginn Press.

Reich, Robert B. 1991. *The Work of Nations: Preparing Ourselves for 21st-Century Capitalism.* New York: Knopf.

Roff, Sandra Shoiock, Anthony M. Cucchiara, and Barbara J. Dunlap. 2000. *From the Free Academy to CUNY: Illustrating Public Higher Education in New York City, 1847–1997.* New York: Fordham University Press.

Roueche, John E., and Suanne D. Roueche. 1999. *High Stakes, High Performance: Making Remedial Education Work.* Washington, DC: Community College Press.

Ryan, William P. 1976. *Blaming the Victim.* New York: Vintage Books.

Sadovnik, Alan R., Peter W. Cookson Jr., Susan F. Semel, and David L. Levinson. 2002. "Educational Reform in the United States: 1980s and 1990s." In *Education and Sociology: An Encyclopedia*, ed. David L. Levinson, Peter W. Cookson Jr., and Alan R. Sadovnik. New York: RoutledgeFalmer.

Schmidt, Benno. 1999. *The City University of New York: An Institution Adrift.* New York: Mayor's Task Force on the City University of New York.

Schneider, Barbara. 2002. "Social Capital: A Ubiquitous Emerging Conception." In *Education and Sociology: An Encyclopedia*, ed. David L. Levinson, Peter W. Cookson Jr., and Alan R. Sadovnik. New York: RoutledgeFalmer.

Seybert, Jeffrey A. 2002. "Assessing Student Learning Outcomes." *New Directions for Community Colleges* no. 117 (Spring).

Steinberg, Jacques. 2002. *The Gatekeepers: Inside the Admissions Process of a Premier College.* New York: Viking Penguin.

Sullivan, Linda. 2001. "Five Models of Integrated Learning Communities." http://www.mcli.dist.maricopa.edu (accessed January 2, 2005).

Traub, James. 1994. *City on a Hill: Testing the American Dream at City College.* Boston: Addison-Wesley.

Tyack, David B., and Larry Cuban. 1995. *Tinkering toward Utopia: A Century of Public School Reform.* Cambridge, MA: Harvard University Press.

University of Phoenix. N.d. "FlexNet® Internet Classes." http://info.university-ofphoenixcampuses.com/online.jsp (accessed November 8, 2004).

U.S. Bureau of the Census. 2003. *Net Worth and Asset Ownership of Households: 1998 and 2000.* Current Population Reports, P70–88, by Shawna Orzechowski and Peter Sepielli. Washington, DC: Government Printing Office.

U.S. Department of Education. 2001. "Overview: Introduction: No Child Left Behind." http://www.ed.gov/nclb/overview/intro/ (accessed November 4, 2004).

———. 2003. *The Conduction of Education 2003.* National Center for Education Statistics, 2003-067. Washington, DC: Government Printing Office.

Waits, Tiffany, and Laurie Lewis. 2003. *Distance Education at Degree-Granting Postsecondary Institutions: 2000–2001.* NCES 2003–17. Project Officer: Bernard Greene. Washington, DC: U.S. Department of Education, National Center for Education Statistics.

Winter, Greg. 2002. "Junior Colleges Try Niche as Cheap Path to Top Universities." *New York Times,* December 15.

Workforce Strategy Center. 2003. *Building Bridges to College and Careers: Contextualized Basic Skills Programs at Community Colleges.* Brooklyn, NY: Workforce Strategy Center.

Young, Michael. 1958. *The Rise of the Meritocracy, 1870–2033: An Essay on Education and Equality.* London: Thames and Hudson.

*Chapter Four*

# ⏎ The Curriculum: Transfer versus Career

## THE HISTORIC CURRICULUM DIVIDE

The term "curriculum" refers to a particular course of study. Typically within higher education a student's specific curriculum—or major and minor fields of study—includes an array of general education courses and specialized, occupationally related courses that are germane to a particular field. By accruing a specific number of credits, usually 60 to 65 for an associate's degree and 120 to 128 for a baccalaureate degree, a student receives a diploma, assuming that he or she has maintained at least a 2.0, or C, cumulative average.

Considerations about curriculum are inextricable from discussions concerning the mission of community colleges. The comprehensive community colleges' mission is all-encompassing: They seek to serve all local constituents. Given the multiplicity of interests and concerns of the population in a given locale, community colleges are, at times, caught in the intersection between conflicting public-sector and private-sector needs. They are continuously engaged in an "environmental scan" to ascertain workforce needs. This is done in consort with program advisory boards that are made up of representatives from business and industry, program faculty, and representatives of state, county, or local government.

Within the public sector, community colleges attempt to address the employment needs of residents by participating on Workforce Investment Boards and social service agencies, along with a wide range of civic associations. Similarly, community colleges are involved with various commerce and industry associations, local employers, and other business interests. Typically, members of a community college's board of trustees are drawn from a wide range of public and private entities, although this will vary depending on whether trustees are elected or appointed.

Historically there has been a great divide in the United States between academic and vocational programs. Academic programs have been oriented toward the traditional student who is ultimately interested in attaining a college degree. Vocational programs provided vocationally-oriented students with a skills-based curriculum devoid of extensive liberal arts courses.

The roots of this bifurcation are quite complex. In part it is due to the initial structure of mass education, which was developed in response to the rapid industrialization of U.S. society in the nineteenth century. The dramatic population boom experienced during this time, along with the rise of manufacturing, placed a number of pressing demands on the New Republic (Katz 1968). The response on the part of the state was to bureaucratize and standardized public education. As stated in Chapter 2, this was done in part to acculturate and assimilate the large numbers of immigrants arriving in the United States, for one of the consequences of immigration at that time was the creation of an industrial workforce. Underlying these changes was the embedding of a socioeconomic structure in which decisions affecting "the masses," especially when it came to education, were promulgated by an elite, as in the case of the abolition of Beverly High School that Michael Katz describes in his book. Katz (1968) argues that laborers at that time resisted the imposition of compulsory public schooling, which he asserts was empirically reflected in the low level of support and ultimate abolition of public high school in Beverly, Massachusetts.

During the Industrial Revolution higher education in the United States took a decidedly pragmatic bent. Unlike higher education in western Europe during that time, which had a classical focus, U.S. higher education exhibited an applied orientation. As Christopher Lucas (1994, 105) notes, the purpose of higher education during colonial times was "educating civic leaders and preparing a learned clergy." He continues (1994, 109):

> The course of study offered by the typical colonial college very much reflected the earliest settlers' resolve to effect a *translation studii*—a direct transfer of higher learning from ancient seats of learning at Queen's College in Oxford and Emmanuel College at Cambridge to the frontier outposts of the American wilderness. The curriculum basically was a combination of medieval learning, devotional studies judged conducive to the preservation of confessional religious piety, and late Renaissance arts and literature.

During this time an explicit connection was made between education and economic development. As depicted by Horace Mann, education played a central role in the development of a productive nascent economy. This utilitarian approach to education was later embodied within the Morrill Acts of 1862 and 1890, which, as discussed in Chapter 2, provided a federalized nationwide system of land grants for the founding of colleges that promoted the applied sciences.

With respect to higher education, this applied focus stood in contradistinction to the classical university model, which was characterized by a "great books" approach to higher education, that is, a tendency to examine the written works of earlier periods in a contemplative, introspective fashion. From 1869 to 1909, under the leadership of Charles W. Eliot, Harvard University underwent a period of dramatic change as its curriculum was transformed from having a classical focus to having an applied one, in part through the introduction of graduate education (Freeland 1992). In fact, it was the movement away from a fixation on the undergraduate curriculum that characterized Harvard's turn toward preparing students for emerging professions.

Although recognizing the importance of the classics, especially in producing a cultivated mind, Eliot was also sanguine about the advances in scientific knowledge that were occurring during that time. He said: "We must extend our training of the imagination beyond literature and the fine arts to history, philosophy, science, government and sociology. We must recognize the prodigious variety of fruits of the imagination that the last century has given to our race" (quoted in Cremin 1988, 385).

Similarly, Richard Freeland (1992, 26) notes:

> Academic change in the age of the university was a multifaceted phenomenon, but two developments stood out: the heightened attention to practical concerns and the expanded importance of graduate instruction and scientific research. The theme of "utility," so expressive of late nineteenth-century preoccupations with industrial growth and social mobility, had been present, of course, long before the Civil War in the technical institutes like Rensselaer, in some of the state universities, and even in traditional offerings in law, medicine and theology. With the Morrill Act of 1862 and the wave of state universities and land-grant colleges that flowed from it, however, industrial and agricultural programs moved to center stage.

This tension between the classical and the applied, between liberal arts study and professional preparation, is an overarching theme that has influenced the development of higher education. Graduate institutions in the early twentieth century were reflective of advanced, specialized study—something that was seized upon during both world wars, when university-military collaborations became the foundation for future domestic economic growth through transfer of militaristic applications to domestic uses.

This endeavor fueled laboratories such as MIT's Lincoln Laboratories in the mid-twentieth century and is still supporting centers of advanced research, in such fields as photonics and biotechnology. Community colleges were left to address what basically became low-level occupational needs. Although there have been some recent efforts to create course work in community colleges to meet high-level scientific needs—such as the Advanced Technology Education program of the National Science Foundation (NSF) (Bailey et al. 2003)—the tendency has been to restrict community colleges to entry-level work. Given this historical trend, creating career pathways that would truly promote an upwardly mobile route for employees became a challenge. This bifurcated structure of training and education is in part an aspect of the "cooling-out" function of community colleges as identified by Burton Clark in 1960.

Community colleges have traditionally divided their credit-bearing instructional offerings into transfer programs and career programs. Transfer programs, which typically feature a relatively high number of general education requirements, are designed to enable a student to transfer easily to a four-year institution. Career programs, however, have traditionally been viewed as providing direct entry into a specific occupation and typically offer only a modicum of general education courses.

However, given that on average Americans change employers every three and a half years and change careers on average three times during a working lifetime, and given the cognitive requirements for employment in the "new economy," gearing education for a terminal occupational experience makes little sense. Importantly, the challenge remains of how to structure educational experiences that will allow students to get a solid foundation of transferable cognitive skills for a range of occupations while attaining some of the specific knowledge base required for immediate employment.

The relationship between school and work in the United States has been historically problematic for a number of reasons. The localized structure of educational policy found in the United States, for example, precludes a strict, centralized ministerial control of curriculum. Moreover, albeit to the chagrin of many, there is relatively little centralized workforce policy planning, which is in part due to the primacy of private market relationships over state planning. Although at times various business and entrepreneurial associations—such as the Business Roundtable and other regional or local associations—have banded together, there remains great resistance to any semblance of centralized planning due in part to the fear that it would be a form of "creeping socialism."

Unlike other advanced industrial nations, the United States does not rigidly determine, through a series of examinations or other assessments, the educational and career pathways of children. Although there is certainly a selection and sorting process at work in primary and secondary education, this process does not parallel the strict and distinct determinacy that operates in other nation-states. Community colleges provide a "second chance" for students who may not have succeeded in their first attempt at college, and they also serve those who wish to change careers or seek a college degree later in life.

Although the curriculum of community colleges has been typically bifurcated between career and transfer programs, many observers assert that the cognitive needs of the knowledge industry require a workforce whose competencies embody attributes that are associated with a college-oriented curriculum. However, there are also those who suggest that the high skill needs of the knowledge economy have been oversold and exaggerated, constituting what some have termed the "great training robbery" (Berg 1970; Livingstone 1998). The complexities of these issues will be discussed in this chapter, and the community college's changing role in these debates will be examined.

Apart from nation-states whose educational systems are more restrictive and pronounced in their linkage of schooling to occupational attainment, the United States maintains a degree of separation between educational opportunities and occupational realities. Although other nations engage in fairly rigid occupational segmentation via restrictive educational opportunities from an early age, the United States is thought to be unrestricted, thereby allowing for the achievement of upward social mobility.

## RESPONDING TO WORKFORCE NEEDS

During the twentieth century there were dramatic changes in the U.S. occupational structure as the nation was transformed from an agrarian to an industrial and then to a service-based society. Similarly, significant technological developments accompanied the expansion of the interdependent global economies of the G-7 nation-states.

Although it is beyond the scope of this work to detail all that was involved in these changes, it is important to note some of its salient aspects. At the start of the millennium, the United States was largely an agrarian society, and what production there was, was manufacturing based. By the end of the twentieth century, the economy was primarily service based, with a strong technological component. Richard Florida (2002) characterizes the salient aspect of the changing occupational structure in the late twentieth century as the rise of the creative class.

Compared to other advanced nations, the United States has an underdeveloped system of vocational education. As James Rosenbaum (2001, 1) reports, the National Educational Longitudinal Survey (NELS 1992), undertaken by the NCES, shows that 95 percent of all high school seniors aspire to attend college. Similarly, Barbara Schneider and David Stevenson (1999) find that although the overwhelming majority of high school students are highly ambitious and desire to attend college, there is a paucity of linkages to channel these desires in an advantageous direction.

Despite these desires, approximately two-thirds of high school graduates do not complete a baccalaureate degree, and about 25 percent seek employment immediately upon graduating from high school. "Nearly half of all high school students and approximately one-third of college students are involved in vocational programs. . . . Perhaps as many as 40 million adults—one in four—engage in short-term, postsecondary occupational training" (Horn, Peter, and Rooney 2002).

The United States lacks an effective mechanism for coordinating aspirations, ambitions, and opportunities. Career advice, and advice about the pathways a student should take in order to prepare for a given profession, often emanates from parents and school counselors. Unfortunately, their knowledge of changing labor market conditions is often poor, largely because of the rapid sequence of developments in the occupational world and because there is little cogent analysis that captures these trends.

### Vocational Education

It was through the growth of proprietary schools that vocational education took off from the 1890s to the 1920s. Joseph Kett (1996, 256) states:

> The bulk of organized vocational education in the United States was conducted in proprietary schools, which mainly targeted employed adults. Proprietary schools, especially those specializing in correspondence instruction, pioneered simplified methods of mass vocational training and attracted clients in astounding numbers. Their success depended not only on their advertising and marketing proficiency but also on the public's increasing association of specialized skills with

middle-class status and on the close ties between leading correspondence schools and corporations.

Apprenticeship programs, often offered in conjunction with trade unions, have been another source of vocational education. There have been a number of such apprenticeship programs, such as those offered by District 1199 Service Employees International Union (SEIU) and the International Brotherhood of Electrical Workers (IBEW). The AFL-CIO has organized a program called Union Summer in which undergraduates experience union organizing in the form of a service-learning project. Since it was launched in 1996, over 3,000 activists have graduated from this program, in which their participation enabled them to develop skills that are important for union organizing (AFL-CIO 2004). In New Jersey, there is presently an effort to develop a statewide model for apprenticeship training that will allow students to accrue college credits in the process of learning a particular trade.

Episodically in the United States, there have been national level efforts designed to forge a tighter fit between higher education and vocational training, beginning with passage of the Smith-Hughes Act in 1917, continuing through passage of the Carl D. Perkins Vocational and Technical Education Act, initially passed in 1990, and extending through a number of revisions to that act, most recently "Perkins III," which was passed in October 1998 (Horn, Peter, and Rooney 2002).

One of the most notable ways community colleges have attempted to create a seamless transfer of students from high schools to community colleges to the workforce has been through "tech prep." As part of the Carl Perkins Vocational and Applied Technology Act Amendments of 1990—known as Perkins II (Orr and Bragg 2002)—federal funds were provided for colleges to establish "2 + 2" agreements. Under this rubric, courses that students take in high school are articulated for college credit. Typically these are found in career-oriented tracks. This legislation was passed in response to a concern that high school graduates lacked the technical sophistication required for employment in an increasingly technologically intensive workplace and global interdependent and competitive economic environment. As Alan Hershey et al. (1998, xiv–xv) state, early proponents such as Dale Parnell (1985; 1992) viewed tech prep as a bona fide alternative to "traditional college prep and general education tracks." They go on to say:

> They [early proponents] envisioned Tech-Prep as a structured, planned program of study that would combine academic and vocational courses

and link high school studies to advanced technical education in community colleges, technical colleges, apprenticeship programs, or other postsecondary institutions. Students would consciously choose Tech-Prep, committing themselves to a program with a broadly defined career focus running through the latter years of high school and two years of more specialized postsecondary education. Tech-Prep programs would include applied academic instruction—teaching academic materials in a practical, hands-on way—and the development of clearly defined technical and academic competencies. Instead of watering down or neglecting academic content, schools were to find effective ways to teach students who learn best through tangible experience.

In an earlier work on tech prep programs, Debra Bragg (2001) found that there are few demographic differentials, other than gender (attributable to male-dominated technical fields), when tech prep students are compared to a general population of high school students. She also states (2002, 3–4), when comparing the tech prep students with the general population of high school students, that:

> the proportion of students in each group that went on to college at the two-year and four-year college levels is astounding. Indeed, the percentage of students attending college at the two-year level was quite high, with over 80% of the tech prep-participants in six consortia and close to that percentage or higher among the non-participant group in five consortia. Tech prep-participants showed a slight preference for attending two-year colleges over their non-participant peers but, again, this is not surprising given the focus of articulated course-taking that emphasizes sequenced course work extending from high school to community colleges. What seems more interesting is the frequency with which tech prep-participants attended both two-year and four-year colleges and four-year only. For all students, however, there was a substantial need to enroll in remedial courses and the relatively low graduation rate among students was a concern.

Furthermore, she reports,

> to date, completion of a college degree (AA, AS, or AAS) or certificate has not been a common occurrence for students in any consortium, regardless of tech-prep status. The median percentage of students earning some credential was only 10.5%, three or four years after high school graduation. Indeed, most consortia reported a modest range of completers at 8.5% to 11.7%.

Over 1,000 local consortia arose to implement tech prep agreements that involved 70 percent of all school districts nationwide and 90 percent of all American high schools (Hershey et al. 1998). As discussed, the Perkins Acts fostered a tighter connection between the last two years of high school and first two years of college. The hope was that students could explore career pathways in high school and concurrently earn college credit that would be articulated with a higher education institution. Community colleges have been the primary higher education providers as part of tech prep. Community colleges were the largest recipient of tech prep funds, receiving about 70 percent of such moneys.

However, federal appropriations for vocational education have not kept pace with other spending priorities. States the U.S. Department of Education (Horn, Peter, and Rooney 2002, 2): "For the past 20 years Perkins has represented a declining share of federal education budgets, but it is still the largest single source of Department funds spent on high schools. . . . In fiscal year 1980, funding for vocational education represented about 6 percent of total ED appropriations; it is now less than 3 percent."

Although Perkins III recognizes that vocational skills extend beyond what had been so narrowly defined and although there is explicit statutory recognition that it is also important to improve academic skills, the states are left to determine which aspects of Perkins (high school completion, postsecondary attainment, and so on) they wish to emphasize. As the U.S. Department of Education (Horn, Peter, and Rooney 2002) observes, this is quite different from the heavily prescriptive measures contained in the No Child Left Behind Act.

### Determining Career Trajectories

Schools play a primary role in selecting and sorting students for the multitude of occupational roles present in a given society. Sociologists of education have demonstrated that tracking clearly exists, with some believing that placement in tracks is based upon a meritorious assessment of students' ability. The likelihood of attending college is based on how students are tracked in high school.

In reviewing existing research on tracking, Amanda Datnow and Robert Cooper (2002, 689) find that "as a result of curriculum differentiation, at the end of high school, high-track students are prepared to attend college, whereas low-track students face much more limited options. Students enrolled in vocational courses seldom acquire the job skills necessary for success in the workplace." They conclude that "tracking serves as the major vehicle to sort and institutionalize the division between the 'haves' and 'have-nots,' resulting in racially identifiable groups of students, with African American, Latino, and low-income students receiving an unequal distribution of educational access and opportunity" (690).

Community colleges are in an awkward position in this scenario. They have little prestige or status in the strata of higher education institutions. Community colleges never appear in *U.S. World and News Reports* college rankings. Nor are they typically viewed as viable options by high school guidance counselors, who shuttle their advisees to higher-status institutions. In fact, ironically, it is community colleges' openness and absence of restrictiveness that relegates them to a low position in the status hierarchy. Although they represent the sine qua non of democracy, community colleges are at times vilified for not being selective.

The rise of the comprehensive high school in the United States embodies a tension similar to that discussed in Chapter 3 affecting the mission of community colleges: the conflict between meritocratic and egalitarian conceptions of schooling (Labaree 1988). According to Labaree's analysis of the founding of Central High in Philadelphia, the resultant structure represented a victory for those who advocated a differentiated curriculum based upon student performance on achievement tests. Expectations about the results of such tests tended to be "self-fulfilling," and those from lower social classes were often relegated to the vocationally oriented track.

Ira Katznelson and Margaret Weir (1985) make a similar point. Jeannie Oakes (1985) finds that tracking is an endemic part of the social organization of schools, reproducing inequality that had been legitimated as being meritocratically based by internal organizational processes. Others have gone so far as to say that such segmentation processes have been implemented to purposely involve mechanisms of social control.

## COMMUNITY COLLEGE CURRICULA

### *General Education*

An important component of education in community colleges—and for that matter, the base of whatever is defined as "higher education"—is "general education." General education refers to the foundation, sometimes referred to as the "core knowledge" a student should learn. A number of ways have been devised to deliver this knowledge base, ranging from the competency-based curriculum at Alverno College and to a stringently prescribed sequence of courses at an institution such as DeVry University. The articulation of what constitutes an appropriate "general education" varies widely among higher educational institutions.

General education in the community college differs depending on the vision and mission of an institution. Cascadia Community College in Bothell, Washington, requires fulfillment of very specific distributed area learning outcomes in communication, quantitative reasoning, technology, cultural competence, humanities, social sciences, and natural sciences prior to graduation (http://www.cascadia. ct.edu). At LaGuardia  Community College in Long Island City, Queens, all students are required to engage in a cooperative education program as part of their degree program (http://www.lagcc.cuny. edu).

As previously stated, the curriculum at community colleges has traditionally been bifurcated in that transfer degree programs (leading to associate of arts and associate of science degrees) and career programs (leading to associate of applied science degrees) have been distinct. Transfer programs are often articulated with baccalaureate institutions so that they provide ready continuation of study, and they typically contain a higher quotient of general education courses than do AAS degree programs. Transfer and articulation still remain formidable challenges in many states. Although in some locations moving to a baccalaureate institution is truly a seamless experience, with two-year and baccalaureate institutions using common numeric and nomenclature designations for courses, in other states it is a bumpier process. To some extent this has to do with whether or not there is a centralized, regulatory agency in place, one that coordinates all sectors of higher education within a state. The state of New Jersey is an interesting case in point. With the demise of the State Department of Education, a looser commission structure has taken hold, resulting in considerable autonomy on the part of baccalaureate institutions. Borrowing from an articulation model implemented in the state of Maryland, New Jersey has engaged in an effort called New Jersey Transfer, which provides a Web-based system for seeing how courses from a specific community college equate to those in a particular transfer institution (NJ Transfer n.d.).

### *Cross-Functional Skills*

When business leaders speak about skills that are necessary for the twenty-first-century workforce, they usually discuss cross-functional and soft skills. Cross-functional skills refer to the realm of reading, writing, and critical thinking; soft skills relate to interpersonal communication. Although technical prowess is required in many occupations, many observers proclaim that the content of a "classic liberal arts" education is also essential. In a 1999 report, "Spanning the Chasm: A Blueprint for Action," the Business–Higher Education Forum states that "America's competitive edge in the 21st century global economy will greatly depend on a healthy spirit of collaboration between business and higher education as colleges and universities prepare graduates to take their place in the nation's workforce" (Business–Higher Education Forum 1999, 1). The report recommends that institutions

- ➨ gear the core curriculum toward helping students develop flexible and cross-functional skills, including leadership, teamwork, problem solving, time management, communication, and analytical thinking;
- ➨ integrate into the core curriculum methods of helping students acquire personal traits such as a positive work ethic, adaptability, self-management, global consciousness, and a passion for life-long learning.

Similarly, in the 1990s the Secretary's Commission on Achieving Necessary Skills (SCANS) reported on the skills needed for successful employment in the current labor market and on how "curriculum and instruction" can procure these competencies. The report identifies three types of foundational competencies (SCANS 1991):

- ➨ *Basic skills:* Reads, writes, performs mathematical operations and computation, listens effectively, and communicates well.
- ➨ *Thinking skills:* Thinks creatively and abstractly, is able to make decisions and solve problems, visualizes, uses reasoning, and knows how to learn.
- ➨ *Personal qualities:* Demonstrates responsibility, self-esteem, sociability, self-management, integrity, and honesty and has developed an ethical and moral code.

The report then recognizes the importance of workplace competencies in five areas—resources, interpersonal, information, systems, and technology—which it describes as follows (SCANS 1991):

- *Resources:* Identifies, organizes, plans, and allocates resources within the areas of time, money, material and facilities, and human resources.
- *Interpersonal:* Works with others as a member of a team, contributes to the group effort, teaches new skills, works harmoniously with customers and clients, exercises leadership, negotiates toward agreements, and works well with individuals from diverse backgrounds and cultures.
- *Information:* Acquires and uses information while evaluating, organizing, interpreting, and communicating; uses computers to process this information.
- *Systems:* Understands complex interrelationships, including social, organizational, and technological systems; monitors and corrects performance of systems operations; suggests modifications to existing systems and designs more effective systems that improve performance.
- *Technology:* Is knowledgeable about a variety of technologies and is able to choose appropriate procedures, tools, or equipment; is able to set up and operate equipment, maintains and troubleshoots equipment.

These foundational and workplace competencies parallel the twenty-first-century learning skills that have been articulated by the League for Innovation in the Community College's Twenty-First Century Learning Skills project (League for Innovation in the Community College n.d.) incorporating the competencies as articulated by the SCANS report. They are communication skills, computation skills, community skills, critical-thinking and problem-solving skills, information-management skills, interpersonal skills, personal skills, and technology skills.

Also emanating from the SCANS report is a process for career transcription, a process in which life skills are translated into proficiencies and then credits. The Career Transcript System (CTS) created at Johns Hopkins University codifies lifelong learning as part of the following objectives (Learning Resources, Inc. n.d.):

> The Career Transcript System (CTS) is a means of changing/shifting the labor market for high school graduates, entry-level workers, and incumbent workers. How? By creating multi-employer career ladders and strengthening internal labor markets for these clients through ten complementary innovations:

1. Leveraging the resources that normally flow through the community colleges.
2. Assessing SCANS competencies through new instruments that include supervisors' and teachers' evaluations as well as employer-validated tests.
3. Maintaining a consistent database of the results through a new computer-based Community-based Human Resource Database.
4. Issuing Career Transcripts that document acquisition of the required/defined SCANS competencies.
5. Using workplace liaisons to help supervisors and employees work together to attain common goals, including acquiring and documenting these competencies and the resulting improved work behavior.
6. Building an Electronic Learning Network so that communities can learn from each other and from experts in order to improve the operation of CTS and other career development and Welfare-to-Work (WtW) programs. These experts include a National Advisory Board with members from employer organizations, human resources and service organizations, and educators, including the National Association of Manufacturers, the National Retail Federation, NAPIC, AACC, NSSB, National Institute for Literacy, the AFL-CIO, and others.
7. Creating a continuous improvement management system for each community.
8. Establishing other feedback loops so that community colleges realign their teaching, supervisors improve their management skills, and workers take responsibility for getting where they want to go on the career ladder.
9. Creating a national model in the WtW arena that has implications for other workforce development programs (WIA and TANF) and the larger issue of moving from low wages to sustainable wages.
10. Making this a win-win situation for college, employer, Workforce Investment Board, and client so that the model is viable without continued federal funding.

### *Vocational Clusters*

In recognition of the array of transferable skills that cut across occupational categories, an increasing number of states are moving toward a system of vocational clusters. On a national level, there has been an attempt to cluster career opportunities in the following areas (States' Career Clusters n.d.):

- Agriculture, Food, and Natural Resources
- Architecture and Construction Arts, A/V
- Technology and Communication
- Business, Management, and Administration
- Education and Training
- Finance
- Government and Public Administration
- Health Science
- Hospitality and Tourism
- Human Services
- Information Technology
- Law, Public Safety, and Security
- Manufacturing
- Marketing, Sales, and Service
- Science, Technology, Engineering, and Mathematics
- Transportation, Distribution, and Logistics

Within each cluster, there is a discernible career path and set of knowledge and skills required in order for a student to progress through each domain. For example, the following skills are identified as necessary to the Transportation, Distribution, and Logistics cluster: communication skills; problem solving and critical thinking; proficiency in information technology applications; leadership and team skills.

An underlying assumption in this discussion of career clustering is that the modern workplace will incorporate a high-performance organizational model. This model is characterized by flexible work structures and streamlined production systems. Under this ideal model, job quality rises and even entry-level jobs offer good wages, autonomy, and skill development because the model relies on human-resource strategies to create high levels of motivation and on mechanisms that channel employee involvement into performance gains. These strategies include participatory management, self-directed teams, job rotation, and more-sophisticated employee incentives. Under this model, everyone wins. The firm's success depends on the skill and creativity of its workforce, and in return it provides high wages and job security.

### Absence of Clear Career Pathways

The absence of clear pathways from school to work in the United States has at times hindered the coordination of educational services with workforce needs. In the hope of remedying this situation, President Bill

Clinton signed the School-to-Work Opportunities Act in 1994. Using federal funds as seed money, this program was an attempt to facilitate coordination between education and employment. All students were to be provided with

●➤ a relevant education, allowing students to explore different careers and to see what skills are required in their working environment;

●➤ skills, obtained from structured training and work-based experiences, including the skills necessary for a particular career as demonstrated in a working environment; and

●➤ valued credentials, establishing industry-standard benchmarks and developing education and training standards that ensure that proper education is received for each career.

## IS THERE A SHORTAGE OF SKILLED WORKERS?

Much of the current discussion of education to promote skill development comes out of human-capital theory. Although there is unanimity concerning the significant transformation in the economy from manufacturing to services, there is hardly a consensus on the impact of this change, especially with respect to the skill level required for the jobs created in a service-based economy.

The first order of concern is whether a shortage of skilled workers actually exists. A driving force in setting the stage for education reform efforts in the 1980s and 1990s was the belief that a dearth of skilled workers, especially in areas such as information technology, engineering, and health care, was inhibiting the ability of the United States to compete globally. Many of the reports issued by organizations such as the Business–Higher Education Forum and the Committee for Economic Development stressed the importance of aligning education to the economic needs of the nation. For example, the Hudson Institute's *Workforce 2000* (Johnston and Packer 1987) suggests that numerous highly skilled jobs will be created in the United States and that this is necessary if the United States is to regain economic competitiveness (Commission on the Skills of the American Workforce 1990; Reich 1991; Thurow 1992). An important issue concerns the bifurcation of job creation that is associated with what some have argued is the lack of a theoretical paradigm for understanding the implications of these economic changes. Reich (1991) argues that "symbolic analysts," who make up about 30 percent of the workforce, are the high-end jobs in a service-based economy. The issue of how to produce more "symbolic analysts" becomes pressing in this perspective.

Ivar Berg (1970) and, more recently, David Livingstone (1988) intimate that much of this emphasis on new, high-skills jobs is mere hyperbole and amounts to what Berg calls the "great training robbery." As Berg argues in *Education and Jobs: The Great Training Robbery* (1970) and Livingstone argues in *The Education-Jobs Gap: Underemployment or Economic Democracy* (1988), it is questionable whether the workplace of the twenty-first century will make adequate use of a workforce with increasing educational and technical needs. Berg documents how existing job opportunities often fail to engage the interests of a more educated workforce. He finds that those with higher educational backgrounds placed in settings requiring relatively low skills express significant job dissatisfaction, which contributes to high employee turnover. Livingstone argues that what is needed is not to reform education in order to meet the growing skill requirements of high-technology production but, rather, to restructure the workplace so as to engage a highly skilled workforce.

The relationship between technology and skills is a topic explored by Claudia Goldin and Lawrence Katz (1998). They find that technological changes in the 1800s actually resulted in a diminution in the need for skilled workers. They do find, however, that "technological-skill and capital-skill complementarities did indeed exist in the early twentieth century, having been effected by an increased usage of electric motors and shifts between certain modes of production."

### Wage Inequality

Thomas Bailey and Annette Bernhardt (1997) suggest that growing inequities in wage earnings have more to do with the increasing absence of well-paying jobs than with a deficit in the skill level in workers that relegates them to low-wage employment. However, they are sanguine that increasing the educational level of workers might place them on the road to higher-wage employment (1997, 180):

> At the peak of industrial capitalism, many low-skill workers found good
> opportunities in the manufacturing sector. But the service sector,
> which has replaced at least half of these jobs, has not proven nearly as
> high tech, high wage, and knowledge intensive as originally hoped.
> Compared to manufacturing, there are many service industries where
> mobility changes are lower and job instability higher, and where low-
> wage business strategies dominate. The concern, then, is that we are

seeing a decline in jobs that offer opportunities for career mobility and earnings growth to workers without a college education.

Yet they offer a number of caveats based upon their examination of how firm restructuring has affected job quality. They conclude from their research that (1) the spread of the high-performance workplace is limited; (2) the low road may be more efficient in some contexts; (3) the high road can still encompass low-wage jobs; and (4) the better jobs go to recruits with more skills and education.

### *Is College for All?*

Analysts question whether it makes sense to recommend college as an option for all. James Rosenbaum (2001) assesses whether community college attendance has resulted in college success. He finds that attending a community college does not necessarily result in success (2001, 56):

> The high level of community college dropouts arises because high schools offer vague promises of open opportunity for college without specifying the requirements for degree completion. . . . Failure in community colleges may stem not from any overt barrier in those institutions but from seeds planted much earlier—when youths are still in high school. Because students usually do not realize that their expectations were mistaken until long after they have left high school, high schools are rarely blamed for their graduates' failures in community college.

Barbara Schneider and David Stevenson report a similar finding in their 1999 work, *The Ambitious Generation: America's Teenagers, Motivated but Directionless.* Thus, the debate as to whether everyone should attend college continues. This issue was addressed in a 1999 NCES report titled *College for All? Is There Too Much Emphasis on Getting a Four Year College Degree?* (Boesel and Fredland 1999). The authors offer an excellent overview of the issues at stake:

> Over the years, larger and larger proportions of high school graduates have enrolled in 4-year colleges. While many people view college as essential to success in the labor market, the movement toward 4-year colleges also has its critics. These critics contend that
>
> ❧ the public has come to believe that almost all high school graduates should go to college;

- this "college movement" is sweeping many marginally qualified or unqualified students into college, and hence the average ability of college students has declined;
- as a result of these declining ability levels, college noncompletion and dropout rates have increased;
- many noncompleters do poorly in the labor market and would have been better advised to pursue other education and training options;
- these noncompleters are also burdened by unnecessary debts from college loans; and
- even college graduates are not doing very well in the labor market.

One factor in the widespread college expectations among high school students may be the increased tendency of high school guidance counselors to encourage students of limited ability to attend college. In fact, the authors of the NCES report suggest that channeling students to two-year program options may be more advantageous, partly because it provides students with a less costly education option. The authors show that students who complete a two-year degree program have higher earnings and far less educational debt than those who do not persist in a baccalaureate program.

Whether college is a worthwhile investment is shown to be related more to issues of wage inequality and market forces that impinge upon employment availability than to level of education per se. The report continues (Boesel and Fredland 1999):

> The large and rapidly expanding literature on wage inequality helps explain the changes in the economic performance of college graduates over time. College premiums—which express the degree of inequality in earnings between college graduates and high school graduates—dropped in the 1970s because of a great increase in the supply of college graduates. Enrollments ballooned in the late 1960s and early 1970s, encouraged by high premiums in the 1960s and pushed up especially by draft deferrals during the Vietnam War. In the 1980s, the college premium increased sharply, in part because of a deceleration in the growth of the college graduate supply. The main cause of the rising premiums, however, was technological change favoring more skilled workers. New technology, including the computer revolution, tended to replace lower-skilled with higher-skilled workers. As demand for less skilled workers dropped and the range of jobs for which they could compete narrowed, their wages went down. The loss of manufacturing jobs to developing countries exacerbated the labor market problems of less skilled workers,

such as high school graduates and high school dropouts, but was not the primary cause. The decline of labor unions and the decline in the real minimum wage in the 1980s also contributed to the growth of wage inequality but were not the primary cause of it.

Michael Handel addresses the growing skills gap in the United States and concludes (2000, 35) that

> the most powerful factors affecting wages would seem to be the recession and trade deficits of the early 1980s, which coincided with the most dramatic growth in wage inequality and the most noticeable change in occupational composition: the sharp decline in blue-collar manufacturing workers. The modest decline in inequality during the expansion of the 1990s also suggests the importance of macroeconomic forces. It appears that the skill requirements of postindustrial technology have had far less influence on wages than the state of the overall macro economy.

## ANTIPATHY TOWARD VOCATIONAL EDUCATION

A liberal arts curriculum has been the foundation of undergraduate study in the United States. Defined in a number of ways, the liberal arts are held to represent a compendium of disciplinary knowledge that a "well-rounded" person possesses. Typically, this includes a basic understanding of the arts, humanities, and natural and social sciences. In contrast, vocational and technical education are often looked down upon. As Christopher Winch (2000, 1) notes: "Anyone interested in promoting vocational education is thought to be a philistine, concerned only with material gain rather than with higher forms of human achievement."

However, vocational education has always been an important aspect of the community college. When community colleges began as a two-year extension of high school, their vocational mission was emphasized. At present, there is a focus on what has been termed the "New Vocationalism" (Hennigan 2001). This encompasses the following (Bragg 2001):

- Career clusters
- Curriculum integration of academic and vocational dimensions
- Integration into K–16
- Active learning strategies
- Holistic instruction

The disdain displayed by many in the United States toward vocational education is in part responsible for its relative neglect and underdevelopment, especially in comparison to western European nations (Glouchevitch 1992). This is especially unfortunate given the U.S. inability to compete well on an international scale in many sectors of skilled manufacturing, for example.

The negative undertones associated with vocational education and the perception that higher-order cognitive skills are required for successful employment in what some have categorized as the post-industrial world are factors that pull students into postsecondary education. In addition, the U.S. Bureau of Labor Statistics repeatedly reports that although the service sector is the fastest-growing sector of the economy in terms of job growth, the occupations in the service sector are primarily low-paying and low career-mobility positions. For many, the "promise" of an upwardly mobile career track is too hard to resist.

Historically, community colleges perpetuated a rigid separation between career and transfer programs. However, such a separation makes little sense given the changing occupational structure and the skills required of workers today. The importance of "symbolic" thinkers and the cognitive requirements of work in the twenty-first-century suggest that such a dichotomy is not productive. Anthony Carnevale and Donna Desrochers (2001, 93) state:

> The academic-versus-vocational problem may seem like an "either/or" choice. Should the community college focus on academic transfers or on a range of work-related programs as its core and quality standard? Some observers view the movement toward providing vocational credentials, certifications and customized training as a process of commercialization. They say it competes with the community colleges' broader social mission to provide access and upward mobility through academic preparation. Viewed from the perspective of the comprehensive community college, however, this seems a false dichotomy. The ability of community colleges to fulfill their broader social mission depends to a large extent on the exchange between academic education and the various forms of vocational education and training—give-and-take that would not exist if either role were compromised.

### Changing the Context of Undergraduate Education

The undergraduate curriculum has varied over time with respect to its prescriptive character. One variant has been highly structured, providing undergraduates with little choice with respect to courses and subject

matter. Such an approach parallels what some have termed a funda-
mentalist or essentialist conception of knowledge, which has been
championed on a K–12 level by Edward Hirsch in his *Cultural Literacy:
What Every American Needs to Know* (1988). This philosophy provided
fodder for the student movement in higher education during the 1960s
and 1970s. Under the rallying cry of relevancy, many people challenged
the established curricular canons of the day. In the infamous Port Huron
Statement, the first official document of Students for a Democratic Society, Tom Hayden described education as a powerful tool for the better-
ment of society. The Port Huron Statement encompassed a philosophy of
activism and community involvement and a focus on such world problems as overpopulation, poverty, and war. Education must be an agent of
"making history" as opposed to merely reading about the past (Hayden
1962).

Another way of delivering the traditional undergraduate curriculum has been through a distributive scheme, in which students select
from a range of courses to fulfill requirements in specific areas. This
smorgasbord approach of course selection became popular as a way of
placating those arguing for choice and relevance within the undergraduate curriculum.

A third model is to package a range of instruction in foundational
courses, often interdisciplinary (such as the already-mentioned University of Chicago's Great Books curriculum or Columbia University's core
curriculum), so that students receive an exposure to a common base of
subject matter.

Much of the way the undergraduate curriculum is organized is
derivative of what is found in high school. Traditionally, the high school
curriculum has been divided into academic and vocational tracts. Those
on the academic side of the house presumably have an aptitude and
ambition to pursue a college education. In contrast, those in vocational
studies are assumed to desire immediate entry into a career, often
viewed as one that centers on some form of manual dexterity.

Looking at the current landscape of high schools in the United
States, one also sees a number of vocational technical secondary schools,
in which the courses of study have changed recently. Adding a technological cachet to what have traditionally been less-prestigious courses of
study provides an alluring incentive. One example of this is Bergen Technical High School in Hackensack, New Jersey, whose organization into
academies and technical institutes is a notable departure from the blue-
collar mechanical pursuits often taught in these institutions.

The U.S. educational system, as discussed in Chapter 2, has historically had a weak link to career opportunities and employment. This lack of correspondence between education and occupational realities has long been a subject of much discussion and debate. For example, Berg (1970) and Livingstone (1998) not only lament the disconnect but charge corporate and industrial leaders with perpetuating a hoax when it comes to workforce needs. Similarly, Stanley Aronowitz and William DiFazio (1994), among other commentators, have discussed the charge that industrialists only want cheap labor, with education and training costs subsumed by community colleges, thereby using public funds for private gain.

The diminishing gap between what had been a stringent bifurcation of vocational and academic tracks is in part a reflection of the changing nature of work in what has often been called our postmodern, postindustrial knowledge-intensive economy. A number of books, such as Robert Reich's discussion of symbolic analysts (Reich 1991) and more recently Richard Florida's *The Rise of the Creative Class and How It's Transforming Work, Leisure, Community, and Everyday Life* (2002), have noted that the ability to think abstractly and to solve problems are central for upwardly mobile employment and career tracks. It has been suggested by Carnevale and Desrochers (2001) and Marshall and Tucker (1992) that contemporary jobs that offer an upwardly mobile career path require high levels of abstract, symbolic thinking. Similar conclusions are reached in the Hudson Institute's *Workforce 2000* (Johnston and Packer 1987) and in *Building a Career Pathway System: Promising Practices in Community College–Centered Workforce Development* (Alssid et al. 2002), which lament the poor state of preparation of many in the workforce.

It makes little sense to continue a rigid separation between vocational and academic pursuits. In some states, such as New York, there has been a movement away from what had been distinct tracks in high school whereby students were either in a college preparatory or vocational curriculum. Similarly, the creation of "middle colleges" and early high school enrichment programs, such as Bard High School in New York City, speak to the desire that college should increasingly be the norm, and not an exception. Such a trend to universal college is seen in the growing number of people enrolling in higher education (Horn, Peter, and Rooney 2002).

Teaching what the League for Innovation in the Community College has called "twenty-first-century skills" has also become the preoccupation of many in K–12 reform efforts. Richard Murnane and Frank Levy (1996), for example, speak about the need to move away from rote learning and toward critical-thinking skills. Beyond the classroom, groups such as the Coalition for Essential Schools have argued for developing an organizational structure of schools to support such activity. Similarly, the New American Schools movement has endorsed such activities.

Community colleges have long grappled with these concerns. Historically, they have embraced the importance of supplying a labor force for emerging industries and have played a prominent role in providing immigrant populations with educational and training opportunities. At the same time, community colleges have a long-standing commitment to providing students with the ability to transfer to baccalaureate institutions. As discussed in Chapter 1, they have been criticized for shortcomings in both of these areas. Critics suggest that often the job training they provide is for low-level, dead-end jobs that offer little possibility of upward mobility. A similar disparaging sentiment is expressed with respect to the transfer role of community colleges, as some critics state that community colleges do poorly in providing transfer opportunities to students. Judith Eaton (1994) observes that community colleges have perpetuated the catch–22 of being unable to do either effectively while perpetuating the gap between the two.

A recent study by the AACC and the American Association of State Colleges and Universities (AASCU) sought to explore the barriers to transfer. In their report "Access to the Baccalaureate," the following barriers were identified:

- Perception that community college graduates are less intellectually challenged than their counterparts in four-year colleges
- Lack of formal articulation agreements; lack of enforcement at the baccalaureate level
- Lack of compliance between statewide general education requirements on the part of baccalaureate institutions; also problems of compliance with respect to four-year accreditation standards (for example, National Council for Accreditation of Teacher Education) on the part of two-year colleges
- Four-year colleges not accepting credits earned at community college
- Belief that through expanded use of technology, these barriers can be reduced via accurate information flow and via Web sites that will function as contracts
- Belief in virtual universities as a way to eliminate geographical barriers

### Workforce Training

Carnevale and Desrochers (2001, 18–19) talk about the multiple credential role of community colleges within the knowledge economy. Quoting from Grubb, they cite the following roles:

- Academic preparation for transfer or terminal academic degrees
- Second-chance remediation
- English language development for non-native students
- Public job training for disadvantaged clientele
- Occupational preparation for public or private credentialing, licensing, and certification
- Worker-initiated short-term training and individual development
- Customized training and certification for employers and equipment vendors

### Separating Technical from Liberal Arts

Historically, community colleges have promulgated a structure that separates career and transfer programs. Associate of applied science (AAS) programs have been designed to provide students with the skills needed to immediately enter the workforce. A number of these programs are common in the fields of allied health and medicine, ranging from nursing and respiratory therapy to sonography and radiography. Given present shortages in nursing and other areas of health care, many of these fields have proven to be lucrative pathways for community college graduates.

There are also a variety of AAS programs in what can be termed service industries. Culinary arts, hospitality, office administration, travel and tourism, and a range of allied business programs such as retail and sales are examples of this category. However, many of these programs have not fared very well of late. For example, activities that previously needed the services of a travel agent can now easily be done on the Internet by anyone. Office administration programs have been subsumed by courses taught at a high school level or in a career academy.

A final category of AAS programs is technology programs, ranging from manufacturing and information technology to automotive technology. Given the higher skill levels involved in many of these occupations, some of these programs are transferable to senior institutions. However, the relative lack of general education requirements that students have to satisfy continues to differentiate these from associate of arts programs.

Many of the AAS programs duplicate outside corporate and business interests. For example, some hospital nursing schools also offer licensed practical nursing programs like those typically found in community colleges. Proprietary institutions have also made a large inroad into these fields. Organizations such as DeVry and Chubb Institute offer courses, often on terms more hospitable for working adults than community colleges can offer. Not wedded to the traditional sixteen-week semester, these and other institutions offer roving starts and extremely flexible schedules. Recent statistics reveal the growth and profitability of many of these ventures.

In contrast to vocational education at the secondary level, occupational program enrollments continue to grow at a rate in keeping with the sub-baccalaureate more generally. As pointed out by the National Assessment of Vocational Education (NAVE), most of the literature shows an economic benefit to attaining vocational training.

An interesting finding is reported by Lisa Hudson and David Hurst (2002) regarding "the persistence of employees who pursue postsecondary study." They conclude (2002, 1) that

> Among those who expect to earn a certificate from their first postsecondary institution, students who define themselves as employees who study seem to do as well as their peers in persisting in and completing their postsecondary programs. But employees who define themselves as students seem to have a more difficult time than all other students in persisting when their expectations are to earn a bachelor's or higher level degree. The persistence problem has many potential causes. Since employees who study are more likely than other students to be full-time workers, they face greater time constraints that may make it more difficult for them to continue their studies. In addition, because their primary role is as an employee rather than as a student, they may be more likely than other students to forgo schooling for work when time (or other factors) becomes an issue. Finally, employees who study are more likely than their peers to have personal backgrounds that are related to lower postsecondary completion and persistence; these background characteristics may also contribute to persistence problems. In short, for a variety of reasons, employees who enroll in college to pursue a degree appear to be a group of postsecondary students who are particularly at risk for not persisting.

There is a long-standing debate within the research literature regarding the appropriate mix of transfer and career programs in community colleges. In light of growing concerns over the shortage of skilled workers in areas such as information technology, some stakeholders are pressing community colleges to focus on workforce development. At the same time, many continue to advocate for a curriculum that provides an exposure to varying fields of inquiry from a "liberal arts" perspective.

## CONCLUSION

The tension between career programs and transfer programs illustrates a number of peculiarities that characterize U.S. higher education in general and community colleges in particular. The United States does not have the highly choreographed relationship that exists in many nations among education, training, and occupational entry, and there has been a long history of concern over the "loose coupling" of education and occupational opportunities in the United States. Not only has this concern been articulated by business and industry, but inside the academy, great antipathy is typically expressed against an insoluble linkage between the liberal arts and vocational education. These tensions are quickly brought to the surface when one examines community colleges, for these institutions are typically called upon to provide an educational experience both for students who wish to transfer to baccalaureate institutions and for those who want to enter the workforce directly. One way that community colleges have tried to bridge this divide is to focus on the attainment of learning competencies, which constitute the bedrock of both liberal education and career preparation.

Related to this is the importance of articulating discernable career pathways so that students can pursue an advantageous trajectory as they engage in the duality of lifelong learning while at times "stopping-out" or reducing involvement in formal learning.

### References

AFL-CIO. 2004. "Union Summer: Questions and Answers." http://www.aflcio.org/aboutunions/unionsummer/ (accessed December 31, 2004).

Alssid, Julian L., David Gruber, Davis Jenkins, Christopher Mazzeo, Brandon Roberts, Regina Stanback-Stroud. 2002. *Building a Career Pathway System: Promising Practices in Community College–Centered Workforce Development.* Brooklyn, NY: Workforce Strategy Center.

American Association of Community Colleges (AACC). 1998. *Responding to the Challenges of Workforce and Economic Development: The Role of America's Community Colleges.* AACC White Paper. Washington, DC: AACC.

————. AACC. N.d. "Access to the Baccalaureate." http://www.aacc.nche.edu/pathtocollege/issue.html.

Aronowitz, Stanley, and William DiFazio. 1994. *The Jobless Future: Science, Technology, and the Dogma of Work.* Minneapolis: University of Minnesota Press.

Bailey, Thomas R., and Annette D. Bernhardt. 1997. "In Search of the High Road in a Low-Wage Industry." *Politics and Society* 25, no. 2 (June).

Bailey, Thomas, Y. Matsuzuka, J. Jacobs, V. Morest, and K. Hughes. 2003. *Institutionalization and Sustainability of the National Science Foundation's Advanced Technological Education Program.* New York: Community College Research Center, Teachers College, Columbia University.

Berg, Ivar. 1970. *Education and Jobs: The Great Training Robbery.* New York: Praeger.

Boesel, David, and Eric Fredland. 1999. *College for All? Is There Too Much Emphasis on Getting a 4 Year Degree?* Washington, DC: U.S. Department of Education, Office of Educational Research and Improvement.

Bragg, Debra D. 2001. "The New Vocationalism in Community Colleges." *New Directions for Community Colleges,* no. 115 (Fall).

————. 2002. "Community College and Beyond: Major Results of a National Evaluation of Tech Prep." OCCRL. Urbana-Champaign: University of Illinois. 14, no. 1 (Fall).

Business–Higher Education Forum. 1999. "Spanning the Chasm: A Blueprint for Action." *Higher Education and National Affairs* 48, vol. 17.

Carnevale, Anthony P., and Donna M. Desrochers. 2001. *Help Wanted . . . Credentials Required: Community Colleges in the Knowledge Economy.* Princeton: Educational Testing Service and the American Association of Community Colleges.

Commission on the Skills of the American Workforce. 1990. *America's Choice: High Skills or Low Wages!* Rochester, NY: National Center on Education and the Economy, June.

Cremin, Lawrence A. 1988. *American Education: The Metropolitan Experience 1876–1980.* New York: Harper and Row.

Datnow, Amanda, and Robert Cooper. 2002. "Tracking." In *Education and Sociology: An Encyclopedia,* ed. David L. Levinson, Peter W. Cookson Jr., and Alan R. Sadovnik. New York: RoutledgeFalmer.

Dougherty, Kevin J. 1994. *The Contradictory College: The Conflicting Origins, Impacts, and Future of the Community College.* Albany: State University of New York Press.

Eaton, Judith S. 1994. *Strengthening Collegiate Education in Community Colleges.* San Francisco: Jossey-Bass.

Florida, Richard. 2002. *The Rise of the Creative Class and How It's Transforming Work, Leisure, Community, and Everyday Life.* New York: Basic Books.

Freeland, Richard M. 1992. *Academia's Golden Age: Universities in Massachusetts, 1945–1970.* New York: Oxford University Press.

Glouchevitch, Philip. 1992. *Juggernaut: The German Way of Business. Why It Is Transforming Europe—and the World.* New York: Simon and Schuster.

Goldin, Claudia, and Lawrence F. Katz. 1998. "The Origins of Technology-Skill Complementarity." *Quarterly Journal of Economics*, August.

Handel, Michael J. 2000. *Is There A Skills Crisis? Trends in Job Skill Requirements, Technology, and Wage Inequality in the U.S.* Levy Institute Public Policy Brief No. 62. Annandale-on-Hudson, NY: Jerome Levy Institute for Public Policy, Bard College.

Hayden, Tom. 1962. "Port Huron Statement." As reprinted on http://www.orlok.com/tribe/insiders/huron.html (accessed November 11, 2004).

Hennigan, Jamie. 2001. *The Business of Vocational Education.* Los Angeles: University of California, ERIC Clearinghouse for Community Colleges, October.

Hershey, Alan M., Marsha K. Silverberg, Tom Owens, and Lara K. Hulsey. 1998. *Focus on the Future. The Final Report of the National Tech Prep Evaluation.* Princeton: Mathematica Policy Research.

Hirsch, Edward. 1988. *Cultural Literacy: What Every American Needs to Know.* Boston: Houghton Mifflin.

Horn, Laura, Katharine Peter, and Kathryn Rooney. 2002. *Profile of Undergraduates in U.S. Postsecondary Institutions: 1999–2000.* NCES 2002–168. Project Officer: Andrew G. Malizio. Washington, DC: U.S. Department of Education, National Center for Education Statistics.

Hudson, Lisa, and David Hurst. 2002. "The Persistence of Employees Who Pursue Postsecondary Study." *Education Statistics Quarterly* 4, no. 1 (June 7).

Johnston, William, and Arnold Packer. 1987. *Workforce 2000: Work and Workers for the 20th Century.* Washington, DC: Hudson Institute.

Katz, Michael. 1968. *Irony of Early School Reform: Educational Innovation in Mid-Nineteenth Century Massachusetts.* Cambridge, MA: Harvard University Press.

Katznelson, Ira, and Margaret Weir. 1985. *Schooling for All.* New York: Basic Books.

Kett, Joseph F. 1996. *The Pursuit of Knowledge under Difficulties: From Self-Improvement to Adult Education in America, 1750–1990.* Stanford, CA: Stanford University Press.

Labaree, David F. 1988. *The Making of an American High School: The Credentials Market and Central High School of Philadelphia, 1838–1939.* New Haven, CT: Yale University Press.

League for Innovation in the Community College. N.d. "Twenty-First Century Learning Outcomes Project." http://www.league.org/league/projects/pew/about.htm (accessed January 11, 2005).

Learning Resources, Inc. N.d. "The Career Transcript System (CTS)." http://www.learning-resources.com/Workforce/CTS.php3 (accessed November 11, 2004).

Livingstone, David W. 1998. *The Education-Jobs Gap: Underemployment or Economic Development.* New York: Westview.

Lucas, Christopher. 1994. *American Higher Education: A History.* New York: St. Martin's.

Marshall, Ray, and Marc Tucker. 1992. *Thinking for a Living: Education and the Wealth of Nations.* New York: Basic Books.

Murnane, Richard J., and Frank Levy. 1996. *Teaching the New Basic Skills: Principles for Educating Children to Thrive in a Challenging Economy.* New York: Free Press.

NJ Transfer. N.d. http://www.njtransfer.org/main.html (accessed January 10, 2005).

Oakes, Jeannie. 1985. *Keeping Track.* New Haven, CT: Yale University Press.

Orr, Terry, and Debra D. Bragg. 2002. "Tech Prep and Postsecondary Education." In *Higher Education in the United States: An Encyclopedia,* ed. J. F. Forest and Kevin Kinser. Denver, CO: ABC-CLIO.

Parnell, Dale. 1985. *The Neglected Majority.* Washington, DC: Community College Press.

———. 1992. "Every Student a Winner: How Tech Prep Can Help Students Achieve Career Success." *Vocational Education Journal* 67, no. 4.

Reich, Robert B. 1991. *The Work of Nations: Preparing Ourselves for 21st Century Capitalism.* New York: Vintage Books.

Rosenbaum, James E. 2001. *Beyond College for All: Career Paths for the Forgotten Half.* New York: Russell Sage Foundation.

Schneider, Barbara, and David Stevenson. 1999. *The Ambitious Generation: America's Teenagers, Motivated but Directionless.* New Haven, CT: Yale University Press.

Secretary's Commission on Achieving Necessary Skills (SCANS). 1991. *What Work Requires of Schools: A SCANS Report for America 2000.* Washington, DC: U.S. Department of Labor.

States' Career Clusters. N.d. "The 16 Career Clusters." http://www.careerclusters.org/16clusters.htm (accessed January 11, 2005).

Thurow, Lester C. 1992. *Building Wealth: The New Rules for Individuals, Companies, and Nations in a Knowledge-Based Economy.* New York: HarperCollins.

U.S. Department of Education. 2001. "Overview: Introduction: No Child Left Behind." http://www.ed.gov/nclb/overview/intro/ (accessed November 4, 2004).

U.S. Department of Education, Office of the Under Secretary, Planning and Evaluation Service. 2002. *National Assessment of Vocational Education:*

*Interim Report to Congress. Executive Summary.* Washington, DC: Office of the Under Secretary.

Winch, Christopher. 2000. *Education, Work, and Social Capital: Towards a New Conception of Vocational Education.* London and New York: Routledge.

Workforce Strategy Center. 2002. *Building a Career Pathways System: Promising Practices in Community College–Centered Workforce Development.* Brooklyn, NY: Workforce Strategy Center.

———. 2003. *Building Bridges to College and Careers: Contextualized Basic Skills Programs at Community Colleges.* Brooklyn, NY: Workforce Strategy Center.

*Chapter Five*

# ⊷ Community Colleges and Lifelong Learning

This chapter begins with a discussion of the increasing importance of education for economic development in a knowledge-based economy, including the rise of professions. Then the provision of education by community colleges at various stages of the life span is discussed, followed by an explication of models for the delivery of education throughout the life span such as distance learning, competency-based learning, and career pathways. Also discussed in this chapter are the seamless tracks that are being proposed for K–16. Finally, factors that inhibit a seamless provision of lifelong learning are discussed.

Adult education and lifelong learning has long been an important component of education in the United States. Some view the desire to continue one's education as emanating from the ideological foundations of the nation. Max Weber long ago ascribed the perception of the importance of self-improvement to the "Protestant ethic" found within capitalist societies. He noted that acquisitive behavior and the relentless desire for advancement were motivating forces in U.S. society. The idea that one should work toward self-improvement is also part of the cultural history of the United States. Joseph F. Kett, in *The Pursuit of Knowledge under Difficult Circumstances: From Self-Improvement to Adult Education in America, 1750–1990*, calls the unmitigated pursuit of education intrinsic to the nation's "democratic idealism." As he observes about the diffusion of knowledge in antebellum America (1994, 75–76):

> Economic development and political democratization shaped the popularization of knowledge in various ways, some straightforward, others tortuous. By 1815 the penetration of the market economy had brought a flourishing book trade to agricultural regions that for most of the eighteenth century had experienced few economic and cultural dealings with urban centers. . . . But the quest for knowledge was more than an instrumental accommodation to new occupational opportunities. In the prevailing view, self-improvement was a disciplined and arduous undertaking that bred a certain detachment from the workaday world

in those who answered its summons. . . . Viewed as a calling, self-improvement simultaneously proved attractive to leaders of growing but vulnerable professionals and occupations, who praised it as a way to spur virtue in young aspirants to law or medicine or commerce. . . . For the most part . . . Americans traced the diffusion of knowledge to liberty and democracy—forces that seemed likely to become universal in their society.

As previously discussed in Chapter 2, the importance of applied knowledge for the successful industrialization of the nation was at the heart of the Morrill Acts of 1862 and 1890. Passage of these acts also marked an important change from the classical model of higher education that had been dominant in the United States until the Civil War. They reflected the weakening apprenticeship system and strengthening industrialization that occurred after the Civil War. As Robert Church (1976, 193) states:

> Between 1865 and 1900 the training of the hand became an increasingly popular responsibility for the school to assume in the United States. *Hand training* comprehends manual training, dexterity training as done in the kindergarten and primary grades, industrial education and vocational training. *Manual training* was training in the use of tools and materials without any vocational goal. *Vocational training* was training in the specific tools and materials used in a specific trade or industry—tool and die making, cloth printing, carriage making, or blueprint reading. *Industrial education* was the most complicated for it included educational programs which taught children work habits and discipline by having them work, usually at profit-making enterprises, and educational programs that trained students in the use of tools and materials to prepare students for general categories of work—farming, woodworking, construction and such.

The rise of professions in the United States is another important cultural component driving lifelong continuing education. Professionalization, defined as the monopolization of a body of knowledge by an occupational group that is self-regulating and that proffers a field of expertise that it dominates and controls, became an important aspect of the changing occupational structure in the United States after the Civil War. As Magali Larson (1977) and Andrew Abbott (1988) suggest, professionalization occurred in a number of fields during the nineteenth and early twentieth centuries. Linked to this was the growing importance of credentialing, which not only provided a prescribed route of entry into a given occupation but allowed professionals to regulate admissions to a select cadre of practitioners.

Education throughout the life span is part and parcel of a knowledge-based society. A fluid occupational structure, in which accelerated technological change quickly alters the structure of daily work and the labor process, is a feature of the global economy (Carnoy 2000). The flexible mode of labor in the "new economy" and that economy's need for a skilled labor force whose competencies cut across rigid occupational lines place a premium on continuous training and development. This situation represents an unprecedented opportunity for community colleges to become involved in occupational growth and economic development (Carnevale and Desrochers 2001).

Education in the United States has become a cradle-to-grave phenomenon, which emulates the social welfare practices found in such nations as Sweden. What is new from earlier periods is not that learning occurs throughout a U.S. citizen's life. Rather, what is new is that continuing learning is now a purposeful, organized activity that begins with increasing use of early childhood education and extends through a burgeoning network of learning in retirement, as exemplified in the growth of Elderhostel. As John Lederer (2003, 1) states: "The case for lifelong learning almost does not need to be stated, it is so ingrained in our current thinking. The knowledge economy, the information society, higher order skills, the knowledge revolution are all buzz phrases describing the same concept: Capital will flow to nations—thereby increasing wealth—that continuously develop and exploit the skills of their workers."

Norton Grubb, Norena Badway, and Denise Bell (2002) point out that the "educational gospel"—the unquestioned belief that education itself will prepare people for jobs in the "new economy"—has taken over and obfuscates the fact that workforce support is crucial if this capital flow is to occur.

As lifelong learning has come to include an increasingly purposeful, organized set of activities, some organizational principles have become commonplace for engendering effective learning throughout the life span. These include:

1.  An emphasis on continuing education to keep abreast of developments in one's occupation (often in the form of so-called continuing education units [CEUs]), and an increasing emphasis on teaching the "soft skills"—which often revolve around interpersonal relationships and which might include communication and working in teams—that employers increasingly consider desirable.

2. Relatively small and nurturing learning structures that respond to the specific needs of the learner, often in a customer-service fashion. Mark Milliron, president and CEO of the League for Innovation in the Community College, terms this "Learning Relationship Management," a spin-off from customer relations management in the business world (Milliron 2001).

3. Education that is not bound by place or by time. The rise of the Internet and global communications allows learning to occur independent of place. The dramatic rise of online learning and the overall expansion of asynchronous education allows for an exponential increase in people's ability to participate in some type of formalized education.

4. The encroachment of formalized learning into all spheres of life, many of which were in the past considered solely leisure or private activities. In addition to being undertaken to earn a degree or to gain specific job training, formal education is on the rise to learn informal leisure activities (e.g., training a dog; finding a mate) and to gain expertise in areas that traditionally were the province of sole practitioners (e.g., learning automotive retail versus wholesale values; financial investing).

5. An increasing number of providers in the marketplace of knowledge. Besides nonprofit institutions, there has been a dramatic increase in for-profit providers, such as Walden University, Capella University, and the University of Phoenix. Networks of for-profit institutions have also been developed, such as Computer Training Schools (http://www.computertrainingschools.com), and there has been a dramatic rise in career institutes, such as Chubb Institute, DeVry Institute, and Katherine Gibbs School.

6. Tremendous growth in noncredit adult education programs, as evidenced by the voluminous bulletins of New York University's School of Continuing and Professional Studies (http://www.nyu.edu/scps.nyu). Organizations such as the Ninety-Second Street Y in New York City (http://www.92y.org) offer large numbers of adult courses, something that is also increasingly common in community education programs sponsored by school districts throughout the nation.

Community colleges are uniquely positioned to providing formalized learning opportunities throughout the life span. They provide early childhood education programs that typically bring infants and toddlers to campus. They are expanding early college initiatives for middle school and secondary school students. They are finding an increasing number of eighteen-to-twenty-year-olds at their doorstep, providing an increasing number of credit programs that go beyond the associate's degree, offering CEUs to those who are seeking currency in their chosen profession, and affording cultural enrichment to members of the community. They also sponsor Institutes for Learning in Retirement for those who have worked in a chosen career.

## EDUCATIONAL INEQUALITY
## THROUGHOUT THE LIFE SPAN

A number of recent reports have shown that social inequality in the United States not only persists but is on the rise (U.S. Census Bureau 2003). The role of education in perpetuating inequality is complex and controversial. Some suggest that the educational system plays a central role in perpetuating social inequality because they provide unequal opportunities, in part because of inequities in school financing. However, there is a body of research in the sociology of education on what are known as "school effects" that asserts that the social background of students' families has more to do with school achievement, and eventual occupational attainment, than does what actually transpires within schools. This line of argument emanates from James Coleman's classic study of school effects, *Equality of Educational Opportunity* (Coleman 1966). According to Roger Shouse (2002, 519), the Coleman report reached the following major conclusions:

1.  Factors related to a student's home environment were the strongest predictors of achievement across all racial groups.
2.  Student composition variables (e.g., a school's percentage of white students, its students' average economic background) were the next strongest predictor of achievement among minority students.
3.  Teacher characteristics (e.g., education, years of experience) had some impact on achievement, but only among southern black children.
4.  After controlling for the effects [already stated], variables related to school physical resources (e.g., curricular or instructional facilities, per-pupil spending) appeared to have little or no effect on school achievement.

Schools are the primary mechanism for selecting and sorting students for occupational attainment slots via their conveyance of the exogenous factors just discussed. Patterns of inequality in educational funding persist across school districts, which leads in poorer districts to a preponderance of out-of-field teachers, crumbling physical plants, large class sizes, and little community outreach. Importantly, parental involvement, crucial for academic success of children, is often nonexistent in schools where there is a large population of disadvantaged children. Jonathan Kozol made similar observations, albeit without social scientific research, throughout many of his works, including *Death at an Early Age* (1967) and *Savage Inequalities* (1991). Valerie Lee and David Burkham (2002) provide social scientific research supporting similar conclusions. And the National Association for the Education of Young Children (NAEYC) has advocates for more early childhood education, pointing to the desirable outcomes that emanate therefrom. According to NAEYC (n.d.), effective early childhood education must encompass the following:

- Developmentally appropriate curricula
- Development of standards through research-based models of "best practices"
- Support of children's growth and learning in ethical ways
- Support of and commitment to early childhood programs, professionals, and families

Lee and Burkham (2002) assert that effective early childhood education is essential to attempt to forestall the ill effects of educational inequity. In *Inequality at the Starting Gate: Social Background Differences in Achievement as Children Begin School*, they offer the following conclusions about the determinacy of social background for educational performance:

1. There are substantial differences by race and ethnicity in children's test scores as they begin kindergarten. Before even entering kindergarten, the average cognitive scores of children in the highest socioeconomic status (SES) group are 60 percent above the scores of the lowest SES group. Moreover, average math achievement is 21 percent lower for blacks than for whites and 19 percent lower for Hispanics.
2. Race and ethnicity are associated with SES. . . . Cognitive skills are much less closely related to race/ethnicity after accounting for SES. Even after taking race differences into account, how-

ever, children from different SES groups achieve at different levels.

3. Socioeconomic status is quite strongly related to cognitive skills. Of the many categories of factors considered—including race/ethnicity, family educational experiences, access to quality care, home reading, computer use, and television habits—SES accounts for more of the unique variation in cognitive scores than any other factor by far. (Lee and Burkham 2002, 2)

Underscoring the relationship between SES and learning, they conclude (2002, 2–3),

> Low-SES children begin school at kindergarten in systematically lower-quality elementary schools than their more advantaged counterparts. However school quality is defined—in terms of higher student achievement, more school resources, more qualified teachers, more positive teacher attitudes, better neighborhood or school conditions, private vs. public schools—the least advantaged U.S. children begin their formal schooling in consistently lower-quality schools. This reinforces the inequalities that develop even before children reach school age.

## HUMAN CAPITAL, LIFELONG LEARNING, AND ECONOMIC DEVELOPMENT

Given the more-advanced skill level needed by the U.S. workforce, career advancement primarily accrues to those with upgraded skills. The "deindustrialization of America" (Bluestone and Harrison 1982) and overall migration of low-skilled jobs to other nations, along with a dramatic decline in the number of well-paying manufacturing-sector jobs, has made it incumbent upon many U.S. workers to "re-skill." The National Commission on the Skills of the American Workforce (1990) calls for a strong connection between labor and education, asserting that it is not possible for the United States to be a "high wage, low-skilled nation." Similarly, Robert Reich (1991) believes that investing in people is the best way to add value to the economy. The nurturing of "symbolic analysts," whose cognitive skills form the base of the knowledge economy, is the key to social and economic prosperity.

In order to gain a competitive edge in a burgeoning global economy, improving the skills levels of workers has become increasingly important.

A number of observers have highlighted the dominance of knowledge-based companies in the global economy and consequently for local economic development (Machlup 1962; Nespoli 1991). In order for knowledge-based enterprises to thrive, they require a constant supply of human capital. "Human capital" refers to the investment in the productive resources of an individual laborer. A number of international organizations, such as the Organization for Economic Co-operation and Development (OECD) and the United Nations Educational, Scientific, and Cultural Organization (UNESCO), assert that lifelong learning and the procurement of human capital is key for sustaining individual and social prosperity.

The term "human capital" was first coined by the economist Theodore Schultz. This concept has become an important construct for understanding how the creation of wealth occurs in a knowledge-based society. In a 1960 presidential address to the American Economic Association, he stated (Schultz 1961, 2):

> The mere thought of investment in human beings is offensive to some among us. Our values and beliefs inhibit us from looking upon human beings as capital goods, except in slavery and this we abhor. . . . To treat human beings as wealth that can be augmented by investment runs counter to deeply held values. It seems to reduce man once again to a mere material component, something akin to property. And for man to look upon himself as a capital good, even if it did not impair his freedom, may seem to debase him. . . . [But] by investing in themselves, people can enlarge the range of choice available to them. It is one way free men can enhance their welfare.

George Psacharopoulos (1995) argues that the increasing investment in human capital by nations throughout the world is responsible for increasing standards of living, decreasing poverty, raising economic levels, and spurring economic growth. The OECD (1997) asserts that an insufficiently educated workforce threatens economic expansion in advanced capitalist societies. The World Bank (2005) contends that investing in education "is crucial for creating, applying and spreading knowledge." In the sequel to its influential *Workforce 2000*, the Hudson Institute argues strenuously in *Workforce 2020* (Judy and D'Amico 1997) that an upgraded educational system is urgently needed to maximize the promise of economic prosperity and upward social mobility in the twenty-first century.

That workers will need to "[think] for a living" (Marshall and Tucker 1992) and that "knowledge is the new basis of wealth" (Thurow

1999) are dominant notions in the current information age. The National Center on Education and the Economy states that "knowledge—and the capacity to put knowledge to good use—is now the only dependable source of wealth all over the world." Throughout the modern educational world it is a deeply held belief that education is the ticket to occupational success, upward social mobility, and national prosperity.

Augmenting the concept of human capital are the constructs of cultural capital and social capital. The notion of cultural capital is typically associated with the work of Pierre Bourdieu, a French social theorist. Cultural capital, according to Bourdieu, is the "cultural practices or dispositions a person acquires, often through disguised or hidden ways, that realizes profits in the economic field primarily through ensuring academic success" (Madigan 2002, 121). Through possession or command of cultural capital, a person knows how to navigate through the cultural norms governing a particular situation. Such things as knowing how to "dress for success," understanding the appropriate code of conduct for networking at a business meeting, or recognizing the nuances of how to approach an instructor about not understanding the content of a particular assignment are all subsumed under the concept of cultural capital.

Social capital, most closely identified with the work of the sociologist James Coleman, can be equated to the social networks that one has at one's disposal. Barbara Schneider states (2002, 546) that "Coleman . . . defines social capital as inhering in the structure of relations between persons and among persons. . . . Social capital exists in social structures, be it the family, school, or community. It facilitates the actions of individuals who are within the structure. Like other forms of capital, such as human and physical capital, it makes possible the achievement of certain ends that would be impossible without its presence."

It is reasonable to generalize that community college students do not have as much access to social capital as do more-advantaged students. Given that community college students generally are poorer and are more likely to be first-generation college students, their "stock of knowledge" does not include some of the social and cultural perquisites available to more affluent students. In fact, one rationale for the importance of efforts to formally introduce students to the college experience, whether it be through courses or workshops, is that such introductions will help them acquire the cultural and social nuances that are already understood by others. Such a deficiency places them at a competitive disadvantage when compared to other students.

## WORKFORCE TRAINING AND
## WORKFORCE INTERMEDIARIES

Community colleges are uniquely positioned in the current workforce-training system found in the United States. As Kevin Dougherty and Marianne Bakia (2000) discuss, over 90 percent of community colleges offer some form of contract training, typically in response to the need of an employer for such things as English as a second language (ESL) training for workers, an upgrade in employee skill levels, or the acquisition of technical skills. Dougherty and Bakia go on to note that contract training is desired by more than just the employers, for it is an avenue of involvement that community colleges are interested in: "The willingness of community colleges to provide contract training was also a product of strong marketing efforts on the part of their national and state associations. These associations have addressed their exhortations about the benefits of having community colleges do contract training as much to community college faculty and staff as to businesspeople and government officials" (2000, 224).

This finding relates back to the point raised in Chapter 2 about professionalization and the need to cultivate a market for professional services. The American Association of Community Colleges, for example, has on its Web site (http://www.aacc.nche.edu/) a number of workforce training initiatives, such as a Workforce Development Institute, and it is also taking an active role in reshaping current federal reauthorizations of the Carl Perkins Act and the Workforce Investment Act.

One of the most advantageous ways of thinking about the role of community colleges in workforce training is through the concept of career pathways, as articulated by the Workforce Strategy Center (http://www.workforcestrategy.org). The intent of this model is to provide workers who are stuck in situations with relatively little upward mobility with an avenue for career placement. According to Sara Rab (2003, 62), research on institutions that have implemented successful career pathways programs reveals that such programs have the following elements:

1. Community outreach to disadvantaged adults
2. Basic skills course work at community-based organizations that serve as branch campuses of community colleges
3. Entry-level training
4. Internship placement
5. Entry-level employment
6. Upgrading training

Key to the notion of a career pathway is that all entities within the community college (academic departments, offering both for-credit and noncredit courses; academic affairs offices; student services offices) work together and provide seamless services to the student. On an internal level, this involves the formation of learning communities and bridge programs that unite traditional, developmental, and noncredit courses. Besides these internal steps, community colleges need to engage the local Workforce Investment Board (WIB), a member of the local One-Stop Center (a key provision under the Temporary Assistance for Needy Families [TANF] Act, centers designed to provide career counseling, training, and placement services within a single location), and other community-based organizations that are linked to those currently employed.

Community colleges can serve as effective workforce intermediaries, as was recently discussed by Richard Kazis (2003), senior vice president at Jobs for the Future. Kazis suggests that community colleges are uniquely positioned as go-betweens for those providing funding for job training and those seeking jobs. However, as Lederer (2003) has noted, the workforce training system that needs to be in place so that community colleges can maximize their potential is in a state of disarray. At present other constituencies—such as One Stop Centers and local social service agencies—eat up the bulk of funds that are available through the Workforce Investment Act (WIA) and other aspects of federal financial support that is given for workforce training. As Richard Kazis, Heath Prince, and Jerry Rubin (2003) suggest, an effective workforce development system would place training providers, employers, and intermediaries such as community colleges at the same table. They also note that there are currently no discernible outcomes measuring the effectiveness of current workforce efforts.

Julian Alssid and colleagues at the Workforce Strategy Center have pioneered a number of efforts to look at career pathways. Such a model requires that all relevant players in the workforce training system work together to provide an upwardly mobile pathway for career development (Alssid et al. 2002).

Recently the Workforce Strategy Center (2003) released a monograph emphasizing the importance of contextualized learning for promoting student achievement. All too often what is taught in the classroom does not resonate with the life experiences of students. In addition, few instructors or institutions take the time to assess the varying learning styles of students and simply employ a pedagogy that fails to account for varying learning needs. With respect to career training, it is urgently important to place learning within a context where students understand by seeing the direct applicability of what is being taught. The use of simulations, for example, is one way of accomplishing this end. The popularity of simulated patients in an allied health program, for example, and other virtual reality approaches is testament to the effectiveness of such approaches. However, these are very costly solutions to what are vexing learning problems.

A companion piece to Workforce Strategy's work on career pathways is the asset development policy research undertake by the Asset Development Institute's Center on Hunger and Poverty at the Heller School for Social Policy and Management at Brandeis University. According to Larry Beeferman (2001, 12–13), "assets refer to the capacities and resources that enable individuals to identify, choose, and carry out projects for their lives. Through these choices, individuals choose what well-being signifies to them, and by these means are enabled to attain it."

Asset development policy can be viewed as a successor to the policy framework ushered in by the New Deal, a set of assumptions that has been transcended (and some would say made obsolete) by social legislation of the past twenty years (Beeferman 2001, 51):

> The economic, social and other realities of the 21st century have overtaken many aspects of the policy framework that served as a keystone since the New Deal. A new policy framework is required, but one which can, in a number of respects, be viewed as extending the vision and expanding the means that were adopted in the New Deal era. To succeed, that new policy framework must be compatible with broadly held American values. . . . Assets are critically important to those goals. Assets are of various kind, both individual and collective, and serve in diverse ways to afford families and individuals economic security and opportunity. In certain respects, asset policies are not novel but, ironically, those that exist largely benefit the more affluent.

An interesting application of assets development to the career ambitions of individuals is contained in the publication *Pathways to Getting Ahead* (Beeferman and Venner 2003), a joint project of the Public and Community Affairs Department of the Federal Reserve Bank of Boston and the Asset Development Institute at Brandeis University. This booklet, designed for a wide audience, provides a step-by-step guide for acquiring the assets needed for career advancement. It discusses a variety of issues, ranging from the economic return of a higher education to savings and investment strategies.

The need for an integrated workforce-development structure is the recent subject of a report coauthored by the National Center on Education and the Economy, Jobs for the Future, and the Council for Adult and Experiential Learning. In *Toward a National Workforce Education and Training Policy*, Ray Uhalde, Marlene Seltzer, Pamela Tate, and Rebecca Klein-Collins (2003) make a number of recommendations for improving the workforce training system in the United States. The report states the following objectives for a revamped workforce training system:

1. Invest in training on a scale that supports the well-being of the nation's economy and so that it is not just a privilege for the lucky few.
2. Expand the scope of all federal training and education programs to reach incumbent workers, particularly those with low skill and income levels, and to help them advance to jobs that pay family-sustaining wages.
3. Use federal resources to leverage state, local, and private investment in education and training.
4. Create stronger linkages with higher education programs and help to improve access, retention, and success for working adults pursuing skills and credentials.
5. Strengthen connections between workforce training and employers, as well as with the economic and community development initiatives/strategies, and fund interventions that engage the private sector. (Uhalde, Seltzer, Tate, and Klein-Collins 2003, executive summary)

## LIFELONG HIGHER EDUCATION ENROLLMENT PATTERNS

It makes sense to think about the educational career of a student in terms of a set of recurrent enrollments in higher education institutions (Adelman 1999). It is no longer common—in fact it is a rarity—for a student to enroll in a single baccalaureate institution, stay continuously enrolled, and graduate from that institution. As Robert C. Dickeson, senior vice president of policy, research, and evaluation at the Lumina Foundation for Education notes (in Ewell, Schild, and Paulson 2003, foreword):

> It is becoming increasingly difficult to understand student retention and educational goal attainment in the United States. The traditional pattern—one student attending one institution and graduating in four years—no longer endures. By contrast, today's college student is more likely than ever to transfer from one institution, enroll in a second or

third school, and simultaneously take distance-learning courses from yet another provider.

Clifford Adelman (1999) notes that community college graduation rates would be far higher if each student's successive enrollments and credits earned were blended into a single academic record. Recognizing the importance of developing such a system, the Lumina Foundation for Education commissioned the National Center for Higher Education Management Systems (NCHEMS) to assess whether such a system could be constructed. In the resulting report—*Following the Mobile Student: Can We Develop the Capacity for a Comprehensive Database to Assess Student Progression?*—NCHEMS did find that over 50 percent of students who eventually earn bachelor's degrees enroll in "two or more institutions, and almost a fifth attended three or more" (Ewell, Schild, and Paulson 2003, 1). NCHEMS did find that thirty-nine states maintained forty-six unit-record databases. With some supplemental data collection those databases could provide the type of coherent system desired by the Lumina Foundation for Education, with some caveats regarding the need to maintain student privacy, that participation should be voluntary, and that a record-keeping architecture needs to be created in order to unify the way data is recorded in these state databases.

### *Creating a Foundation for Lifelong Learning*

As previously discussed in this volume, the release of *A Nation at Risk* in 1983 sounded an alarm about what was alleged to be the deteriorating foundation of elementary and secondary education throughout the United States. With literally hundreds of reports on the sorry state of U.S. education being released in its aftermath, education reform went through a number of phases, ranging from initial efforts focused on macro-structural issues of accountability and achievement to later responses that focused on local reforms (Sadovnik, Cookson, Semel, and Levinson 2002).

One of the well-publicized federal initiatives was passage of Goals 2000 during the administration of George H. W. Bush in 1990 and continuing throughout the administration of Bill Clinton. The six articulated goals underscore the importance of learning throughout the life span.

1. Goal 1: By the year 2000, all children will start ready to learn.
2. Goal 2: By the year 2000, the high school graduate rate will increase to at least 90 percent.

3. Goal 3: By the year 2000, American students will leave grades 4, 8, and 12 having demonstrated competency in challenging subject matter, including English, mathematics, science, history, and geography, and every school in America will ensure that all students learn to use their mind well, so they may be prepared for responsible citizenship, further learning, and productive employment in our modern economy.
4. Goal 4: By the year 2000, U.S. students will be first in the world in mathematics and science achievement.
5. Goal 5: By the year 2000, every adult American will be literate and will possess the skills necessary to compete in a global economy and exercise the rights and responsibilities of citizenship.
6. Goal 6: By the year 2000, every school in America will be free of drugs and violence and will offer a disciplined environment conducive to learning. (Sadovnik et al. 2002, 228)

### *Factors That Inhibit Lifelong Learning*

As stated in Chapter 1, the typical college student in the United States is no longer an eighteen-to-twenty-two-year-old undergraduate who resides at a baccalaureate institution and attends college full-time. Although the dominance of this mythical depiction overstates its empirical reality, it continues to influence higher education policy in the United States. For example, many federally funded financial aid programs continue to be tailored to the full-time undergraduate and not to the part-time student, who is often also working full-time. In addition, many colleges are still structured as though they continue to serve a full-time, day-student body, even though this group has precipitously shrunk in numbers. It is not unusual to find support services such as academic advisement, counseling, and student services lacking for the part-time evening student.

## INCREASE IN CONTINUING AND PROFESSIONAL EDUCATION ENROLLMENTS

Adult participation in education is steadily rising in the United States: In 1999, 46 percent of adults participated in some form of adult education, representing an increase from 33 percent in 1991. In many ways, this phenomenon is inseparable from the overall growth of higher education in the past thirty years. From 1970 to 1998, enrollments in public higher education increased from 6,428,000 to 11,176,000. Private higher education enrollments increased from 2,153,000 to 3,373,000 during this time. All told, the number of people enrolled in higher education increased from 8,581,000 to 14,549,000 during this period, or approximately 59 percent (National Center for Educational Statistics 2002, 10–13). With respect to adult learners, the U.S. Department of Education (2002, v) reports that

> the overall increase in participation in adult education between 1991 and 1999 was widespread, occurring among virtually every group of adults examined in this report. Specifically, participation rates increased among the following: all age groups except those ages 35–44, both men and women, all racial/ethnic groups, all educational levels, all labor force groups, and all occupation groups except those in professional or managerial positions. The groups that did not increase their participation rates had some of the highest initial participation rates in 1991 and constant rates of participation thereafter.

An increase in the number of adult learners has changed the complexion of higher education. Whereas in 1970, 28 percent of those enrolled in higher education were twenty-five years of age or older, this figure had increased to 45 percent by the year 2000 (Aslanian 2001, 4). One aspect of this trend is that there has been a concomitant increase in noncredit enrollments. Carol Aslanian (2001, 132) attributes this increase to the additional desire on the part of adult Americans to enhance training for a job or career advancement:

> A myth about noncredit instruction and noncredit students has been that the curriculum focuses on the avocational, recreational, and personal needs of the learning. . . . Noncredit instruction in this nation— that is, instruction that the student selects and pays for (or gets reimbursement or funding for from another)—is all about career preparation. Noncredit students in this study specifically talked about jobs—ones they had or wanted—as the reasons for taking courses or workshops, enrolling in special institutes or seminars, or doing whatever was needed to acquire the competencies required.

### *Perfecting Adult Learning: CAEL and*
### *Adult Learning–Focused Institutions*

One organization that has championed the cause of adult learning is the Council for Adult and Experiential Learning (CAEL). CAEL has identified eight principles that are important for effective adult learning. Taken in their composite, these principles catalog the attributes of an Adult Learning Focused Institution (ALFI). According to Thomas Flint and Associates (1999), such institutions will

1. provide outreach to students so that they have lifelong access to educational opportunities;
2. provide life and career services to students;
3. offer a variety of options to adults for financing their learning;
4. define and assess learning outcomes;
5. base teaching upon a diverse set of instructional strategies that recognize diverse learning styles and biographical experiences;
6. offer services to assist students in becoming self-directed learners;
7. provide technology that will facilitate and enhance the learning experience; and
8. engage in "strategic partnerships with employers and other organizations."

Another important initiative undertaken by CAEL is the promotion of lifelong learning accounts (LiLAs): "self-managed educational advancement accounts for adult workers. They are universal, portable and funded by the workers, themselves, and matched to an established cap by employers and third-party sources" (CAEL n.d.). Employees have the opportunity to draw upon their accounts to fund educational advancement.

In many professions and occupations, practitioners must keep up with emerging knowledge. Through the requirement of attaining a specified number of continuing education units (CEUs) during a given time period, professions create a market for lifelong learning. Although CEUs and the need for continuing professional education was first associated with the health professions, other occupational groups are now requiring such continuing education credits for renewal of certifications. Recently, many states have mandated that teachers acquire a specific number of professional development hours in order to renew their licenses. Through this measure, school districts attempt to ensure that teachers stay current with emerging pedagogical practices and are aware of new regulations and mandates.

### University Extension and Continuing Education Programs

University extension programs began a period of formidable expansion during the 1980s. U.S. institutions took their cue from what was occurring at elite universities such as Oxford and Cambridge in the United

Kingdom (Cremin 1988, 243–245). William Rainey Harper, president of the University of Chicago at the turn of the twentieth century, was a strong proponent of extension services. Harper was a strong proponent of community colleges and was instrumental in the development of two-year colleges. University extension programs also grew quickly in the Midwest as the University of Wisconsin and the University of Kansas zealously developed programs to support agricultural interests.

The increasing importance of industrialization and of corporations in U.S. economic life also drove the development of extended education, since the mechanical arts and engineering were important for the industrialization of the United States during this period. According to Joseph Kett (1994, 234), "during the 1870s and 1880s the corporate revolution forged new bonds between higher education and the higher levels of business enterprise."

Correspondence schools, which offered distance learning via the U.S. Postal Service, came into being during this period of time. Again according to Kett, "The growth of correspondence schools also coincided with the quantum leap in public high-school enrollments from under 250,000 in 1890 to over 4,000,000 by 1930. . . . each successive surge in school enrollments left an army of stragglers, those too old to attend or too poor to persist beyond a few grades, and these stragglers, in turn, sought surrogates for the education denied them" (1994, 236).

Organized labor also played an important role in the development of "nonmatriculated" adult learning. As Kett (1994: 189–199) states, labor leaders at that time felt it was important for constituents to know about larger macro-structural issues that had an impact on their working lives.

Another boost for adult learning came through the importance attached to education by eastern European émigrés, many of whom were Jewish, who were fleeing the oppressive conditions of that time. German Jews formed the Educational Alliance, which was modeled on the work of Jane Addams at Hull House and on the settlement-house movement. Besides offering a range of educational programs, such associations provided Jewish immigrants with important avenues of social support (Howe 1976).

In 1926, the American Association for Adult Education was formed, signaling the formalized beginning of what can euphemistically be termed the "adult education movement" (Heaney 1996). Also around this time, philanthropic foundations, notably the Carnegie Corporation of New York, began to play an important role in adult education. "In 1924 the corporation summoned its first conference on the education of adults and in the next ten years made grants totaling just under $3,000,000 to organizations that engaged in adult learning" (Kett 1994,

335). The founding of the New School for Social Research also represents an important moment in the creation of opportunities for adult learning. As Peter Rutkoff and William Scott (1986) note, the adult education classes at the New School were much more successful than had been anticipated when the school opened its doors in 1919. Throughout the century, the New School became a leader in providing adult education to millions of New Yorkers.

Certainly passage of the Servicemen's Readjustment Act of 1944, commonly known as the GI Bill, provided an enormous boon to colleges and to the notion of lifelong learning. Returning servicemen populated the nation's higher education classrooms as never before. The post–World War II era also ushered in a new wave of prosperity and expansion of the population through a boom in home ownership and suburbanization. During this period community colleges also expanded greatly.

### Learning Competencies

In tandem with the need for higher-order skills, there has been a growing emphasis on the importance of learning competencies. This is related to the increasing concern about accountability within higher education and its importance is being championed by the six regional educational accrediting agencies that have been empowered by the federal government to regulate institutional quality in the United States.

Alverno College in Milwaukee, Wisconsin, has been a leader in the nation with respect to restructuring a curriculum based on the mastery of an array of college-wide and discipline-specific competencies. In addition, there has been a growing emphasis on awarding credits based on an assessment of lifelong learning. The College of Public and Community Service (CPCS) at the University of Massachusetts in Boston has structured a competency-based experience for adult learners. Competency-based experience is also at the center of Cambridge College's curriculum, and it is becoming common within community colleges. The Community College of Vermont, which is noteworthy for its lack of a campus, has developed an elaborate system for awarding credit for prior learning.

## COMMUNITY COLLEGE AND
## COMMUNITY BUILDING

In providing lifelong learning, community colleges are increasingly involved in efforts designed to make education "seamless." At present there are significant barriers to collaboration between community colleges and K–12 schools. Although community colleges in part evolved from secondary schools, administratively they are typically under separate oversight. However, there is a growing movement to unite K–14 under one umbrella. As Margaret Orr and Debra Bragg (2001, 102) observe,

> Community college and public school systems are well positioned for system integration. They are the two largest, and most broad serving, public educational systems in the United States. . . . Community colleges are well suited to work closely with school districts because of their similar public education mission, specializing in transfer and technical education, low costs and accessibly. . . . both systems are pressured by similar public expectations about the role and function of public education for social equity and workforce development.

In the words of Horace Mann, education is "the great equalizer of the conditions of men" (quoted in Gwynne, 693). In this regard, community colleges could be doing a better job with respect to economic development and promoting self-sufficiency on the part of the poor (Kazis and Liebowitz et al. 2001). Career pathway models as previously discussed and developed by Workforce Strategies, a nonprofit research organization based in Brooklyn, New York, provide an avenue for mobility. A career pathways model organizes the resources of a community college to bridge what are often disparate and self-contained organizational entities. Within many community colleges, credit and noncredit classes are offered by separate and distinct entities; ESL and developmental instruction is not offered by the same departments that offer credit-bearing instruction. A career pathways model unites these disparate parts by focusing on how an institution's resources can be marshaled to promote students' success as they navigate through the educational process.

## RECENT GROWTH IN ADULT EDUCATION

### *Proprietary and For-Profit Institutions*

Adult learning occurs within a variety of contexts. First, there are the industry-based venues and learning that occurs literally on the job. Organizations such as McDonald's, through McDonald's University, and other corporate entities comprise a sector that continues to enlarge. In addition, companies such as Disney offer extensive internship opportunities, which also constitutes an example of corporate learning.

Another important force in the adult learning world are the proprietary institutions that offer noncredit, career-directed opportunities. Various programs based on information technology, such as Computer Learning, and information technology training are linked to companies—such as Chubb Institute and Gibbs—that offer instruction at times that are often more responsive than traditional higher education institutions to the scheduling constraints facing adults.

For-profit universities have grown tremendously. The behemoth in this category is the University of Phoenix, which has become the largest university in the world. Owned by the Apollo Group, the University of Phoenix has developed a nationwide network of didactic instruction providers who are linked with an online component. Although such universities are scorned by many in the academic world, they have been extremely effective in partnering with two-year colleges to offer students anytime-anywhere credit-bearing educational opportunities.

### Distance Learning and Cyberschools

The rise of distance learning is endemic to community colleges in the twenty-first century. A recent report by the National Center for Education Statistics underscores the rise in this form of learning. The overwhelming majority of community colleges now offer some form of distance learning.

In the 1990s a number of attempts were made to launch for-profit distance-learning facilities, such as Fathom at Columbia University. In addition, the Open University of the United Kingdom attempted to market an array of online learning opportunities. However, these ventures have largely failed because the potential profitability of these ventures was severely overestimated.

One of the problems of distance learning has been the high attrition rates associated with these courses. Attrition rates of 50 percent have been the norm. In addition, many universities have had to deal with intellectual property issues stemming from distance learning regarding the "ownership" of the product of these courses. Another concern centers on the pedagogy that instructors use for online courses. Simply transferring the instructional strategies utilized in didactic classes to the screen is not an effective pedagogical technique, since most of those depend on and assume student participation and group interaction or discussion.

## INSTITUTES FOR LEARNING IN RETIREMENT

A major force in the growth of lifelong learning has been the learning in retirement movement, which is closely associated with Elderhostel. Based in Boston, Elderhostel has grown from 220 participants to over 200,000 yearly. Founded in 1975, with five colleges in New Hampshire offering programs to adults over age fifty-five, it has grown to offer more than 10,000 programs in one hundred countries.

Norwalk Community College in Connecticut has close to eight hundred students enrolled in their Lifetime Learners Institute. The institute offers peer-taught courses, and adult learners can enroll in undergraduate credit-bearing courses on a space available basis (Cantor, 2003). Besides making an immense contribution to the intellectual vitality of the college, institute-affiliated learners provide one-to-one mentoring for ESL students and actively participate in the college's foundation to raise funds for the college.

## CONCLUSION

Given the burgeoning cognitive requirements of a knowledge-based society, lifelong learning is increasingly a ubiquitous feature of everyday life. Community colleges are ideally structured to provide learning throughout the life span in that they typically house programs ranging from early childhood education, which often features a laboratory school that provides child care to infants and toddlers, to programs that engage learners in retirement. One of the challenges is to create a seamless educational system in which K–14 is an integrated experience. Besides the need to transcend educational segmentation in order for this to occur, there needs to be a common platform for lifelong learning so that learning outcomes are portable throughout the life course of the learner. This can be done through the use of electronic portfolios that capture the competencies attained by learners beginning in pre-K and continuing throughout college.

### References

Abbott, Andrew. 1988. *The System of Professions: An Essay on the Division of Expert Labor.* Chicago: University of Chicago Press.

Adelman, Clifford. 1999. *Answers in the Toolbox: Academic Intensity, Attendance Patterns, and Bachelor's Degree Attainment (PLLI 1999–8021).* Washington, DC: U.S. Department of Education, Office of Educational Research and Improvement.

Alssid, Julian L., David Gruber, Davis Jenkins, Christopher Mazzeo, Brandon Roberts, and Regina Stanback-Stroud. 2002. *Building a Career Pathways System: Promising Practices in Community College–Centered Workforce Development.* Brooklyn, NY: Workforce Strategy Center.

Aslanian, Carol B. 2001. *Adult Students Today.* New York: College Board.

Bailey, Thomas, and Elliot Weininger. 2002. "Educating Immigrants and Native Minorities in CUNY Community Colleges." *Community College Research Center Brief.* No. 13. New York: Columbia University.

Beeferman, Larry W. 2001. *Asset Development Policy: The New Opportunity.* Waltham, MA: Asset Development Institute, Center on Hunger and Poverty, Heller School Social Policy and Management, Brandeis University.

Beeferman, Larry W., and Sandra H. Venner. 2003. *Pathways to Getting Ahead.* Joint Project of the Public and Community Affairs Department of the Federal Reserve Bank of Boston and the Asset Development Institute. Boston and Waltham, MA: Brandeis University.

Berg, Ivar. 1970. *Education and Jobs: The Great Training Robbery.* New York: Praeger.

Bluestone, Barry, and Bennett Harrison. 1982. *The Deindustrialization of America: Plant Closings, Community Abandonment, and the Dismantling of Basic Industry.* New York: Basic Books.

Cantor, Jeffrey A. 2003. "Bridging Generations: A 'Community' College Imperative." *Leadership Abstracts* 16, no. 10 (October). Online edition, http://www.league.org/publication/abstracts/leadership/labs1003.htm (accessed January 12, 2005).

Carnevale, Anthony, and Donna M. Desrochers. 2001. *Help Wanted . . . Credentials Required: Community Colleges in the Knowledge Economy.* Washington, DC: Educational Testing Service and the American Association of Community Colleges.

Carnoy, Martin. 2000. *Sustaining the New Economy: Work, Family, and Community in the Information Age.* Cambridge, MA: Harvard University Press.

Church, Robert L. 1976. *Education in the United States.* New York: Free Press.

Coleman, James. 1966. *Equality of Educational Opportunity.* Washington, DC: U.S. Department of Health, Education, and Welfare.

Council for Adult and Experiential Learning (CAEL). N.d. http://www.cael.org/lilas.asp (accessed December 30, 2004).

Cremin, Lawrence. 1988. *American Education: The Metropolitan Experience, 1876–1980.* New York: Harper and Row.

Delano Abbott, Andrew. 1988. *The System of Professions: An Essay on the Division of Expert Labor.* Chicago: University of Chicago Press.

Dougherty, Kevin, and Marianne Bakia. 2000. "Contract Training and the Community College: Origins and Impacts." *The Teachers' College Review.* New York: Teachers' College Press.

Eaton, Judith S. 1994. *Strengthening Collegiate Education in Community Colleges.* San Francisco: Jossey-Bass.

Ewell, Peter T., Paula R. Schild, and Karen Paulson. 2003. *Following the Mobile Student: Can We Develop the Capacity for a Comprehensive Database to Assess Student Progression?* Indianapolis, IN: Lumina Foundation for Education.

Flint, Thomas A., and Associates. 1999. *Best Practices in Adult Learning: A CAEL/APQC Benchmarking Study.* New York: Forbes Custom Publishing.

Grubb, W. Norton, Norena Badway, and Denise Bell. 2002. *Community Colleges and the Equity Agenda: The Potential of Non Credit Education.* Boston: Jobs for the Future.

Gwynne, Julia. 2002. "Urban Schools." In *Education and Sociology: An Encyclopedia,* ed. David L. Levison, Peter W. Cookson, and Alan R. Sadovnik. New York: RoutledgeFalmer.

Heaney, Tom. 1996. *Adult Education for Social Change: From Center State to the Wings and Back.* Columbus, OH: ERIC Monograph.

Hoffman, Nancy. 2003. "College Credit in High School: Increasing College Attainment Rates for Underrepresented Students." *Change Magazine,* July/August.

Howe, Irving. 1976. *World of Our Fathers.* New York: Harcourt Brace Jovanovich.

Judy, Richard W., and Carol D'Amico. 1997. *Workforce 2020: Work and Workers in the 21st Century.* Indianapolis, IN: Hudson Institute.

Kazis, Richard. 2003. "The Emergence of Regional Workforce Intermediaries and the Implications for Community Colleges." In *Building a Workforce System through Partnering,* ed. Norm Nielsen, Dee Baird, Boo Browning, Mark David Milliron. Tempe, AZ: League for Innovation in the Community College.

Kazis, Richard, and Marty Liebowitz. 2003. "Changing Courses: Instructional Innovations that Help Low-Income Students Succeed in Community College." MDRC. http://www.mdrc.org/publications/349/overview.html (accessed February 13, 2005).

Kazis, Richard, Heath Prince, and Jerry Rubin. 2003. *Employer Use of the Publicly Funded Workforce Development System: Perceptions of What's Working and What's Not, and Recommendations for Improvements—Summary of Findings and Recommendations.* Boston: Jobs for the Future.

Kett, Joseph F. 1994. *The Pursuit of Knowledge under Difficulties: From Self-Improvement to Adult Education in America, 1750–1990.* Stanford, CA: Stanford University Press.

Kozol, Jonathan. 1967. *Death at an Early Age: The Destruction of the Hearts and*

*Minds of Negro Children in the Boston Public Schools.* Boston: Houghton Mifflin.

———. 1991. *Savage Inequalities: Children in America's Schools.* New York: HarperPerennial.

Larson, Magali Sarfatti. 1977. *The Rise of Professionalism: A Sociological Analysis.* Berkeley and Los Angeles: University of California Press.

Lavin, David E., and David Hyllegard. 1996. *Changing the Odds: Open Admissions and the Life Changes of the Disadvantaged.* New Haven, CT: Yale University Press.

Lederer, John. 2003. "Broken Promises: Lifelong Learning, Community Colleges, and the Sad State of Incumbent Worker Training." http://success.shoreline.edu/shoreline/research/Broken_Promises_John_Lederer.pdf (accessed January 2, 2005).

Lee, Valerie E., and David T. Burkham. 2002. *Inequality at the Starting Gate: Social Background Differences in Achievement as Children Begin School.* Washington, DC: Economic Policy Institute; Ann Arbor: University of Michigan.

Machlup, Fritz. 1962. *The Production and Distribution of Knowledge in the United States.* Princeton: Princeton University Press.

Madigan, Timothy J. 2002. "Cultural Capital." In *Education and Sociology: An Encyclopedia,* ed. David L. Levinson, Peter W. Cookson Jr., and Alan R. Sadovnik. New York: RoutledgeFalmer.

Marshall, Ray, and Marc Tucker. 1992. *Thinking for a Living: Education and the Wealth of Nations.* New York: Basic Books.

Mazzeo, Christopher, Sara Y. Rab, and Julian L. Alssid. 2003. *Building Bridges to College and Careers: Contextualized Basic Skills Programs at Community Colleges.* New York: Workforce Strategies.

McCabe, Robert H., and Phillip R. Day Jr., eds. 1998. *Developmental Education: A Twenty-First Century Social and Economic Imperative.* Mission Viejo, CA: League for Innovation in the Community College.

Meier, Deborah. 2002. *In Schools We Trust: Creating Communities of Learning in an Era of Testing and Standardization.* Boston: Beacon.

Milliron, Mark David. 2001. "Touching Students in the Digital Age: The Move toward Learner Relationship Management (LRM)." *Learning Abstracts* 4, no. 1 (January). Online edition, http://www.league.org/publication/abstracts/learning/lelabs0101.htm (accessed January 12, 2005).

National Association for the Education of Young Children (NAEYC). N.d. http://www.naeyc.org/resources/position_statements/creating_conditions.asp (accessed December 23, 2004).

National Center for Education Statistics. 2002. "Participation, Trends, and Patterns in Adult Education: 1991–1999." *Statistical Analysis Report.* Washington, DC: U.S. Department of Education, February.

National Center on Education and the Economy. N.d. http://www.ncee.org (accessed December 30, 2004).

National Commission on Excellence in Education. 1983. *A Nation at Risk.* Washington, DC: Government Printing Office.

National Commission on the Skills of the American Workforce. 1990. *America's Choice: High Skills or Low Wages!* Rochester, NY: National Center on Education and the Economy.

Nespoli, Lawrence A. 1991. "Investing in Human Capital: State Strategies for Economic Development." *New Directions in Community Colleges,* no. 75 (Fall).

Nielsen, Norm, Dee Baird, Boo Browning, and Mark David Milliron, eds. 2003. *Building a Workforce System through Partnering.* Tempe, AZ: League for Innovation in the Community College.

O'Banion, Terry. 1999. *Launching a Learning-Centered College.* Mission Viejo, CA: League for Innovation in the Community College.

Organization for Economic Co-operation and Development (OECD). 1997. *Thematic Review on Adult Learning in Canada: Background Report.* Paris: OECD.

Orr, Margaret, and Debra Bragg. 2001. "Policy Directions for K–14 Education: Looking to the Future." In *Educational Policy in the 21st Century,* vol. 2, *Community Colleges: Policy in the Future Context,* ed. Barbara K. Townsend and Susan B. Twombly. Westport, CT: Ablex.

Psacharopoulos, George. 1995. *The Profitability of Investment Education: Concepts and Methods.* Washington, DC: World Bank.

Rab, Sara. 2003. "Building a Career Pathways System: Promising Practices in Community College–Centered Workforce Development." *Educause Quarterly,* no. 1.

Reich, Robert B. 1991. *The Work of Nations: Preparing Ourselves for 21st Century Capitalism.* New York: Vintage Books.

Rutkoff, Peter M., and William B. Scott. 1986. *New School: A History of the New School for Social Research.* New York: New York Free Press.

Sadovnik, Alan R., Peter W. Cookson Jr., Susan F. Semel, and David L. Levinson. 2002. "Educational Reform in the United States: 1980s and 1990s." In *Education and Sociology: An Encyclopedia,* ed. David L. Levinson, Peter W. Cookson Jr., and Alan R. Sadovnik. New York: RoutledgeFalmer.

Schneider, Barbara. 2002. "Social Capital: A Ubiquitous Emerging Conception." In *Education and Sociology: An Encyclopedia,* ed. David L. Levinson, Peter W. Cookson Jr., and Alan R. Sadovnik. New York: RoutledgeFalmer.

Schultz, Theodore. 1961. "Investment in Human Capital." *American Economic Review,* LI. American Economic Association Presidential Address, March.

————. 1963. *The Economic Value of Education.* New York: Columbia University Press.

Shouse, Roger C. 2002. "School Effects." In *Education and Sociology: An Encyclopedia,* ed. David L. Levinson, Peter W. Cookson Jr., and Alan R. Sadovnik. New York: RoutledgeFalmer.

Thurow, Lester. 1999. *Building Wealth: The New Rules for Individuals, Companies, and Nations.* New York: HarperCollins.

Uhalde, Ray, Marlene Seltzer, Pamela Tate, and Rebecca Klein-Collins. 2003. *Toward a National Workforce Education and Training Policy.* Washington, DC: National Center on Education and the Economy.

U.S. Census Bureau. 2003. *Poverty, Income See Slight Changes; Child Poverty Rate Unchanged, Census Bureau Reports.* Washington, DC: U.S. Department of Commerce, September 26.

U.S. Department of Education. 2002 *Participation Trends and Patterns in Adult Education: 1991–1992,* by Sean Creighton and Lisa Hudson. Washington, DC: National Center for Education Statistics.

Weber, Max. 1976. *The Protestant Ethic and the Spirit of Capitalism.* Translated by Talcott Parsons. London: Allen and Unwin.

Workforce Strategy Center. 2003. *Building Bridges to College and Careers: Contextualized Basic Skills Programs at Community College.* Brooklyn, NY: Workforce Strategy Center.

World Bank. 2005. Education: Overview. http://www.worldbank.org (accessed February 12, 2005).

Young, Michael. 1958. *The Rise of the Meritocracy 1870–2033.* London: Thames and Hudson.

*Chapter Six*

# ✦ The Future of the Community College

The dramatic growth of community colleges during the twentieth century was an important part of the expanding universality of higher education opportunities in the United States. By the end of the twentieth century, community colleges were in easy reach of virtually all U.S. residents, either in traditional brick-and-mortar form or via cyberspace. The growth of private, profit-making providers of higher education—such as the University of Phoenix, whose size eclipsed all existing universities by the end of the millennium—was also an important part of this expansionary story. This chapter assesses the present and future challenges facing community colleges as this sector enters its second century of existence.

## THE VISION OF COMMUNITY COLLEGE LEADERS

The hundredth anniversary of the community college was celebrated at the 2001 annual meeting of the AACC. In recognition of this occasion, Bergen Community College's president, Judith K. Winn, and former academic vice president, David L. Levinson, organized a plenary session at which the following leaders in the community college movement participated: George Boggs, president of the AACC; Mark David Milliron, former president and CEO of the League for Innovation in the Community College; John Roueche, the Sid W. Richardson Regents' Chair in Community College Leadership and professor and director of the Community College Leadership Program at the University of Texas at Austin; Jerry Sue Thornton, president of Cuyhauga Community College; and Leo Chavitz, former chancellor of Foothill-Dianza Community College District. These participants identified twenty-one maxims to guide community colleges in strengthening and expanding their effectiveness for the twenty-first century. What follows is an explication of these maxims, both as the community leaders identified them at the plenary session and as they have been developed in the further discussion that has ensued since the AACC meetings.

1. *Be responsive to a rapidly changing world.* As sociologists have long argued, change is part and parcel of any social order. Key for the vitality of any society is the civic engagement of its citizenry. Community colleges have the potential to be primary institutions for engendering civic engagement in demographically diverse communities (Levinson 2004).

For many communities throughout the United States, community colleges constitute a central site for public interactions. AACC estimates that over 10 million Americans have direct contact with a community college in the course of a single year. Literally every citizen in the United States is within the reach of a community college, for there are 1,171 community colleges in the United States. Beyond being in close physical proximity, an increasing number of people enjoy a cybernetic connection with a community college.

Community colleges came into fruition during a time of tremendous alterations in the nation's occupational structure, demographic composition, labor force, and residential patterns. Community colleges have consistently attempted to respond to changing local conditions. Given their connections to intermediaries involved in workforce training—such as the Worker Investment Boards that were created as part of the Workforce Investment Act (WIA)—and their growing participation in customized, corporate training, community colleges are constantly poised to seize upon new markets for training. A dramatic example of this is the current wave of contracts being issued as part of fortified homeland security initiatives in the United States after the events of September 11, 2001. Confronted with the need to train thousands of newly federalized Transportation Security Administration (TSA) workers in a short period of time, the U.S. Department of Homeland Security turned to community colleges as the preferred vendor of this training.

Another aspect of this changing world is the growing globalization of the economy and the growing attention that U.S. community colleges are paying to international student recruitment, expansion of study abroad programs, and overall internationalization of the curriculum. The AACC has been aggressively organizing international recruitment opportunities for community colleges. Recognizing the international dimensions of business and other fields, such as information technology, community colleges are paying increased attention to incorporating disciplinary learning with global dimensions, such as courses in international business and finance and an increasingly robust offering of modern languages.

A dramatically changing occupational structure, which is in part due to the internationalization of production that has resulted in manufacturing and service-sector jobs going overseas, represents a challenge to community colleges on a number of levels. One dimension concerns the nature of associate of applied science (AAS) programs, long the bread and butter of community colleges, whose mission is to produce credentialed workers for immediate entry into the labor force. Unfortunately, some of the skills acquired in such programs are not transferable across occupational sectors and therefore do not provide students with transferable skills, inhibiting easy migration across occupational sectors.

Another challenging aspect of the rapidly changing U.S. occupational structure is its cyclical nature. The demand for workers in particular fields, such as allied health and nursing, gyrates in often unpredictable ways. Thus, for example, although an institution might enlarge its nursing program in response to an existing labor market need, by the time the participants in the expanded program graduate, the specific need might have receded.

However, whether incessant job training is actually needed is a point that has been debated. As previously discussed, Ivar Berg (1970) and David Livingstone (1998) assert that the obsession with skills training constitutes the "great training robbery," and at times, a surplus of trained workers for a given industry is produced, resulting in depressed wage levels. Moreover, they suggest that such programs are tantamount to "corporate welfare" in that companies often do not pay, or are given reduced rates, for such programs. Another criticism is that such skill training is excessively narrow and does not impart skills that are useful across industrial sectors. Given the high frequency with which people change jobs and careers, many observers consider this last problem to be a fatal flaw. A suggested corrective to this problem is to instill a strong general education, with a liberal arts foundation, into workforce training so that people attain transferable skills.

2. *Cater to the increasing need for lifelong learning.* The centrality of lifelong learning for everything from the economic health of the nation (thought to rest on worker productivity and employability) and the burgeoning human-capital needs of the twenty-first century (including the constant need to upgrade skills because of relentless technological innovation) is at the heart of many contemporary workforce-training efforts. Providing lifelong learning usually falls within the province of particular professional associations whose licensure requirements require their practitioners to acquire a specific number of continuing education units (CEUs) in order to maintain currency. Although in some settings it is common for the employer to pay for such training, in others it is the responsibility of the individual worker. Often strapped for cash, those

who work on the lower rungs of the occupational ladder find it difficult to afford this training, a problem that organizations such as the Council for Adult and Experiential Learning (CAEL), through its Lifelong Learning Accounts (LiLA) initiative (an initiative similar to the productive work of the Center for Poverty and Hunger), have attempted to address. LiLAs are an initiative pioneered by the CAEL, intended to be individual learning accounts, to which an employer makes contributions to provide funding for lifelong education.

Many community colleges provide lifelong learning through a Division of Continuing and Professional Studies, which often organizationally exists as an entity separate from credit-bearing instructional programs. Although at times faculty on the instructional side of the house teach in a college's noncredit division, such teaching is generally not part of their contractual workload and is assumed as additional work. The continuance of this chasm between the credit and noncredit sides of community colleges is problematic, for it does not allow for easy internal transfer from noncredit to credit worlds. It also skirts the issue of competency-based learning, which theoretically can occur within either credit or noncredit programs.

Community colleges can foster communication on pressing social issues by bringing constituents together for days of dialogue. The National Issues Forum is a project designed to support such an initiative. The forum provides reading materials presenting all perspectives on controversial issues. In addition, training is offered to facilitators who wish to promote continued discourse relevant to these issues. Dialogue training, a mode of engaging in public conversation where participants listen and validate opposing viewpoints, is a method endorsed by the forum.

A recent thematic issue of the *Community College Journal of Research and Practice* titled "Community Colleges as Civic Institutions" highlights the civic capacity and community-building potential of community colleges (Levinson 2004). A wide range of initiatives designed to foster civic engagement are described in this issue of the journal, including a community-based theater program, service-learning initiatives, a criminal justice program in which members of the law enforcement community comprise a community advisory board, a variety of efforts designed to positively connect to a multicultural student population, and a survey of community college chief executive officers discussing the civic engagement challenges that lie ahead.

3. *Extend the mission of community colleges to include applied baccalaureate preparation.* Given the workforce's need for what many perceive as more advanced and refined skills and given the limited capacity of some states to offer baccalaureate degrees, legislating that

community colleges offer applied baccalaureate degrees is becoming increasingly popular. In states such as Florida, which ranks third in the nation in associate degrees awarded but only forty-seventh in baccalaureate degrees awarded (Evelyn 2003), the idea of offering applied baccalaureate degrees is catching on. Miami Dade Community College and two-year colleges in Arkansas, Nevada, and Utah are offering applied baccalaureate degrees (Evelyn 2003). Many assert that a baccalaureate degree is perfect for community colleges, given that they are attuned to applied academic needs. The community college also provides a province of academic activity that it can call its own.

4. *Enhance open access and provide support to students so that all succeed.* As discussed in Chapter 3, perhaps the greatest challenge facing community colleges is attaining and realizing the twin pillars of their foundation: access and excellence. As open admission institutions, community colleges accept all who apply, often resulting in a need to supply heavy remedial needs and a last-minute scramble to accommodate all who enter in a given semester. Unlike many residential colleges, which know the number of students returning months before the beginning of a semester, community colleges literally accept those coming through the doors until the first day of classes and sometimes beyond.

An immediate challenge for community colleges is to provide the assessment, advising, and placement services that these students need. Given that a large number of community college students are first-generation college attendees, many of them natives of other nations, there is a great need to help students acclimate to the college experience. Often a student will begin the enrollment process by taking a placement exam that assesses his or her reading, writing, and mathematical abilities. The results of this assessment are then used to place him or her in the proper level of courses in English or mathematics or possibly in courses for adult basic skills or ESL. With the results of the placement exam in hand, the student is then advised as to what would be an appropriate course of study, with respect to his or her aspirations and the results of the exam. Some type of orientation typically follows, with advisement, supplemental instructional support (for example, tutoring), and career services available to students throughout their enrollment. In addition, many community colleges offer a robust student activities program, which features a variety of student clubs, guest speakers, and other cultural events. A key dimension for students' success is their integration into the life of the college.

One challenge that community colleges face are high attrition rates, something that is complicated further by the multiplicity of reasons students attend community colleges. Gary Hoachlander, Anna

Sikora, and Laura Horn (2003) find that 58 percent of those attending a community college desire a credential or transfer, 23 percent desire job skills, and 19 percent enroll for other reasons, including personal enrichment. Reviewing existing studies on attrition, Michael Summers (2003) notes that studies have found that approximately 50 percent of students who begin their studies during a given term fail to re-enroll. Upon an extensive review of research on attrition, Summers notes that "early warning" monitoring has proven to be effective and that students who display "at risk" characteristics at the outset should be followed by the institution.

5. *Embrace the challenge of remediation, in terms of both the costs and the problems of integrating remedial students into the larger institutional curriculum.* Forty-two percent of community college students enrolled in at least one remedial course in 2000 (Parsad and Lewis 2003). Although some observers lament the omnipresence of remedial courses in community colleges, until secondary schools graduate students who have achieved competencies in mathematics, reading, and writing, this situation will probably remain the norm. In addition, an increasing number of four-year institutions are withdrawing from the remedial education business, for better or worse, and sending students with developmental needs to the community college. And in some public higher education systems, such as City University of New York (CUNY), remedial education has become the role of community colleges by fiat.

One of the challenges and controversies surrounding developmental education is how to structure it within the larger institutional context. Although it has been common practice to administratively separate it from the mainstay credit-bearing academic programs, some analysts (Roueche and Roueche 1999) argue against this practice. Creating bridges between developmental and credit-bearing courses poses a significant challenge, for faculty often see developmental learning as the responsibility of a learning specialist or whoever is assigned to this task. To embrace it as part of the mainstream instructional missions engenders some concern that it will dilute the intellectual caliber of credit instruction. In addition, to be a successful developmental instructor requires a good deal of training and expertise, something that is often rejected by those teaching within the academic area.

6. *Respond to the growing market need for increasing skill certifications.* Skill certifications have become a mainstay of information technology training. Many community colleges offer Cisco Systems, Microsoft, Oracle, and other certifications. Similarly, many allied health professionals must complete continuing education units (CEUs) in order to maintain licensure. And given the current widespread concern

with the quality of teachers, and in order to develop a more accountable process for teachers' skill development, many states now require completion of a specific number of professional development points (PDPs) from school teachers.

Although community colleges are not often heavily engaged in teacher training, in states such as New Jersey, state statutes limit community college involvement in teacher education to six credits. However, given the current shortage of teachers and preponderance of those who teach out of their field of undergraduate preparation—especially in the sciences and mathematics (Ingersoll 1996, 1999; Seastrom et al. 2002)—the viability of community colleges as a valuable pipeline for certified teachers is being increasingly explored.

However, some observers are not convinced of the wisdom of focusing on skill certifications. One drawback is that vendors may impart primarily proprietary knowledge through such programs, so that students may be stuck with knowledge that is not transferable across companies. Many suggest that students would benefit more from attaining a strong foundation in a particular industry's base of knowledge and then getting vendor-specific training upon employment.

7. *Expand the scope and variety of noncredit offerings.* Community colleges typically offer a wide range of noncredit courses or events to residents in their catchment area. These courses range from culinary arts to basics of home repair, from children's academic enrichment offerings to courses in theater and the creative arts. Another area of noncredit offerings is the customized and workforce training provided to companies.

Besides being valuable in and of themselves, such offerings also, by bringing these constituents to campus, may enable the college to recruit them for other experiences, all part of lifelong learning.

It is also important that there be organizational linkages between noncredit and the credit sides of the college. This involves offering courses that are concurrently credit and noncredit using noncredit courses as a pipeline for entry into credit-bearing programs, and envisioning all components of the college as providing a lifetime continuum of learning.

8. *Offer credit instruction in different forms: modular, intensive, and cyber.* Most colleges are still focused on an agrarian-based calendar that makes little sense for the high-tech world of today. To be current and relevant to the needs of learners, community colleges must offer instruction at any time and place so that potential students are able to fit course work into their busy schedules. The demands on the community college student may include family, work, and child care. Proprietary

schools are successful partly because of their customer-service orientation, and it would behoove the community college to be mindful of this important factor. In this regard, community colleges need to be more flexible in the ways they deliver instruction, because there will be a tremendous growth in and need for distance learning. Again, because so many potential students are engaged in some form of employment, the community college should offer a variety of instructional alternatives.

The current format of semester-long courses equated to a specific number of credits is a by-product of "Carnegie Units" and the influence of the Carnegie Foundation on the structure of higher education at the turn of the twentieth century (Lagemann 1983), a time when agrarian rhythms of production influenced the setting of academic calendars. Given the current structure of everyday life, in which the number of working hours has expanded as parents increasingly attempt to balance work and family and in which both parents in intact family units work (Schor 1993), flexibility with regard to course scheduling is a necessity. Within this context, the need for learning that is 24/7—anytime and anyplace—becomes paramount. Of all higher education sectors, community colleges are the largest providers of online learning.

9. *Implant the paideia of a "learning college" in an institution's culture.* According to Terry O'Banion, the concept of a learning college provides a unifying set of institutional values, similar to the idea of the "paideia principle" that Morton Adler proposed. The paideia proposal (Adler 1982) is based upon twelve principles that are designed to create a nurturing and democratic educational atmosphere. These principles encompass the following beliefs about children and learning:

- All children can learn.
- All children deserve the same quality of schooling.
- The quality of schooling to which students are entitled is what the wisest parents would wish for their own children.
- Schooling is preparation for becoming generally educated in the course of a whole lifetime.
- Schools should prepare all Americans to be good citizens of the nation and world, to earn a decent living, and to make a good life for themselves.
- Genuine learning is the activity of a learner's own mind.
- Three types of teaching should occur in schools: didactic teaching of subject matter, coaching that produces the skills of learning, and the Socratic method of questioning.
- The goals of teaching should be the acquisition of organized knowledge, skills in the use of language and mathematics, and

the growth of the mind's understanding of basic ideas and issues.

•• The assessment of a student's achievement should not be carried out by comparing him or her to other students.

•• The principal of a school should be a teacher, as should the administrator, and they should work with faculty to plan, reform, and reorganize the school community.

•• The principal and faculty of a school should be actively engaged in learning.

•• Those who dedicate their lives to education should be motivated by their own desire for lifelong learning.

Many of these principles are embodied in O'Banion's concept of a learning college. All of a learning college's operations should be centered on the goal of enhancing student learning. An important component is to focus on active learning and pedagogical strategies that are customized to the needs of the learner. Administrative processes should be transparent and should not detract from the institution's primary mission.

In many ways, community colleges extend the learning principles of progressive education, whose hallmark is a focus on the needs of the individual student. Terry O'Banion, president emeritus of the League for Innovation in the Community College, has promulgated the concept of a learning college, which embodies many of these principles.

In order for community colleges to play a truly transformative role in higher education, they must embrace the principles of a learning college (O'Banion 1997) that promotes the democratic underpinnings of our society. Most important, they have to provide a "high-trust," nurturing learning environment that embodies many of the best principles found in K–12 reform.

10. *Serve a growing disabled student population.* The Individuals with Disabilities Education Act (IDEA) assures an appropriate education for those ages three to twenty-two. An Individual Education Plan (IEP) is written when a student's disability can be documented and when the disability affects his or her ability to learn or even the way he or she learns. When a student with an IEP graduates from high school, the community college is often his or her choice for higher education. At times, the community college may even become the site of deinstitutionalization, that is, a person's leaving a therapeutic school or hospital and entering the mainstream. Challenges arise when the service delivery plan that has been implemented at a student's secondary school is not in place at the community college. Whereas a student with an IEP

may have enjoyed much individual attention in secondary school, the services at a community college may not provide for this scenario. This is challenging for many reasons, not the least of which is the high cost to the college to provide for those students who require a great deal of academic support.

11. *Transcend the social and technical divide.* As previously discussed, the distribution of wealth in U.S. society is skewed. A ramification of this is that low-income citizens lack access to information technology. Transcending the digital divide has been an important objective of the League for Innovation in the Community College, as written about by Gerardo de los Santos, Alfredo de los Santos, and Mark Milliron (2003). Community colleges are engaged in a number of proactive efforts to acquire technology for the disenfranchised. However, when it comes to pedagogy and instructional effectiveness, simply introducing information technology is no panacea. Critics such as David Noble (2002) suggest that there are commercial interests behind the proliferation of instructional technology. He alleges that marketing strategies gloss over the centrality of learning and sidestep the question of whether distance learning enhances critical inquiry. A number of recent analyses of higher education, most notably by Derek Bok, the former president of Harvard University, in his *Universities in the Marketplace: The Commercialization of Higher Education* (2003) and by David L. Kirp in his *Shakespeare, Einstein, and the Bottom Line: The Marketing of Higher Education* (2003), point to the phenomenon of profit as a propelling force for change in higher education, as opposed to policies that are formulated with academic excellence as a motivator. Two recent studies have revealed that ever-expanding instructional technology is not tantamount to educational attainment (Moss and Mitra 1998). In addition, a recent report by the NCES reveals inequities in access to instructional technology (Cattagni and Farris 2001).

Nevertheless, community colleges provide a valuable service in offering industry-specific information technology training for those seeking certification in the information technology field. Although many community colleges offer Microsoft, Cisco Systems, Oracle, and other vendor-certified training programs, there is concern that vendor-specific training limits the employability of students.

12. *Strive for ethnic and racial diversity, advocating for affirmative action and equal opportunity.* The 2000 census shows an upswing in the number of immigrants who have entered the United States compared to the census of 1990. Cities such as New York, for example, whose population is now at 8 million, include tremendously large pockets of immigrant populations (Lehrer and Sloan 2003). For many of these people,

the community college plays an important role in their acclimation to the United States by providing occupational training and instruction in ESL, both credit and noncredit, and in adult basic skills. In fact, many programs, such as medical laboratory technology, are utilized by immigrant populations to gain access into potentially lucrative allied health careers. At the current time, community colleges and other higher education sectors are facing problems, emanating from the U.S. Department of Homeland Security, with implementation of the SEVIS system for tracking foreign students who study in the United States. Because of implementation glitches, the processing of foreign nationals coming to study in the United States has been encumbered, resulting in numerous cases of students not being able to continue their studies.

Another problem has been the persistence of low rates among Hispanics of entry into higher education and of graduation from higher education institutions. Although Hispanics make up 17 percent of the eighteen-to-twenty-three-year-old population, Alberto F. Cabrera and Steven M. La Nasa (2002, 308) report that "they currently account for only 9 percent of total college enrollment." They go on to state that "when compared to those of whites, Hispanics' chances of dropping out from college are 13 percent higher" and conclude that "if these college participation and dropout rates continue, Hispanics will be less likely than whites to secure the social and economic benefits associated with a college degree" (308).

Federal support to Hispanic-serving institutions was affirmed by Title V of the 1998 amendment to the Higher Education Act. Hispanic-serving institutions are defined as higher education institutions whose student body is comprised of at least 25 percent or more Hispanics, with at least 50 percent coming from low-income backgrounds. Title V provided over $42 million of direct federal aid to such institutions in 2000 (Flores 2002).

Perceiving an attack by the Bush administration on such initiatives, which were designed to bolster equal opportunity and affirmative action in higher education, a number of higher education institutions recently banded together to submit a joint amicus brief to the U.S. Supreme Court in support of the University of Michigan Law School's affirmative action policy. The American Association of Community Colleges, along with other organizations, was concerned that the Supreme Court would negate an institution's ability to consider affirmative action goals in admissions and employment.

13. *Provide effective and contextually appropriate ESL instruction to an increasingly multilingual population.* As noted throughout this book, a diverse student population is enrolling in community colleges.

One of the challenges colleges face is how to provide instruction to a populace for whom English is a second language. A particular challenge concerns how to overcome this linguistic challenge while at the same time bringing ESL students into credit-bearing programs. A notable characteristic of many of these ESL learners is that they were highly educated in their native countries, yet this fact is often hidden because of their language challenges.

The Workforce Strategy Center (Mazzeo, Rab, and Alssid 2003) talks about the importance of "contextualizing" learning in order to address developmental needs of students. Using a career pathway model (Alssid et al. 2002), the authors cite a number of effective programs in which students with little English-language skills enter career tracks in which further language instruction was embedded in the content area. This enables the student to learn English in the process of acquiring job-related content knowledge.

Rather than being an impediment to the delivery of learning, diversity among the student body provides enhanced educational opportunities for all concerned. The linguistic diversity of a multicultural student body is a simulated microcosm of global diversity and brings out the importance of the acquisition of world languages. It has been shown that the study of world languages enhances learning throughout the life span. One of the most promising features of community college education in the United States has been the increasing number of world languages that are offered as part of the instructional program.

14. *Transcend the hierarchical segmentation of U.S. higher education, which often tends to place a glass ceiling on transfer opportunities for community college students.* As previously discussed in this volume, the lack of a coordinated system of transfer has been underscored by Clifford Adelman (1999), who demonstrates that students often amass credits at several institutions. At times this number is more than the total needed for a degree, but because these credits cannot be counted cumulatively, students nevertheless fall short of graduation. Although this results in low graduation rates on the part of community college students, the situation could be remedied by common curricular protocols among institutions.

The issue of transferability of credit has recently received national attention through hearings concerning reauthorization of the Higher Education Act. As the Council for Higher Education Accreditation (CHEA) notes (2003), there is a movement in Congress to address problems regarding transfer on a federal level, in large part because of constituent interest. However, CHEA believes that transferability should be left as an institutional prerogative, not mandated by the federal government.

15. *Integrate the Internet and technology into all facets of the college.* Information technology and the use of the Internet have become ubiquitous within higher education. Although technology has advanced rapidly in the past few decades, there has not been a correspondence with respect to organizational processes within higher education institutions. Often, the problem is that although information technology can give administrators a large amount of data about their organization's effectiveness, it is not being used to its maximum potential. Increasingly, higher education institutions are looking to industry-based models of quality; an example is the current focus on the Baldrige Criteria, a matrix of "quality measures" intended to assess how effectively an organization delivers its services. Regional accrediting agencies are increasingly mandating outcome-based measures of student learning and institutional effectiveness. In order to amass the data required for successful accreditation, community colleges are contracting with private vendors such as PeopleSoft/Oracle, Datatel, SCT, and other producers of management information systems to make data gathering part of all institutional processes. One of the challenges posed by this development is the ability of institutions to adequately train personnel in the use of what are often complex software operations. Thus, colleges are not only faced with the high cost of management information systems, but they must dedicate a large proportion of their operating budgets for training.

Information technology has also become pervasive in teaching. Internet-based instruction occurs on a number of levels. Textbooks commonly used for instruction often come with a CD-ROM that directs students to Web sites that contain supplemental information. Within the classroom itself, instructors have increasing access to the Internet, which then becomes integrated into lectures and presentations. More and more instructors are offering Web-enhanced courses in which the traditional didactic class is supplemented by electronic discussion communities and similar venues for instructional support.

Over 90 percent of community colleges offer some form of pure distance learning, allowing asynchronous discussion to occur 24/7. These courses are extremely popular for the working adult student. Distance learning courses have high attrition rates: Typically, about 50 percent of those who enroll do not complete them. In order to address this problem, colleges increasingly offer special online orientation sessions for students enrolled in these courses, along with faculty development for those teaching distance-learning courses. For example, Bergen Community College in Paramus, New Jersey, has developed the Online Professor's Program (TOPP), which gives faculty members release time for training in online instruction. It is interesting to note, however, that often a student enrolls in traditional and distance learning courses at the same time.

The University of Phoenix, the largest higher education institution in the world, uses a combination of online learning and face-to-face meetings in many of its courses. They have pioneered a system for creating cybernetic learning communities that are fortified by in-person social interactions.

16. *Customize and individualize learning plans for all students.* Technology enhances the ability of institutions to offer individualized instructional plans to each student. By using a battery of online assessment tools for incoming students, along with electronic portfolios (Cambridge et al. 2001) that allow students to create a digital repository of their academic work, higher education institutions can customize an educational experience for the individual learner. LaGuardia Community College in Long Island City in New York, for example, is using electronic portfolios for assessing student learning. Particularly interesting is LaGuardia's diverse student body and innovative cooperative education program that is tied to a student's program of study. In addition, LaGuardia Community College creates cohorts of students who engage in learning communities, thereby providing peer support across cultures. Another model of electronically mediated learning is that developed by Valencia Community College in Orlando, Florida, a program called Lifespan.

The use of "smart cards"—student identification cards with a magnetic strip that can contain information—is valuable in enabling a student to "own" a mobile dossier of his or her learning. SUN Microsystems (which is entering higher education through the dissemination, for free, of its Star Office software, which emulates the functions of Microsoft Office) is a system predicated on "dumb terminals" linked into a high-capacity network (that is, a system in which students have access to a high-capacity computer network through terminals that do not themselves have much computing ability). This system has been designed to work with smart cards held by students.

17. *Procure sufficient resources during a time of fiscal austerity.* Community colleges are faced with a growing fiscal crisis. Federal and state subsidies are on the wane, local support is diminishing as municipalities find themselves strapped for cash, and affordability for students becomes a concern as community colleges resort to raising tuition and fees in order to remedy budget deficits.

Community colleges are increasingly turning to in-house foundations for raising revenues. Such a foundation, which is constituted as a separate entity from the board of trustees, is typically incorporated as a nonprofit 501C3. As such, it is empowered to be a depository of funds ranging from those used to provide scholarship assistance for students to those raised in capital campaigns for building construction. Unlike many private and an increasing number of public higher education institutions, whose development offices, alumni fund-raising, and capital campaigns have become a mainstay of operations, community colleges are relatively new to the fund raising scene, in large part because of their historic dependence on public appropriations. The need to raise funds, moreover, has also transformed the role of the community college president into one that increasingly involves cultivating donors and seeking new sources of fiscal support.

One area that is relatively virgin territory for community colleges is what is known as academic pork. These are projects, often funded through a specific line item appropriation, that are designated for a specific institution and are not competitive. According to the *Chronicle of Higher Education,* academic pork exceeded $2 billion in fiscal year 2003 (Brainard and Borrego 2003). However, community colleges have yet to emerge as players on this scene, where they have been usurped by four-year and research institutions. In 2001, for example, community colleges received only $48 million in federal earmarked funds (Evelyn 2001).

18. *Search for the optimal mix of didactic "bricks-and-mortar" and cybernetic instruction; students often use both concurrently.* Recent studies show that the majority of students enrolled in online courses at community colleges also engage in traditional didactic learning. In addition, online courses are delivered in a variety of ways. Some are carried out entirely over the Internet and do not involve any face-to-face meetings; others are taught in a hybrid fashion in which "seat time" is 50 percent of that of a traditional course.

Online learning, however, is no panacea. A typical course that is totally delivered electronically has a 50 percent attrition rate. In addition, the pedagogical skills required to successfully teach online courses differ from those used in a bricks-and-mortar setting. Online course content needs to be dynamic and engaging, using hyperlinks and threaded discussion. Simply posting a syllabus that guides a traditional course on a Web site and engaging in episodic e-mail with students does not constitute effective online teaching.

19. *Effectively compete with the growing behemoth of private educational providers.* For-profit providers are assuming an ever-increasing role in higher education. They are typically viewed as being more cus-

tomer-oriented than public providers and as willing to provide classes on a schedule and within a time frame more convenient to adult learners. For example, their courses' starting dates are not restricted to the beginning of fall, spring, and summer semesters; many proprietary providers start courses throughout the year and are willing to deliver instruction through weekend immersion colleges and in other delivery modes that are convenient for adult learners. However, the growth of proprietary providers raises some issues of concern, such as the standardization of curriculum design and what some observers have suggested is the usurpation of faculty governance and of faculty's role in curriculum formation.

20. *Optimize the protocol for responsive learner relationship management.* Mark Milliron (2001) applied the concept of customer relationship management to educational institutions by articulating the idea of learner relationship management. Focusing on the importance of providing optimal customer (learner) service, Milliron develops an organizational model for serving the learning needs of students. Utilizing this framework, he asks community college leaders to envision how students enter the institution, how their needs are addressed once admitted, and what can be done to make them "repeat customers." With respect to entry, it is crucial that students experience entrance and admission as a seamless process. Milliron suggests that rather than subjecting students to long registration lines and a lack of academic counseling services, colleges must become more responsive to satisfying students' needs, just as a vendor would do in the private sector. Similarly, it is important to emphasize that a student's initial experience in an institution will color his or her future relationship with that institution. Students who experience poor customer service will go elsewhere for their educational needs. This is especially true in an era when private, for-profit proprietary providers are an option and have developed protocols for serving students in a solicitous manner.

21. *Respond to the faculty and administrative retirement challenge by actively cultivating new leaders.* According to a recent study commissioned by the AACC, a majority of chief executive officers are expected to retire by 2010. As a result, there has been a noticeable effort to increase the number of executive leadership programs to train emerging community college leaders. These include the League for Innovation's Executive Leadership Institute, which emanated from an earlier grant provided by the W. K. Kellogg Foundation; a similar program offered by the AACC; and higher education leadership programs such as the Community College Leadership Program at the University of Texas at Austin.

### Additional Prospects and Challenges
### Facing Community Colleges

Recently Mark Milliron and Gerardo de los Santos (2004) reported on a survey of community college chief executive officers regarding their perception of the greatest challenges they face in the future. Their report shows the following seven themes emerging:

- *Learning swirl.* Community colleges will face a number of countervailing enrollment trends, such as the need for lifelong learning, education for workers displaced by a down economy, and increasing number of baby-boom echo students.
- *Partnership programs.* Colleges will enter into alliances with business and industry, One-Stop Career Centers, and vendors offering computer certification training.
- *Funding agony.* Tuitions will increase in an era of state fiscal constraints.
- *Teaching and leadership transitions due to retirement.* In 2001 it was predicted that 45 percent of community college presidents would retire by 2007 and that another 34 percent would retire in the following seven to ten years (Evelyn 2001).
- *High-tech and high-touch connectivity.* There is a relentless demand for information technology and other technologically mediated tools that deliver "high-touch" or visualization, such as multimedia and hologram, which provide learners with a visceral experience. Given the relatively short life cycles for these instructional tools, the cost of providing this technology becomes a ceaseless challenge for chief executive officers.
- *Courageous catalysts.* Advocating for the dispossessed is a challenge that many presidents undertake as they attempt to broaden the mission of their institutions.
- *Learning dialogues and accountability.* Increasingly, community colleges are being held to accountability standards that, although normative for other realms of academe, are not the most relevant for judging success in a community college setting.

The growing universality of community colleges, and the multiplicity of constituents who utilize community colleges for numerous reasons, constitute a major challenge facing them today. Analyzing the National Education Longitudinal Survey (NELS 1988) NCES longitudinal cohort data set, whose reach includes the years 1992–2000, Clifford Adelman (2003, 26–30) reports the following notable findings:

•• Sixty percent of those in the data set attended a community college at some point in their educational careers.
•• In 1992, 59 percent of those who entered higher education in the year they graduated from high school began at a community college.
•• Forty-seven percent of those who attended community colleges enrolled in more than one undergraduate institution.

This information, along with that in other work by Adelman (1999), illustrates the nuanced pathway of students' utilization of community colleges during their undergraduate careers. Given that enrollment patterns are no longer uninterrupted or entirely sequential, since students may participate in more than one learning program simultaneously, it becomes incumbent upon higher education institutions to create educational pathways that acknowledge all the college credits accrued by a student. As Milliron and de los Santos (2004) note, over 25 percent of those currently attending community colleges have previously earned baccalaureate degrees. Multi-institutional attendance, which Peter Ewell (2002) categorizes as an "enrollment swirl," creates an urgency to think about competency-based curriculum. By articulating desired outcomes of student learning, higher education institutions can engage in a common discourse enabling them to construct a course of study in which all the components resonate. However, such a system requires an entirely new way of thinking about what constitutes a bona fide higher education experience. Rather than regulating access and essentially selling students a complete "package deal," institutions will need to individualize the process by focusing on each student's learning outcomes. Given the market pressures being placed on higher education institutions to attract and retain students, moving into such a system is a formidable challenge.

An important aspect of changing community college utilization patterns concerns the reemergence of the full-time student. In its 2003 edition of *The Condition of Education,* the NCES notes an elliptical pattern when it comes to full-time and part-time enrollments. It notes (NCES 2003, 22):

> In the past, more undergraduate students were enrolled full-time than part-time in degree-granting 2 and 4 year postsecondary institutions. This pattern is expected to continue in the future. In the 1970s, part-time undergraduate enrollment increased at a faster rate than full-time undergraduate enrollment, but the majority of students were still enrolled full-time. During the 1980s, growth slowed for both groups. In the

1990s, full-time undergraduate enrollment increased at a faster rate, while part-time undergraduate enrollment remained fairly constant. In the present decade, full-time undergraduate enrollment is expected to increase at a faster rate than part-time undergraduate enrollment.

This dovetails with Adelman's recent findings (2003) that there is a growing percentage of students under twenty-two years of age attending community colleges. Examining Integrated Postsecondary Education Data System (IPEDS) data from 1991 to 1999, he finds that the percentage of students enrolled who are under twenty-two grew from 32 percent to 42 percent during this time period. Concurrently, the median age of a community college student decreased from 26.5 in 1991 to 23.5 in 1999.

## MISSION AND FINANCES

The changing ways people attend community colleges and the wide range of services that are being demanded suggest a number of implications for the mission and operating costs of these institutions. One of the challenges facing community colleges concerns whether they will be able to maintain their *comprehensiveness*. In an era of significant fiscal constraints, it is difficult for community colleges to secure adequate funding to support high-cost programs like allied health and nursing. Another cost-related phenomenon concerns developmental education, which is commonly being localized within community colleges. In the CUNY system, the board of trustees decided to rid baccalaureate institutions of remedial instruction and to make the community colleges the site for developmental education. A number of states are exploring the question of whether there can be consolidation or specialization within the publicly funded community college sector. Recently, for example, Governor Mitt Romney of Massachusetts floated a plan to consolidate existing public higher education institutions, calling for some of the community colleges to merge with baccalaureate institutions. Related to this is a call for community colleges to differentiate themselves via their mission. In Massachusetts, for example, the Board of Higher Education required that all fifteen community colleges develop specialized mission statements.

### Practicing an Engaged Pedagogy

One of the challenges facing community colleges is to effectively instruct diverse learners. Community colleges cater to a wide spectrum of students, from those for whom English is a second language and those with developmental learning needs to those in honors programs, along with a growing population of students who have already completed a baccalaureate degree. Besides coming with a variety of intentions and goals, community college students present a variety of other cognitive nuances, such as varying learning styles and multiple intelligences (Gardner 1983).

There is a substantial amount of literature on the "first-year experience." John Gardner and his colleagues at the University of South Carolina have done much exploration concerning what "hooks" a student into his or her learning environment. They find that engagement is largely dependent on an institution's ability to establish a close connection with the student through an individualized program of academic advisement and career counseling that begins the moment a student enters the institution. Tailoring an effective first-year experience for students is key for retention and academic success (Gardner and Jewler 1992).

However, as revealed in the results of the 2003 Community College Survey of Student Engagement (CCSSE 2003, 14) only 23 percent of community college students have taken an orientation or "college success" course.

Arthur Chickering and Zelda Gamson's seven principles of effective learning, discussed in Chapter 3, have become a guidepost for developing effective pedagogical strategies. A similar phenomenological perspective is advocated by Parker Palmer (1998), who states:

> The dominant pedagogy in higher education today is objectivity and analysis. The problem with this pedagogy is that it is untruthful to the way that we come to learn. We have come to know this through our personal association with the subject. Unfortunately, we are guided away from the intuitive, subjective ways of knowing because such behavior may spill over on the subject to be learned, thus, fouling or contaminating it.

The practice of an engaged pedagogy goes beyond the classroom, for it assumes that the entire organizational structure is a learning center. Mark Milliron's concept of "learner relationship management" (Milliron 2001) is based on the practices of customer relationship management utilized by private industry. Essential to such a model is an organization's willingness to engage in relationships whereby constituents are served in a seamless fashion.

For a community college, following such a model means that intake and admission processes are personalized and that adequate support is provided for the learners, who may be the first in their families to attend college or may have educational careers peppered with failure.

Throughout the twentieth century and into the twenty-first century, community colleges have extended the reach of higher education to millions of students. They have also played an important role as the linchpin of cultural and noncredit educational opportunities in many communities throughout the nation. In an era in which the "fiscal crisis of the state" (O'Connor 2001) increasingly prevails, resulting in reduced appropriations for public higher education, a number of fiscal and operational challenges confront community colleges as they enter their second hundred years.

### Organizational Challenges Facing Community Colleges

As discussed throughout this book, community colleges are operating under increasing fiscal constraints. Given their multifaceted mission, it is a challenge to provide a sufficient number of personnel and to engage in "smart processes" that allow for the management of complex organizations. Applying the conceptual precepts of what Paul DiMaggio and Walter Powell (1991) have termed "the new institutionalism in organizational analysis" is a useful entry point for constructing optimal processes. This body of theory focuses on the importance of symbolic processes that unite members around a central mission and the importance of legitimacy for effective leadership. Applying the precepts of the new institutionalism leads to an understanding of how effective organizations cultivate engagement by resonating with the values of participants.

Sanford Schugert, president of Valencia Community College in Orlando, Florida, believes that community college leaders should engage in "servant leadership," which he describes as defining their primary task as facilitating the realization of participants' goals (Schugert 2000). He suggests that micromanaging all aspects of an organization can be deleterious to the organization's mission.

The transformation movement in the community college, a set of practices developed by the Dallas, Texas, community college district, focuses on the writings of Parker Palmer (1998) and centers on the importance of creating organizations whose values unite all in a common pursuit. Palmer's treatise—*The Courage to Teach*—constitutes the bedrock of this movement's pedagogical philosophy which, like that of Terry O'Banion and others, centers on active learning and learner-centered pedagogical strategies.

Community colleges, like other institutions, have been swept up by various reform movements aimed at dispersing and flattening organizational decision making and providing frontline workers with input. Total Quality Management (TQM) and Constant Quality Initiatives Network

(CQIN) represent two nationwide embodiments of this endeavor. Much of this work emanates from Tom Peters's and Robert Waterman's *In Search of Excellence* (1982), where they assert that frontline employee involvement in decision making is the hallmark of the best-run corporations in the United States. Flattened organizational structures, which engender widespread participatory decision making, are also the hallmark of organizations that comply with Baldrige criteria. "Since 1988, the President and Secretary of Commerce have presented the Malcolm Baldrige National Quality Award for excellence and quality achievement. This award, named after the 26th Secretary of Commerce, recognizes U.S. organizations demonstrating excellence in quality and performance. Award categories originally included manufacturing, service, and small business. Beginning in 1999, the categories of education and health care were added" (Peters and Waterman 1982).

Perhaps the overarching issue to be faced in addressing the organizational challenges confronting community colleges concerns the definition of the mission of the community college. Commonly, they have been viewed as comprehensive institutions, sort of jacks-of-all-trades. However, to be everything to everyone may not be feasible or desirable. As already mentioned, critics of community colleges have suggested that they have neglected their academic rigor in part by being complicit with every educational, managerial, or industrial fad that appears. Notes Irwin Sperber (1989, 13) about what he calls the "fashion process":

> The *fashion process* refers to the preoccupation with keeping in step with the times; second, to following the example of prestigious opinion leaders who crystallize and reinforce the vaguely expressed collective tastes of the public; admiring proposals for adoption when they are in "good taste" and new, and discarding them when they are in "bad taste" and old; opposing the weight of tradition in general while rediscovering and modifying old proposals as though they were unprecedented, daring and modern; ignoring or downgrading the importance of explicit criteria by which competing proposals for adoption can be rationally evaluated.

Critics of community colleges suggest that by jumping on every industrial bandwagon that appears and by uncritically adopting the latest managerial fashion, community colleges undermine themselves as they eschew the scholastic foundations of academia.

Another important property of successful schools is that they provide a trusting environment. Deborah Meier focuses on the impact of this concept when she discusses how schools are a substitute for the natural learning communities of yesterday (2002, 11):

> In seeking a substitute for the natural learning communities of yesterday, we invented schools and then systematically began to downgrade anything learned in nonschool ways. Schools bore the burden of replacing many if not most of the functions of those former multiage communities—and at increasingly earlier ages. In a daunting but perhaps not surprising twist of fate, the schools that replaced those natural learning communities simultaneously underwent a transformation too—toward greater depersonalization.

Meier goes on to say that the key building block for a relationship between teacher and student is trust (13). She then defines seven conditions that must be present in order for effective learning to occur:

- Schools must be safe.
- Schools must have a ratio of experts to novices that allows for successful learning.
- Schools should make it possible for experts to strut their stuff and to demonstrate their passion.
- Schools that work offer a range of ways for learners to find a way around any new domain of knowledge, and more than one way to become good at science or history.
- Schools must offer plenty of time for ideas to grow and should not set rigid timetables.
- Schools built around an engaging pedagogy make learning fun.
- What one is learning must have hooks to other things, such as to other events that are transpiring in the world (Meier 2002, 11–21).

### Certifications and Credentials

There seems to be an ever-expanding desire and market for credentials. As already mentioned, one of the ways that professions regulate themselves is by restricting admission to the select group of purveyors of a given body of knowledge. Credentialing is also an important way to legitimate a particular body of knowledge. The need to obtain a credential, whose acquisition is controlled by a closed circle, is an effective way of creating a monopoly over a given body of knowledge.

Students face a danger of falling victim to cycles in employment, of being trapped by the latest occupation wave; the recent dot-com bust is a useful case in point. Certainly there will continue to be a need for an information technology workforce. Information technology employment is predicted by the U.S. Bureau of Labor Statistics to continue to grow through 2012. However, at the same time, training for narrow specializations and industry-specific applications whose skills and proficiencies cannot be cross-utilized by other companies has left some people who have invested substantial sums in IT training with little to show. Thus, the fixation with industry-based certifications must be examined in a critical and rational way.

As technology has become diffuse and ubiquitous, there has been an explosion in the number of IT certifications offered. Many of the large IT firms have developed elaborate certification programs, which have become a prerequisite for employment in these areas. However, the industry has gone through a significant retrenchment in which thousands of workers lost their jobs as companies restructured their operations, and the importance of company-specific certifications may be questioned. Certifications that provide students with technical competencies that are not company specific, however, continue to be useful in an era when the centrality of information technology will be prolonged.

### Corporatization of Higher Education

Another factor affecting community colleges, as well as other segments of higher education, is what some critics have called the overall "corporatization" of higher education (Slaughter and Leslie 1997). Many observers have raised questions about how education will be affected by its commercialization.

Within K–12, these concerns have been most glaring with respect to Channel 1—a ten-minute news program pumped into high schools—corporate sponsorship of athletic events, and the overall proliferation of corporate marketing within schools, such as Coke machines in the cafeteria. Related to the corporatization phenomenon are the for-profit companies that run and administer schools, discussed in Chapter 3. In contrast, at the Somerville School in Ridgewood, New Jersey, fourth- and fifth-grade students participate in "TV Studio," where they discuss school news and events as well as world news. This is broadcast to all the classrooms each morning according to my fifth-grade daughter, Emily Levinson.

Given that community colleges have long, strong connections to industry (as perhaps they should), questions arise as to what type of partnerships should be developed and supported. The Committee for Economic Development (CED) and other prominent educational organizations have historically sponsored educational partnerships. As in any other negotiation, it is important for community colleges to receive their fair share of the bargain. All too often, many critics assert, community colleges uncritically sell out to corporate interests and do not keep student needs in mind.

Giroux (2002) and Bok (2003) have recently commented on the impact of commercialization on higher education. Giroux speaks of the dangers of neoliberalism and of its embracing the "market as the arbiter of social destiny" (2002, 429). Giroux is concerned that this lowers the values of higher education that are taken as sacrosanct by such commentators as Richard Hoftstadter. According to Giroux, Hoftstadter argued for the support of higher education because "it was the values of justice, freedom, equality, and the rights of citizens as equal and free human beings that were at the heart of what it meant for higher education to fulfill its role in educating students for the demands of leadership, social citizenship and democratic public life" (Giroux 2002, 433).

The growth of the for-profit sector of higher education has been in the news because of the noteworthy financial and enrollment gains made by these institutions. Their focus on customer-friendly service, along with market-based responsiveness, has increasingly caught the attention of educators. Assessing the impact of the proprietary sector on community colleges, Thomas Bailey, Norena Badway, and Patricia Gumport (2001) note that community college leaders do not find the relatively small proprietary sector to be a threat. Proprietary institutions focus on relatively few areas, most notably business and information technology, and have a specific career focus and do not seek to emulate the comprehensive focus of many community colleges. In fact, some proprietary schools are four-year institutions. However, as Bailey, Badway, and Gumport note, community colleges could learn from the strong customer-service ethos of proprietary institutions.

### *Distance and Online Learning*

Community college students are more likely than their baccalaureate or graduate-degree counterparts to participate in distance learning. Institutions that offer associate's degrees are more likely to offer distance learning than are other types of institutions. Faculty at two-year colleges are much more likely than their counterparts to teach distance learning courses. As the U.S. Department of Education (Sikora 2002, 8) notes: "The participation rates of undergraduates attending public 2-year institutions and those seeking associate degrees also tend to be higher than those of their counterparts in other types of institutional degree programs." This report goes on to state that "nontraditional students (those who are older, married, parents and who have greater financial responsibilities) tend to enroll in 2-year institutions and seek associate's degrees at greater rates than do their more traditional peers" (9). However, there are also a number of countervailing tendencies that undermine student success. As the Department of Education notes in the same report (8–9), these observations are

> consistent with the finding that older students who delayed entry into postsecondary education more than 2 years were more likely to participate in distance education than those who did not delay. Students who attended part-time, full year were more likely to participate in distance education classes than those with other attendance patterns, including those who attended full-time, full year, full-time, part year, and part-time, part year. . . . Taken together, most of these findings suggest that students who might be hindered in their ability to complete college— such as those who have taken remedial courses and those who are more likely to be at risk of not completing postsecondary education— participate in distance education at greater rates than their peers with fewer persistence risk factors or who need less remediation upon postsecondary enrollment.

The "risk factors" referred to in the above quotation are listed in a footnote as including delayed enrollment, no high school diploma (including those who received a GED), part-time enrollees, financial independence, having dependents other than a spouse, single-parent status, and working full-time while enrolled.

Some analysts see the growth of online learning as evidence of the expansion of private market forces into academia. David Noble (2002) is concerned that the profitability of online learning is its real attraction to administrators and that it will supplant critical exchanges that often occur in the classroom. Others suggest that the lack of dialogue in a collective setting individualizes what is thought to be an important social and interactive experience. There is also evidence of student disenchantment with distance learning. As the U.S. Department of Education (Sikora 2002, 23) reports: "A higher proportion of undergraduates reported being less satisfied with distance education courses (30 percent) than reported being more satisfied (23 percent)."

Web-enhanced, or hybrid, courses are another variant of distance learning. Hybrid courses are typically a combination of regular bricks-and-mortar didactic practices with online meetings in lieu of some traditional settings. Thus, Web-enhanced courses are traditional courses supplemented by cybernetic discussions outside the classroom.

### Entrepreneurialism

It is crucial for community colleges to raise funds from outside the college. Although outside fund-raising has long been practiced by colleges and universities, which have bolstered their development and sponsored-research activities in recent years, this is a relatively new activity for community colleges. As Roueche, Johnson, and Roueche (1997) note, with respect to higher education in general, there has been a reduction in public support and a concomitant rise in foundation support, endowed professorships, and the like, which have been a norm within other sectors of higher education but are quite new to community colleges.

The community college foundation has found an increasingly important role. As the fund-raising arm of the community college, foundations are involved in a plethora of activities from raising money for scholarships to securing private donations for construction projects. Created as 501C3 nonprofit organizations, community college foundations can also partake in competing for grant funding that is typically restricted to nonprofits.

As Mark Milliron and Gerardo de los Santos (2004) discovered in their survey of community college leaders, presidents envision spending a large amount of time raising money. This has transformed the role of the community college president to one that parallels that of heads of other higher education institutions. Community colleges are at a competitive disadvantage compared to four-year institutions, in part because of the underdeveloped nature of their alumni relations and their list of prospective donors. Alumni associations are a relatively new phenomenon for community colleges, just as community colleges are relative newcomers to higher education. In addition, community colleges are thought not to have an affluent client base, as colleges and universities do. However, community colleges have produced a number of very successful alumni who in turn have served as ambassadors for the sector.

Compared to other segments of education, community colleges are viewed as being entrepreneurial, in that most feature some degree of corporate contract training and constantly market their services to an array of constituents. They are also known as institutions that incubate new programs in ways that bring them into the curriculum more quickly.

## COMMUNITY COLLEGES
## AND THE AMERICAN DREAM

As already mentioned, community colleges have functioned as gateways for immigrant populations entering the United States. The number of foreign nationals entering community colleges has steadily risen, even though there are some concerns that provisions of the USA Patriot Act, most notably SEVIS, will reverse this trend. Associations such as the AACC have argued vehemently against constructing barriers to international student access, with various groups asserting that the true lesson of 9/11 is that we must understand and embrace the world's diversity, something that is hindered when national borders become impermeable.

Transcending the barriers of social class and racial inequality is a formidable task for community colleges. Under the mantle of such organizations as the American Association of Colleges and Universities (AAC&U), community colleges are engaged in trying to bring about a more equitable world, one in which intercultural understanding leads to creating, in the words of Paul Goodman, a true "communitas" (Goodman and Goodman 1990). An example of this is a campus diversity initiative funded by the Bildner Foundation that currently involves eight New Jersey colleges and universities, two of which are the County College of Morris and Bergen Community College. Bergen Community College's project focuses on its Center for the Study of Intercultural Understanding, created in the wake of 9/11 to promote intercultural dialogue within Bergen County's diverse population. As described by Carol Miele (2004), the center has brought together a wide range of participants who are in the process of creating a common ground for understanding the immense changes occurring among the dramatically diverse student body of this community college.

### *The Challenge of Serving Diverse Populations*

Community colleges are currently encountering a "baby boomlet," what Clark Kerr calls "Shock Waive II" (2002). Increased capacity may very well be needed as a new blip of students come through. In addition, community colleges will be serving a growing minority population, and for many of them English is a second language. How best to respond to English Language Minority Students (ELMS) is a challenge that all community colleges are facing. The past practice of segregating these students within restrictive enclaves that prohibited them from taking college-level credits appears to be an ineffective approach with respect to language instruction.

Another factor that community colleges need to address is the growing racial segmentation that has been occurring in education. As the Harvard Civil Rights Project has recently reported, segregation within schools is on the rise. In their report, *A Multiracial Society with Segregated Schools: Are We Losing the Dream?* Erica Frankenberg, Chungmei Lee, and Gary Orfield (2003: 6–8) find the following:

- According to statistics from the 2000–2001 school year, white students attending public schools in the United States are the most segregated.
- Approximately 40 percent of the students attending public schools in the United States are members of a minority group. (In the West and South that percentage increases to 50 percent.)
- Latinos display the highest high school dropout rates, are the most segregated minority group, and are segregated by both race and poverty.
- Asians are the most well-educated racial group, live in the nation's most integrated communities, and are the most integrated in schools.
- The phenomenon of "apartheid schools," comprised of a totally nonwhite population, is emerging.
- Three-fourths of Asian students, but only 14 percent of Caucasian students, attend multiracial schools.
- The country's largest twenty-seven urban school districts are largely nonwhite and increasingly segregated internally.
- The Supreme Court's 1974 *Milliken v. Bradley* decision, blocking city-suburban desegregation efforts, has contributed to the Detroit Public School's becoming the most segregated of all districts in the United States in 1994.
- The country's largest suburban school systems were largely all white in 1967; patterns of segregation have emerged in these systems despite an influx of minority students since the middle of the 1980s.
- Countywide school districts that encompass both urban and suburban schools, found mostly in the South, showed extensive patterns of desegregation as well as opportunities for minority students to cross racial and class barriers for their education.
- Federal court decisions appear to be a major obstacle when it comes to desegregation efforts, in contrast to the court's earlier reputation as an enabler of desegregation.
- In high schools where the majority population is white, the percentage of black students has decreased 13 percent.

### Forging Closer Linkages to K–12

A challenge for community colleges is to attempt to address the growing segregation in U.S. education by becoming more involved in K–12 schooling. There is a movement afoot to extend the reach of community colleges into primary and secondary schools. One way that community colleges have achieved this is to offer early college experiences for high school students, which at times involves sponsoring or administratively overseeing a high school.

The Middle College National Consortium (http://www.lagcc.cuny.edu/mcnc/) is an organization made up of twenty-four institutions throughout the United States. The organization states:

> Middle College High School Consortium members share the fundamental belief that collaboration between high schools and colleges provides both institutions with the ability to develop a seamless educational continuum that benefits the student as (s)he moves from one level to the next. The collaboration forces two traditionally closed institutions to examine the assumptions that have allowed each to exist as if the other does not. The freedom of the college campus provides at-risk youth with the environment to develop a sense of responsibility for their own education. The location of a high school on a college campus symbolically signals the students that a college education is possible and in fact a natural next step. The college environment provides an academically enriched setting for students who would probably be lost in the larger, traditional educational system. Collaboration between a high school and a college can also result in a cost effective sharing of resources (http://www.doe.mass.edu/charter/reports/2004/annual) (accessed February 11, 2005).

The consortium represents high schools from throughout the nation, most of them located on community college campuses. Its members are

- The Academy at Illinois Central College, East Peoria, Illinois
- Benjamin Mays Academy at Kennedy-King College, Chicago, Illinois
- Boyce Campus Middle College High School at Community College of Allegheny County, Monroeville, Pennsylvania
- Brooklyn College Academy at Brooklyn College, Brooklyn, New York
- College of San Mateo, California

- Community College High School at Community College of Southern Nevada, North Las Vegas, Nevada
- Hostos Lincoln Academy of Science at Hostos Community College, Bronx, New York
- International High School at LaGuardia Community College, Queens, New York
- Lowell Middlesex Academy Charter School at Middlesex Community College, Lowell, Massachusetts
- Middle College High School at Contra Costa College, San Pablo, California
- Middle College High School at El Centro Community College, Dallas, Texas
- Middle College High School at LaGuardia Community College, Queens, New York
- Middle College High School at Olive Harvey City College, Chicago, Illinois
- Middle College High School at Orange Coast College, Costa Mesa, California
- Middle College High School at Santa Ana College, Santa Ana, California
- Middle College High School at Shelby State Community College, Memphis, Tennessee
- Middle College High School at Truckee Meadows Community College, Reno, Nevada
- Mott Middle College High School at Mott Community College, Flint, Michigan
- Robert F. Wagner, Jr. Institute for Arts and Technology at LaGuardia Community College, Queens, New York
- Seattle Central Middle College High School at Seattle Central Community College, Seattle, Washington
- Truman Middle College High School at Truman City College, Chicago, Illinois
- University Heights High School at Bronx Community College, Bronx, New York

With these institutions placed under the aegis of community colleges, students can get a head start on a higher education that will help propel them out of the segregated environments that increasingly pervade schools, as described by the Harvard Civil Rights Project.

Related to this, community colleges are playing a growing role in reinvigorating the senior year of high school. The National Commission on the High School Senior (2001) discusses the transformative experience that a rigorous high school experience can play. As part of its research, the commission advocated creating seamless K–16 systems in which a challenging educational experience is charted for all students, regardless of socioeconomic status. In this way, a rigorous educational experience can counteract the formidable barriers to success that disadvantaged students encounter. New Jersey has taken the lead in creating a sector-wide effort to involve community colleges to revitalize the senior year. In partnership with Governor James McGrevy and Education Commissioner William Librera, the nineteen county colleges have created a sector-wide response to this problem.

### Competition from For-Profit Providers

There has been a dramatic increase in the for-profit and proprietary sector of higher education in the United States. The Futures Project, based at Brown University under the leadership of Frank Newman, has done considerable research on the competitive challenges currently facing higher education. The Futures Project (2002) reports that since the mid-1990s, the number of for-profit two-year institutions grew by 78 percent; the number of four-year for-profit institutions grew by 266 percent. In 2002, there were 625 for-profit institutions enrolling 365,000 students, which represented about 3 percent of total higher education enrollment in the United States.

The University of Phoenix, operated by the Apollo Group, is the clearest example of this growth: It has mushroomed to over 100,000 students throughout the nation. Proprietary institutions have made tremendous inroads in higher education by offering educational services that are often not bound to a particular place or time and that are scheduled for the convenience of the customer. Abandoning the usual model of offering instruction based on the traditional fourteen- or fifteen-week fall and spring semesters—which are based on a schedule that fit an agrarian society—many of these providers offer courses in concentrated segments in locations that are dispersed throughout the United States. The University of Phoenix, for example, often utilizes space in office parks and other facilities that are within easy reach for working students.

### Cultivating Human, Social, and Cultural Capital

One of the "deficiencies" of community college students is that they lack the role models and traditions of higher education to which many successful students have access. It is also important for community colleges to provide access to social and cultural networks (Barabasi 2002) that are not easily accessible to many community college students. The absence of cultural or social capital is an obstacle when it comes to workforce readiness, opportunities, and education. As has been demonstrated, community college students often do not have family members who have gone to college whom they can call on for help in understanding college life. Similarly, they do not have access to the informal or hidden networks that are often the purveyors of jobs and employment.

## CONCLUSION

As community colleges enter their second century, they are poised to carve out an ever-expanding role in higher education and in civic life. The founding generation of community college presidents and chancellors has provided an organizational imprint that has set the tone for the years to come. Embracing the inclusive mission of the community college, community college leaders have set forth a number of organizational principles that have defined an ethos that will create a nurturing and democratic educational atmosphere in these institutions. If there is one organizing ethos for community colleges, it is that everyone is capable of learning with the proper social and pedagogical supports. Community colleges in the United States embody the inclusive ideals of the "New Republic," representing a much-needed correction to the seemingly rampant fragmentation and divisiveness of the contemporary social world.

### *References*

Adelman, Clifford. 1999. *Answers in the Toolbox: Academic Intensity, Attendance Patterns, and Bachelor's Degree Attainment.* Washington, DC: U.S. Department of Education.

———. 2003. "A Growing Plurality: The 'Traditional Age Community College Dominant' Student." *Community College Journal,* April/May.

Adler, Morton. 1982. *The Paideia Proposal.* New York: Macmillan.

Alssid, Julian L., David Gruber, Davis Jenkins, Christopher Mazzeo, Brandon Roberts, and Regina Stanback-Stroud. 2002. *Building a Career Pathways System: Promising Practices in Community College-Centered Workforce Development.* Brooklyn, NY: Workforce Strategy Center.

Bailey, Thomas. 2002. "Community Colleges in the 21st Century: Challenges and Opportunities." In *The Knowledge Economy and Postsecondary Education: Report of a Workshop,* ed. Albjerg Gram and Nevzer Stacey. Washington, DC: National Academy Press.

Bailey, Thomas, Norena Badway, and Patricia Gumport. 2001. "For-Profit Higher-Education and Community Colleges." National Center for Postsecondary Improvement. Stanford, CA: Stanford University Press, March.

Barabasi, Albert-Laszlo. 2002. *Linked: The New Science of Networks.* Cambridge, MA: Perseus.

Bellah, Robert N., Richard Madsen, Ann Swidler, William M. Sullivan, and Steven M. Tipton. 1996. *Habits of the Heart: Individualism and Commitment in American Life.* Berkeley and Los Angeles: University of California Press.

Berg, Ivar. 1970. *Education and Jobs: The Great Training Robbery.* New York: Praeger.

Bok, Derek. 2003. *Universities in the Market Place: The Commercialization of Higher Education.* Princeton: Princeton University Press.

Brainard, Jeffrey, and Anne Marie Borrego. 2003. "Congress Directs Millions to College Projects on Security and Terrorism." *Government and Politics* 50, no. 5 (September 26).

Cabrera, Alberto F., and Steven M. La Nasa. 2002. "Hispanics in Higher Education." In *Higher Education in the United States: An Encyclopedia,* ed. J. F. Forest and Kevin Kinser. Santa Barbara, CA: ABC-CLIO.

Cambridge, Barbara L., Susan Kahn, Daniel P. Tompkins, and Kathleen Blake Yancey, eds. 2001. *Electronic Portfolios: Emerging Practices in Student, Faculty, and Institutional Learning.* Washington, DC: American Association for Higher Education.

Cattagni, Anne, and Elizabeth Farris. 2001. *Internet Access in U.S. Public Schools and Classrooms: 1994–2000.* Washington, DC: U.S. Department of Education, National Center for Education Statistics.

Chickering, Arthur W., and Zelda F. Gamson, eds. 1991. *Applying the Seven Principles for Good Practice in Undergraduate Education.* San Francisco: Jossey-Bass.

Community College Survey of Student Engagement (CCSSE). 2003. *Engaging Community Colleges: A First Look.* Austin: Community College Leadership Program, University of Texas, Austin.

Council for Higher Education. 2003. *CHEA 2003 Almanac.* Washington, DC: Council for Higher Education Accreditation.

de los Santos, Gerardo E., Alfredo G. de los Santos Jr., and Mark David Milliron, eds. 2003. *From Digital Divide to Digital Democracy.* Phoenix, AZ: League for Innovation in the Community College.

DiMaggio, Paul J., and Walter W. Powell. 1991. "The Iron Cage Revisited: Institutional Isomorphism and Collective Rationality in Organizational Fields." In *The New Institutionalism in Organizational Analysis,* ed. Paul J. DiMaggio and Walter W. Powell. Chicago: University of Chicago Press.

Elsner, Paul A. and Janet Beauchamp Clift. 2002. *Community Building: The Community College as Catalyst.* Washington, DC: Community College Press.

Evelyn, Jamilah. 2001. "Community Colleges Face Retirements." *Chronicle of Higher Education.* April 6, p. 36.

———. 2003. "Two-Year Colleges Step Up Lobbying." *Chronical of Higher Education.* August 3, p. 23.

Ewell, Peter T. 2002. "Three 'Dialectics' in Higher Education's Future." Working Papers No. 2, Project on the Future of Higher Education. http://www.pfhe.org/ (accessed January 5, 2005).

Flores, Antonio. 2002. "Hispanic Serving Institutions." In *Higher Education in the United States: An Encyclopedia,* ed. J. F. Forest and Kevin Kinser. Santa Barbara, CA: ABC-CLIO.

Frankenberg, Erica, Chungmei Lee, and Gary Orfield. 2003. "A Multiracial Society with Segregated Schools: Are We Losing the Dream?" The Civil Rights Project. Cambridge, MA: Harvard University Press.

Futures Project. 2002. *An Update on New Providers.* Providence, RI: Brown University.

Gardner, Howard. 1983. *Frames of Mind: The Theory of Multiple Intelligences.* New York: Basic Books.

Gardner, John N., and A. Jerome Jewler, eds. 1992. *Your College Experience: Strategies for Success.* Belmont, CA: Wadsworth.

Giroux, Henry. 2002. "The Corporate War Against Higher Education." *Workplace 5.1. A Journal for Academic Labor.* October.

Goodman, Percival, and Paul Goodman. 1990. *Communitas: Means of Livelihood and Ways of Life.* New York: Columbia University Press.

Hoachlander, Gary, Anna C. Sikora, and Laura Horn. 2003. *Community College Students: Goals, Academic Preparation, and Outcomes, NCES 2003–164.* Project Officer: C. Dennis Carroll. Washington, DC: U.S. Department of Education, National Center for Education Statistics.

Ingersoll, Richard. 1996. *Out-of-Field Teaching and Educational Equality.* NCES 96–040. Washington, DC: U.S. Department of Education, National Center for Education Statistics.

———. 1999. "The Problem of Underqualified Teachers in American Secondary Schools." *Educational Researcher* 28, no. 2.

Kerr, Clark. 1972. *The Uses of the University.* New York: Harper Torchbooks.

———. 2001. "Shock Waive II: 21st Century in American Higher Education." *International Higher Education, Spring 2001.* Center for International Higher Education, Boston College, Chestnut Hill, MA. http://www.bc.edu/bc_org/ (accessed February 13, 2005).

Kirp, David. L. 2003. *Shakespeare, Einstein, and the Bottom Line: The Marketing of Higher Education.* Cambridge, MA: Harvard University Press.

Lagemann, Ellen Condliffe. 1983. *Private Power for the Public Good: A History of the Carnegie Foundation for the Advancement of Teaching.* Middletown, CT: Wesleyan University Press.

Lehrer, Warren, and Judith Sloan. 2003. *Crossing the Blvd: Strangers, Neighbors, Aliens in a New America.* New York: Norton.

Levinson, David L. 2004. "Community Colleges as Civic Institutions." *Community College Journal of Research and Practice* 28, no. 2 (February).

Livingstone, David W. 1988. *The Education-Jobs Gap: Underemployment or Economic Democracy.* New York: Westview.

Mazzeo, Christopher, Sara Y. Rab, and Julian L. Alssid. 2003. *Building Bridges to College and Careers: Contextualized Basic Skills Programs at Community Colleges.* Brooklyn, NY: Workforce Strategy Center.

Meier, Deborah. 2002. *The Power of Their Ideas: Lessons from America from a Small School in Harlem.* Boston: Beacon.

Miele, Carol. 2004. "Building Community by Embracing Diversity." *Community College Journal of Research and Practice* 28, no. 2 (February).

Milliron, Mark David. 2001. "Touching Students in the Digital Age: The Move toward Learner Relationship Management (LRM)." *Learning Abstracts* 4, no. 1 (January). Online edition, http://www.league.org/publication/abstracts/learning/lelabs0101.htm (accessed January 12, 2005).

Milliron, Mark David, and Gerardo E. de los Santos. 2004. "Making the Most of Community Colleges on the Road Ahead." *Community College Journal of Research and Practice,* February.

Moss, Mitchell L., and Steve Mitra. 1998. "Net Equity: A Report on Income and Internet Access." *Journal of Urban Technology* 5.

National Center for Education Statistics (NCES). 2003. *The Condition of Education.* Washington, DC: U.S. Department of Education.

National Commission on the High School Senior. 2001. *Raising Our Sights: No High School Senior Left Behind.* Princeton: Woodrow Wilson National Fellowship Foundation.

Noble, David F. 2002. *Digital Diploma Mills: The Automation of Higher Education.* New York: Monthly Review Press.

O'Banion, Terry. 1997. *A Learning College for the 21st Century.* Washington, DC: American Council on Education and Oryx Press.

O'Connor, James. 2001. *The Fiscal Crisis of the State.* Somerset, NJ: Transaction.

Palmer, Parker. 1998. "Comments to the Conference on 'Education as Transformation: Religious Pluralism and Spirituality of Higher Education.' Massachusetts, Wellesley College." In *Authenticity and Leadership: Integrating Our Inner Lives with Our Work,* ed. Paul A. Elsner. Tampa Bay, FL: The International Chair Academy.

Parsad, Basmat, and Laurie Lewis. 2003. *Remedial Education at Degree-Granting Postsecondary Institutions in Fall 2000.* NCES 2004–010. Project Officer: Bernard Greene. Washington, DC: U.S. Department of Education, National Center for Education Statistics.

Peters, Thomas J., and Robert H. Waterman Jr. 1982. *In Search of Excellence.* San Francisco: Harper and Row.

Roueche, John E., Laurence F. Johnson, and Suanne D. Roueche. 1997. *Embracing the Tiger: The Effectiveness Debate and the Community College.* Washington, DC: Community College Press.

Roueche, John E., and Suanne D. Roueche. 1999. *High Stakes, High Performance: Making Remedial Education Work.* Washington, DC: Community College Press.

Schor, Juliet. 1993. *The Overworked American: The Unexpected Decline of Leisure.* New York: Basic Books.

Schugert, Sanford C. 2000. "A Brief Philosophy of Community College Leadership." Occasional Papers. Orlando, Florida: Valencia Community College, January 18. http://www.valenciacc.edu/president/papers (accessed January 2, 2005).

Seastrom, Marilyn McMillen, Kerry J. Gruber, Robin Henke, Daniel J. McGrath, and Benjamin A. Cohen. 2002. *Qualifications of the Public School Teacher Workforce: Prevalence of Out-of-Field Teaching, 1987–88 to 1999–2000.* Washington, DC: U.S. Department of Education, National Center for Education Statistics.

Sikora, Anna Cy. 2002. *A Profile of Participation in Distance Education.* NCES 2003–154. Project Officer: C. Dennis Carroll. Washington, DC: U.S. Department of Education, National Center for Education Statistics.

Slaughter, Sheila, and Larry L. Leslie. 1997. *Academic Capitalism: Politics, Power, and the Entrepreneurial University.* Baltimore: Johns Hopkins University Press.

Sperber, Irwin. 1989. *Fashions in Science: Opinion Leader and Collective Behaviour in the Social Sciences.* Minneapolis: University of Minnesota Press.

Summers, Michael D. 2003. "Attrition Research at Community Colleges." *ERIC Review.* Washington, DC: U.S. Department of Education, Office of Educational Research and Improvement.

## Chapter Seven

# ❧ Organizations, Associations, and Government Agencies

**American Association for Higher Education**
One Dupont Circle
Suite 360
Washington, DC 20036-1143
202-293-6440
http://www.aahe.org

The American Association for Higher Education (AAHE), whose membership includes over 9,000 faculty members, administrators, and students, aspires to be the organization that best enables those interested in higher education to learn, organize for learning, and contribute to the common good. Addressing the challenges that higher education faces, through meetings, conferences, projects, research, and publications, AAHE is a wonderful resource for those interested in the change and growth of higher education at the individual, campus, state, and national levels.

**American Association of Colleges and Universities**
1818 R Street NW
Washington, DC 20009
202-387-3760
http://www.aacu-edu.org

The American Association of Colleges and Universities (AAC&U), representing two-year and four-year public and private institutions, is the leading national association devoted to advancing undergraduate liberal education. AAC&U fosters connections among college and university presidents, academic administrators, faculty members, and national leaders who are committed to academic excellence.

**American Association of Community Colleges**
One Dupont Circle NW
Suite 410

Washington, DC 20036
202-728-0200
http://www.aacc.nche.edu

The American Association of Community Colleges (AACC), the primary advocacy organization for community colleges in the United States, represents more than 1,100 institutions that grant associate degrees. AACC serves as a national information resource for community colleges, creates opportunities for networking, facilitates collaboration and teamwork among staff and others with an interest in community colleges, and offers leadership and career development opportunities.

**American Council on International Intercultural Education**
One Dupont Circle NW
Washington, DC 20036
202-728-0200
http://www.aacc.nche

The American Council on International Intercultural Education (ACIIE) is an affiliate council of the American Association of Community Colleges. Its focus is to provide information relating to international and intercultural education and to facilitate programs within this arena.

**Association of Community College Trustees**
1233 20th Street NW
Suite 605
Washington, DC 20036
202-775-4667
http://www.acct.org

The Association of Community College Trustees (ACCT) is a nonprofit educational organization of governing boards that represents elected and appointed trustees of over 1,200 two-year colleges in the United States, England, and Canada. ACCT offers training and professional development programs and educational programs, supports research, publishes, and provides public policy advocacy to college trustees.

**Center for Academic Transformation**
Rensselaer Polytechnic Institute
Vice Provost Office
4th Floor, Walker Lab
110 8th Street

Troy, NY 12180-3590
518-276-6519
http://www.center.rpi.edu/

The Center for Academic Transformation provides expertise and support for those in higher education who wish to take advantage of the capabilities of information technology to transform their academic practices.

**The College Board**
45 Columbus Avenue
New York, NY 10023-6992
212-713-8000
http://www.collegeboard.com

The College Board is a national nonprofit association whose goal is to prepare, inspire, and connect students to college opportunities. Founded in 1900, it is composed of more than 4,200 schools, colleges, universities, and other educational organizations. It assists over 3 million students and their parents, 22,000 high schools, and 3,500 colleges through programs and services relating to college admission, guidance, assessment, financial aid, enrollment, and teaching and learning.

The College Board's higher education products, services, and solutions address a broad range of strategic and operational enrollment needs. The Board integrates the data, functionality, and services colleges need to characterize their incoming classes, to implement effective pricing and financial aid strategies, and to enhance their advising and placement decisions.

**Community College Leadership Program**
Department of Educational Administration
The University of Texas at Austin
1 University Station D5600
Austin, TX 78712-0378
512-471-7545
http://www.utexas.edu/academic/cclp

The Community College Leadership Program (CCLP) is the oldest graduate program focusing primarily on preparing its participants to become community college leaders. Since its establishment in 1944, more than 550 students have graduated. The CCLP has produced more community college presidents and more university professors with community college specialties than any other university program.

**Community College Research Center (Teachers College)**
Box 174
525 West 120th Street
New York, NY 10027
212-678-3091
http://www.tc.columbia.edu/~iee/ccrc

The Community College Research Center (CCRC), housed at the Institute on Education and the Economy (IEE) at Teachers College, Columbia University, carries out and encourages research on major issues affecting community colleges in the United States. CCRC is committed to attracting new scholars to the field and offers four research fellowships each year to graduate students who are committed to writing dissertations on community college topics.

**Cornell University Leadership Program**
Discovering Leadership
Cornell University
B20 Day Hall
Ithaca, NY 14853-2801
607-255-7259
http://www.sce.cornell.edu/exec/discleadership.php

The Cornell Leadership Program is designed for senior and midlevel academic administrators of colleges and universities. It focuses on the development of the leadership skills necessary to guide colleges and universities through change. The program enables its participants to expand their skills through developmental exercises based on assessment, challenge, and support. Small groups allow individuals to practice developing and leading effective teams.

**The Council for Adult and Experiential Learning**
55 East Monroe Street
Suite 1930
Chicago, IL 60603
312-499-2600
http://www.cael.org

The Council for Adult and Experiential Learning (CAEL) is an international nonprofit organization whose goal is to create and implement learning strategies for working adults through connections with employers, higher education, government, and labor.

## The Council for Higher Education and Accreditation
One Dupont Circle NW
Suite 51
Washington, DC 20036
202-955-6126
http://www.chea@chea.org

The Council for Higher Education and Accreditation (CHEA) is a private nonprofit national organization whose members include 3,000 colleges and universities. CHEA coordinates accreditation activities in the United States and is the primary conduit for voluntary accreditation and quality assurance to the U.S. Congress and the U.S. Department of Education.

## Education Commission of the States
Center for Community College Policy
700 Broadway
Suite 1200
Denver, CO 80203-0898
801-466-0898
http://www.communitycollegepolicy.org

The Community College Policy Center (CCPC), established by the U.S. Department of Education and the Education Commission of the States, provides information to state policymakers on issues of community college policy. The CCPC contends that state policymakers need much more information than is currently available to them if community colleges are to reach their potential in helping meet the country's postsecondary education needs. To this end, the center is committed to conducting research and analysis; serving as a clearinghouse on issues of community college policy at the state level; establishing a Web-based electronic database of community college policy; organizing national, regional, and state-level workshops around relevant issues; and providing technical assistance.

## Education Resources Information Center
2277 Research Boulevard
MS 6M
Rockville, MD 20850
800-538-3742
http://www.eric.ed.gov

Established in 1966, the Education Resources Information Center (ERIC) is supported by the U.S. Department of Education's Office of Educational

Research and Improvement and is administered by the National Library of Education (NLE). This national information system provides access to a wealth of education-related literature. ERIC's database, the largest education database in the world, contains more than 1 million records of articles, reports, curriculum guides, and teaching guides. Conference papers, books, directories, journals, and reference services are also included to support ERIC's mission of improving education by increasing and facilitating the use of educational research. Its goal is to support positive changes in education that improve practice in learning, teaching, educational decision making, and research.

**Educational Testing Service**
Rosedale Road
Princeton, NJ 08541
609-921-9000
http://www.ets.org/commun.html

Educational Testing Service (ETS) is the world's largest private educational testing and measurement organization. It aims to advance quality and equity in education. Dedicated to the needs of students, educational institutions, and government bodies in almost two hundred countries, it provides fair and valid assessments, research, and related services. Traditionally, ETS's primary purpose has been the development of tests and assessment tools to provide information to test takers and educational institutions. ETS has broadened its scope to include occupational testing, training, and assessments that focus on placement and instruction in the United States, Europe, Asia, and Latin America.

**EDUCAUSE**
1150 18th Street NW
Suite 1010
Washington, DC 20036
303-449-4430
http://www.educause.edu

EDUCAUSE is a nonprofit association devoted to advancing higher education by encouraging the intelligent use of information technology. Members of EDUCAUSE include more than 1,800 colleges, universities, and education organizations. It offers professional development opportunities, produces publications, generates strategic policy initiatives, conducts research, presents awards for leadership and best practices, and provides online information services.

**The Futures Project**
A. Alfred Taubman Center for Public Policy and American Institutions
Brown University
Box 1977
Providence, RI 02912
401-863-9582
http://www.futuresproject.org/

Established in 1999, the Futures Project focuses on evaluating the impact of competitive market-based values on the goals of higher education. The project looks at the role of higher education within the context of the modern global society and the challenges presented in the areas of access to education. Through research, advocacy, and direct action, the Futures Project works to find policy solutions that will maintain the public mission of higher education, ensuring that it will not become subjugated to a focus on revenue and prestige through the impact of market forces.

**Jobs for the Future**
88 Broad Street
Boston, MA 02110
617-728-4446
http://www.jff.org/jff/

The premise of Jobs for the Future (JFF) is that all young people are entitled to a high school and postsecondary education of good quality and that all adults deserve a job that pays well enough to support a family. To this end, marketable skills are needed. JFF, a nonprofit organization that engages in research, consulting, and advocacy for the goals described above, works to create educational and economic opportunities for those most in need.

**League for Innovation in the Community College**
4505 East Chandler Boulevard
Suite 250
Phoenix, AZ 85048
480-705-8200
http://www.league.org

The League for Innovation in the Community College, an international organization, is committed to improving community colleges through experimentation, innovation, and institutional transformation. The league hosts conferences and institutes, develops Web resources, conducts research, produces publications, and leads projects and initiatives with member colleges and corporate partners. The league is the leading community college organization in the use of information technology to improve teaching and learning, student services, and institutional management.

## Lumina Foundation for Education
30 South Meridan Street
Suite 700
Indianapolis, IN 46204
317-951-5300
http://www.luminafoundation.org

The Lumina Foundation for Education is a private foundation that funds grants for research in education focusing on innovation, communication, evaluation, policy, and leadership development. The foundation's mission underscores the importance of increasing access to higher education, particularly for those who are underserved.

## The Middle College National Consortium
LaGuardia Community College
3110 Thomson Avenue
Long Island City, NY 11101
718-609-2025
http://www.lagcc.cuny.edu

The Middle College National Consortium is a professional development organization for secondary and postsecondary educators who work in public education. The consortium provides expertise in the areas of technical assistance and support to new and established middle college high schools. An important focus of the consortium is its work with underperforming students to help them meet mandated academic standards.

## National Association for Tech Prep Leadership
http://www.natpl.org

The National Association for Tech Prep Leadership espouses the idea that every student is entitled to an opportunity to participate in a system that results in the attainment of academic and technical knowledge required for workforce readiness. The association advocates for the growth and improvement of tech prep programs and supports the development of a consistent tech prep model. It works to increase the awareness of the concept of tech prep at the federal, state, and local levels and to generate legislation and financial support from same.

**National Center for Education and the Economy (NCEE)**
555 13th Street NW
Suite 500 West
Washington, DC 20004
202-783-3668
http://www.ncee.org

The National Center for Education and the Economy (NCEE) is an organization that has completed extensive research in twenty countries to evaluate successful educational and job-training programs. With the findings from this research, NCEE has created the America's Choice School Design program, which supports schools to ensure that students are adequately prepared for college upon graduation; Workforce Development programs, which provide government, states, and localities with the knowledge and designs needed to implement successful workforce development programs; and the National Institute for School Leadership, which provides training for principals and school leaders.

**National Center for Education Statistics (NCES)**
Institute of Education Sciences, U.S. Department of Education
1990 K Street NW
Washington, DC 20006
202-502-7300
http://nces.ed.gov

Falling under the auspices of the U.S. Department of Education, the National Center for Education Statistics (NCES) was established to comply with a congressional mandate to collect, collate, analyze, and report detailed statistics on the condition of U.S. education. The NCES conducts and publishes reports and reviews educational activities internationally. Its Statistical Standards Program consults and advises on methodological and statistical aspects involved in the design, collection, and analysis of statistical data collections in the center and provides consultation and advice to offices within the U.S. Department of Education.

**National Institute for Staff and Organizational Development**
University of Texas at Austin
CCLP/NISOD
1 University Station D5600
Austin, TX 78712-0378

518-471-7545
http://www.nisod.org

The National Institute for Staff and Organizational Development (NISOD) is the outreach organization of the Community College Leadership Program (CCLP) in the Department of Educational Administration in the College of Education at the University of Texas at Austin. Entering its fifty-fifth year, the CCLP is the oldest graduate preparation program of its kind in the nation and has produced more community college presidents and more university professors with community college specialties than any other university program. NISOD grew out of the research and development activities of this doctoral-level leadership program and is now its primary connection with college faculty and administrators who support teaching and learning. NISOD contends that teaching excellence is a result of concerned and focused leadership, increased awareness and use of adult learning principles further strengthened by exemplary teaching practices and technologies, and a profound commitment to teaching excellence and student success.

**New England Resource Center for Higher Education**
University of Massachusetts
180 Morrissey Boulevard
Boston, MA 02125-3393
617-287-5000
http://www.nerche.org

The New England Resource Center for Higher Education (NERCHE) is dedicated to improving colleges and universities as workplaces, communities, and organizations through think tanks, research, consulting, professional development, and publications. Such NERCHE publications as *The Academic Workplace* and the Working Papers Series address general education, the faculty labor market, professional service, and organizational change. Meeting five times a year, think tanks for faculty and administrators discuss important questions facing higher education. NERCHE also conducts major studies on key issues in higher education.

**New Jersey Virtual Community College Consortium**
609-343-5612
http://www.njvccc.cc.nj.us

The New Jersey Virtual Community College Consortium allows students to take courses at any participating community college, either online or on campus. Completed credits appear on a student's transcript without the necessity of transferring credits.

**Office of Vocational and Adult Education**
U.S. Department of Education
400 Maryland Avenue SW
Washington, DC 20202
800-USA-LEARN (800-872-5327)
http://www.ed.gov/about/offices/list/ovae/resource/index.html

The Office of Vocational and Adult Education (OVAE), a division of the U.S. Department of Education, provides information relating to adult education, career and technical education, and high school and community colleges. Its focus is on research and resources within the realm of postsecondary education that will lead to productive careers.

**Phi Theta Kappa**
Center for Excellence
1625 Eastover Drive
P.O. Box 13729
Jackson, MS 39236-3729
http://www.ptk.org

Phi Theta Kappa is the oldest, largest, and most respected honor society serving two-year colleges around the world. The purpose of Phi Theta Kappa is to acknowledge and encourage scholarship among two-year college students. Phi Theta Kappa provides opportunities for the development of student leadership and service and the promotion of an intellectual climate. It connects scholars and stimulates interest in continuing academic excellence.

**Western Governors University**
4001 South 700 East
Suite 700
Salt Lake City, UT 84107
801-274-3280
http://www.wgu.edu

Western Governors University (WGU) was founded by nineteen governors of western states to serve the academic needs of busy adults who desire to pursue a college degree. WGU is nonprofit, and it is the only accredited online university offering competency-based degrees.

*Chapter Eight*

# ►◄ Selected Print and Nonprint Resources

## PRINT RESOURCES

Adelman, Clifford. "A Growing Plurality: The Traditional Age Community College Dominant Student." *Community College Journal*, April-May 2003.

Discussion of the shift in the student population in community colleges, which is swinging back to students in the traditional eighteen-to-twenty-two-year-old age group.

Adelman, Clifford. *Principal Indicators of Student Academic Histories in Postsecondary Education, 1972–2000.* Washington, DC: U.S. Department of Education, 2004.

Detailed discussion of changes in postsecondary attendance patterns, suggesting that although students increasingly attend a multiplicity of educational institutions in their lifetimes, there is no effective mechanism for applying all credits earned toward degree attainment.

Adelman, Clifford. *The Way We Are: The American Community College as American Thermometer.* Washington, DC: Office of Education Research and Improvement, 1992.

Presentation of the development of community colleges in the United States within the context of larger socioeconomic changes during the twentieth century.

Alssid, Julian L., David Gruber, Davis Jenkins, Christopher Mazzeo, Brandon Roberts, and Reginald Stanback-Stroud. *Building a Career Pathways System: Promising Practices in Community College Centered Workforce Development.* Brooklyn, NY: Workforce Strategy Center, 2002.

Useful model for workforce development, including a report on results of demonstration projects throughout the nation.

Aslanian, Carol B. *Adult Students Today.* New York: College Board, 2001.

Comprehensive demographic portrait of adult students seeking higher education.

Baker, George A., ed. *Handbook on the Community College in America: Its History, Mission, and Management.* Westport, CT: Greenwood, 1994.

Comprehensive single-volume reference work on community colleges that features an array of articles by leaders in the community college movement.

Bradburn, Ellen M., and David G. Hurst. *Community College Transfer Rates to Four-Year Institutions Using Alternative Definitions of Transfer.* Washington, DC: U.S. Department of Education, National Center for Education Statistics, 2001.

Expansive and novel conceptualization of how to measure the transfer of students from two-year to four-year colleges.

Brint, Steven, and Jerome Karabel. *The Diverted Dream: Community Colleges and the Promise of Educational Opportunity in America, 1900–1985.* New York: Oxford University Press, 1989.

Critical interpretive history that argues that as community colleges developed during the twentieth century, they tended to concentrate on vocational, career-oriented educational programs.

Carnevale, Anthony P., and Donna M. Desrochers. *Help Wanted . . . Credentials Required: Community Colleges in the Knowledge Economy.* Princeton: Educational Testing Service, 2001.

Cogent argument for the centrality of community colleges in the information age.

Center for Community College Policy. *State Funding for Community Colleges: A Fifty-State Survey.* Denver, CO: Education Commission of the States, 2000.

Comprehensive comparative data on public appropriations for community colleges throughout the nation.

Clark, Burton. **"The Cooling-Out Function Revisited."** In *Questioning the Community College's Role.* New Directions for Community Colleges, no. 32. San Francisco: Jossey-Bass, 1980.

Amended presentation of Clark's classic thesis that community colleges marginalize students, keeping them away from mainstream avenues of success.

Cohen, Arthur M., and Florence B. Brawer. *The American Community College.* 4th ed. San Francisco: Jossey-Bass, 2003.

The latest incarnation of a seminal reference work on community colleges.

Colcy, Richard J. *The American Community College Turns 100: A Look at Its Students, Programs, and Prospects.* Princeton: Educational Testing Services, 2000.

Brief and informative overview of how community colleges developed during the twentieth century.

de los Santos, Geraldo, Alfredo de los Santos, and Mark Milliron. *From Digital Divide to Digital Democracy.* Phoenix, AZ: Innovation Press, 2003.

Comprehensive discussion of the digital divide and strategies that can be adopted for closing this abyss.

Dougherty, Kevin J. *The Contradictory College: The Conflicting Origins, Impacts, and Futures of the Community College.* Albany: State University of New York Press, 1994.

Seminal critical work that captures the conflicting and at times irreconcilable sociocultural tensions that have an impact on community colleges.

Grubb, W. Norton, and Associates. *Honored but Invisible: An Inside Look at Teaching in Community College.* New York: Routledge, 1999.

Detailed look at pedagogical practices used by community college instructors, often raising questions about the efficacy of time-honored teaching strategies for community college students.

London, Howard. *The Culture of the Community College.* New York: Praeger, 1978.

Outstanding ethnographic study of life in a community college.

McCabe, Robert H. *Yes We Can! A Community College Guide for Development of America's Underprepared.* Washington, DC: Community College Press, 2003.

Comprehensive and upbeat analysis of strategies for guiding remedial learning.

McGrath, Dennis, and Martin B. Spear. *The Academic Crisis of the Community College.* New York: State University of New York Press, 1991.

Insightful treatise on the challenges of instructing underprepared learners.

Milliron, Mark, and Geraldo de los Santos. "**Making the Most of Community Colleges on the Road Ahead.**" *Community College Journal of Research and Practice,* February 28, 2004: 105–122.

Report on a survey of community college presidents regarding challenges they expect in the twenty-first century.

Nielsen, Norman, Dee Baird, Boo Browning, and Mark Milliron, eds. *Building a Workforce System through Partnering.* Phoenix, AZ: League for Innovation in the Community College and Microsoft Corporation, 2003.

Insightful collection of essays on the challenges and opportunities facing community colleges as they address workforce needs of the twenty-first century.

O'Banion, Terry. *A Learning College for the Twenty-First Century.* Phoenix, AZ: American Council on Education and Oryx Press, 1997.

Classic statement on how best to structure community colleges so that the needs of learners are central.

Phillipe, Kent A. *National Profile of Community Colleges: Trends and Statistics.* 3rd ed. Washington, DC: American Association of Community Colleges, 2000.

The definitive statistical compendium on community colleges, containing data on topics ranging from enrollments to transfer rates.

Phipps, Ronald A., Jessica M. Shedd, and Jamie P. Merisotis. *A Classification for Two-Year Postsecondary Institutions.* NCES 2001-167. Washington, DC: U.S. Department of Education, National Center for Education Statistics, 2001.

Innovative schema for categorizing divergent two-year colleges throughout the nation.

Roueche, John E., and Susan D. Roueche. *High Stakes, High Performance: Making Remediation Work.* Washington, DC: Community College Press, 1999.

Cogent statement on how to promote exemplary academic standards when designing developmental education programs.

## NONPRINT RESOURCES

### Web Sites

**American Association of Community Colleges**
http://www.aacc.nche.edu

The principal advocacy organization for community colleges in the United States. This Web site provides a search tool for community colleges by zip code, access to statistical information about community colleges, and access to briefs on governmental relations. On the Web site one can purchase recent publications produced by their Community College Press and learn about job opportunities in community colleges throughout the nation.

**Center for Community College Policy,**
  **Education Commission of the States**
http://www.communitycollegepolicy.org/

Source for "best practices" in public policies to assist state higher education officials improve the efficacy of community colleges. The center's Web site inventories "best practices" in the following categories: access and participation; community colleges' role in teacher preparation; dual and concurrent enrollment; finance; governance; leadership; remedial education; transfer and articulation; and workforce development.

**Center for International Education—Boston College**
http://www.bc.edu/bc_org/avp/soe/cihe/

The premier electronic center for information on international dimensions of higher education. The center's quarterly newsletter can be accessed through this site, which also provides entrée to a number of worldwide higher education partner organizations.

**Community College Research Center (CCRC),**
  **Teachers College, Columbia University**
http://www.tc.columbia.edu/~iee/ccrc/

Organization whose mission is to "carry out and promote research on major issues affecting the development, growth, and changing roles of community colleges in the United States." The center's Web site features recent research, a list of current projects, and links to other sites relevant to community colleges.

**League for Innovation**
http://www.league.org/welcome.htm

International organization dedicated to "catalyzing the community college movement." The league hosts a number of annual conferences and institutes; conducts research on numerous issues pertaining to learning, leadership, and administration; and champions the use of technology to enhance the efficacy of community colleges. Through "I-Stream" one can electronically subscribe to all league publications and conferences.

**National Center for Education Statistics**
http://nces.ed.gov/

Site containing a wealth of information on the state of education in the United States. In addition to digital versions of *The Condition of Education* and *Digest of Education Statistics,* the Web site provides access to numerous reports on community colleges and longitudinal databases that have been used to assess educational attainment in the United States.

**National Information Center for Higher**
  **Education Policymaking and Analysis**
http://www.higheredinfo.org/

Web site created by the National Center for Higher Education Management Systems (NCHEMS) providing detailed information on state-by-state comparisons on the following indices of educational quality: student preparation; student participation; affordability; student learning; completion rates; benefits of education; employment finance; and "cross-cutting" issues such as poverty, minority-group representation, and so on. The information is elegantly presented in the format of maps, graphs, and data comparisons.

**University of California at Los Angeles (UCLA)**
  **Community College Studies**
http://www.gseis.ucla.edu/ccs/

Site containing some of the resources formerly housed at the Education Resources Information Center (ERIC) Clearinghouse on Community Colleges, which was also housed at UCLA. In December 2003, all of the ERIC clearinghouses were subsumed by the new ERIC Web site (http://www.eric.ed.gov/), which is funded by the U.S. Department of Education Institute of Education Sciences.

### *Online Periodicals and Publications*

*Change Magazine*
http://www.aahe.org/change/

Magazine published bimonthly that features articles on a wide array of topics germane to higher education.

*Chronicle of Higher Education*
http://www.chronicle.com

The premier authoritative review of higher education in the United States, published weekly. Besides its print edition, the *Chronicle* also provides weekly updates of breaking news to subscribers. The *Chronicle* also features a weekly electronic summary of issues pertinent to community colleges and has a special search engine for community college jobs.

*Community College Journal*
http://www.aacc.nche.edu

Bimonthly publication of the American Association of Community Colleges. It typically features an ensemble of articles on a thematic topic of salience to community colleges.

*Community College Journal of Research and Practice*
http://www.tandf.co.uk/journals/

Multidisciplinary journal published ten times a year that "promotes an increased awareness of community college issues by providing an exchange of ideas, research, and empirically tested educational innovations."

*Community College Times*
http://www.aacc.nche

Biweekly newspaper published by the American Association of Community Colleges. It "provides coverage of community college news and issues—from fundraising, strategic planning, and accountability to current legislation, cutting-edge technology, and institutional development."

*Community College Week*
http://www.ccweek.com

Independent biweekly publication that features in-depth analyses of issues pertaining to community colleges.

*Journal of the American Indian Higher Education Consortium*
http://www.tribalcollegejournal.org

Official voice of the thirty-one U.S. tribal colleges, which are two-year colleges on Native American reservations throughout the nation.

**League for Innovation in the Community College,
Leadership Abstracts**
http://www.league.org/publication/abstracts/leadership/labs0405.htm

Monthly abstracts of articles highlighting leadership issues in the community college.

**League for Innovation in the Community College, Learning Abstracts**
http://www.league.org/publication/abstracts/learnab_main.htm

Monthly abstracts of articles highlighting pedagogical innovations.

**National Institute for Staff and Organization Development (NISOD)
Innovation Abstracts**
http://www.nisod.org/publications/abstracts.html

Weekly publication written by community college practitioners that spotlights innovations in teaching and learning in the community college.

**New Directions in Community Colleges**
http://www3.interscience.wiley.com

Monograph series of books published periodically. Its books center on a selected theme relevant to community college educators.

# •◆ Glossary

**Access versus excellence**   the dilemma of trying to maintain high academic standards while opening admissions to anyone regardless of past academic proficiency. Typically, open access admissions processes are seen as undermining high academic standards.

**Articulation agreement**   an agreement forged between a community college and a baccalaureate institution that allows for the seamless transfer of credits between institutions.

**Asynchronous education**   form of delivering education in which, typically, a question or comment is posted in an electronically mediated fashion not intended for a spontaneous response. This communication does not occur in "real time" and therefore is not dependent upon the simultaneous presence of sender and receiver.

**Baldrige Criteria**   a matrix of "quality measures" developed under the aegis of the Baldrige Institute to assess the effectiveness of an organization's delivery of services. Originally developed for the corporate world, such measures have been extended to other organizations.

**Bridge programs**   programs that attempt to span what are currently discrete educational venues. Community colleges have traditionally pioneered a number of such initiatives, for example, granting college credits to high school students through "tech prep" programs and offering high school students the opportunity to enroll in courses that earn college credit while simultaneously fulfilling high school requirements.

**Career pathways model**   a model articulated by the Workforce Strategy Center that provides a clear schema for charting advancement opportunities within a given industry or profession. Such depictions often specify the educational and experiential background needed for upward mobility.

**Charter school**   an independent public school created by teachers, parents, and community leaders that is exempt from many state and local regulations. Although independent, the schools are supported by taxes and are monitored by local or state organizations.

They are designed to promote a specialized and sometimes experimental approach to learning.

**Common schools** the early antebellum formation of what are now known as elementary schools. Common schools were created to assure that schooling was available and equal for all. Horace Mann used the term the "great equalizer" when referring to and advocating the expansion of common schools.

**Continuing education units** (CEUs) supplementary educational units that many professions require in order to maintain licensure. CEUs are often provided through continuing or extended studies divisions of community colleges.

**Contract training** a practice in which community colleges tailor worker training to meet the specific needs of an employer.

**Cooling-out function** a formulation originally advanced by Burton Clark (1962) that refers to the practice of "dumbing down" or downgrading the quality or difficulty of education for community college students.

**Credentialing** the practice of sanctioning, through a common standard or matrix, the attainment of a particular skill or expertise. Examples range from degree-related credentialing (such as a PhD or AA degree) to skill certification within a given industry (for example, CISCO corporation–certified training).

**Cultural capital** cultural differences that reproduce social class division. The term was coined by French sociologist Pierre Bourdieu, who expanded the idea of economic capital to include such "immaterial" forms of capital as cultural and symbolic capital, suggesting that the structure and distribution of all forms of capital have an impact upon the understanding of the social world.

**Developmental education** in college, education for students who need remedial assistance or academic support.

**Digital divide** the division of the world into groups that have access to and capability to use modern information technology and those that do not. The division exists between cities and rural areas, between educated and noneducated populations, between economic classes, and, globally, between industrially developed and underdeveloped nations.

**Elderhostel** a Boston-based organization that acts as a sponsor and clearinghouse for learning opportunities, including travel, offered to those over age fifty-five.

**Electronic portfolios** an electronic extension or medium for keeping or archiving students' achievements. Such portfolios typically include qualitative assessments of students' work. The American

Association of Higher Education (AAHE) has spearheaded an effort to create electronic depositories that can then be transportable and stored at virtually no cost.

**English as a Second Language (ESL)** the instruction of English to those for whom English is not their first language. In contrast to bilingual education, in which both English and the student's native language are used, ESL programs use only English as the instructional language.

**High-stakes testing** the practice of using standardized achievement tests to determine eligibility for promotion or graduation.

**Higher Education Act (Public Law 89-329)** Act whereby the federal government committed to strengthening the educational resources for colleges and universities and created financial assistance programs to students in higher education. The act is undergoing reauthorization.

**Human capital** the attributes of an individual that are ultimately economically productive to the individual or to society. Formal education, for example, may be viewed as an example of human capital whereby a diploma or degree is an "investment" with the return of a salary or other compensation.

**Individual Education Plan (IEP)** a plan outlining the educational goals and services, as well as the location of those services, developed by an educational team for a student with a disability.

**Individuals with Disabilities Education Act (IDEA) (Public Law 105-17)** act passed in 1997 that assures that students with disabilities receive a free education in the most appropriate and least restrictive environment. The act requires the student's local educational agency (LEA) to develop an appropriate Individual Educational Plan (IEP) for each student and holds the LEA accountable for the student's success.

**Knowledge economy** an economic system in which economic wealth is increasingly the product of higher-order cognitive processes. In a knowledge economy, knowledge has a commodifying effect and adds value to production analogously to manufacturing or capital inputs.

**Land-grant colleges** colleges founded under the auspices of the Morrill Act of 1862, whereby the federal government literally allocated land for the public provision of higher education.

**Learner relationship management** a construct modeled after the concept of customer relationship management in business. This construct sensitizes providers of higher education to treat relationships with learners in a way that is analogous to the way effective businesses retain customers. Providing "customer service" to learners that allows for easy access and quick response to individual concerns is key to the model.

**Learning college**   a college structured in such a way as to rid the organization of the "silo effect" and to create cross-functional teams that are centered on promoting student learning.

**Learning community**   a community of students purposefully formed around a specific curriculum or course of study.

**Learning competencies**   a standard expression of some body of knowledge, as actually acquired by a student, that is comparable across institutions and that enables a student to use his or her knowledge in related or advanced courses. The concept arose as part of the general accountability movement in education, where it is increasingly argued that education should be organized in the form of a "deliverable," that is, that a student must demonstrate mastery of a subject that can be expressed in universal terms.

**Lifelong learning**   an array of educational programs, typically offered by community colleges, that are available to students throughout their lives, rather than just during traditional college-age years.

**Meritocracy**   a system where advancement is based upon some objective measure of attainment.

**Middle college**   the placement of high schools on college campuses to offer an early college experience.

**Nontraditional students**   college students older than the "traditional" age range (eighteen to twenty-three years) or attending college as part-time students. The passing of the baby boom and increasing use of higher education by a populace in need of supplemental skills training has led to an increase in the number of nontraditional students.

**One-Stop [Career] Centers**   part of the Workforce Investment Act (WIA) of 1998, centers designed to provide career counseling, training, and placement services within a single location in order to maximize ease of access and utility.

**Online or distance learning**   learning that is electronically mediated and does not necessarily involve any didactic, face-to-face instruction.

**Open admission**   the practice of admitting all who apply to a specific institution. Open admission is typically the practice of community colleges, which usually admit all those who have completed a high school degree. However, high-demand programs such as nursing and other sought-after programs often impose some type of admissions requirement.

**Pell program**   the primary financial aid program offered by the federal government, named after Claiborne Pell, former senator from Rhode Island.

**Perkins Acts**   a series of federal legislative initiatives—Perkins I, II, and III—designed to bolster the quality of vocational education in the United States.

**Politics versus markets**   a contrasting pair of organizing principles that guide social policy. With respect to schools, "politics" refers to government control or agency in schools, as is typical of schools in the public domain (for example, public schools); "market" refers to private control of schools, which is subject to such market-driven controls as school choice.

**Proprietary schools**   for-profit institutions such as the University of Phoenix, the largest such institution.

**Reverse transfer**   the movement of students from baccalaureate or doctoral institutions to community colleges, a phenomenon that some suggest accounts for 25 percent of all community college enrollments today.

**School choice**   a market-driven solution for school improvement that is based on the belief that parents' ability to choose the school where their children will attend will place market pressure on weak schools, which will thus either improve or be eliminated.

**Service learning**   a form of experiential learning in which the student is involved in an activity that incorporates community service and classroom learning. This hands-on experience is usually community based and implemented in areas that address human or environmental needs.

**Service sector**   a category of occupations such as education, retail, or tourism. The service sector is one of the three primary industrial categories in a developed economy, the others being manufacturing and primary goods production.

**Social capital**   social networks among community members and their attitude, desire, and spirit in engaging in collective activities and problem solving.

**Soft skills**   interpersonal and critical-thinking capabilities that are increasingly important for the service economy. Many observers have suggested that critical-thinking skills and communication skills are as important as general job readiness.

**Tracking**   the practice of placing students into classes based upon a perceived difference in academic ability, often determined by the results of standardized achievement or aptitude testing; often referred to as homogeneous grouping.

**Traditional students**   students eighteen to twenty-three years old and enrolled in college full-time. With increasing college enrollments as a result of the baby boom following World War II, such students came to be seen as the norm. However, with the passing of the baby boom, the proportion of students who are in this traditional age range has diminished.

**Vocational training**   programs that are oriented toward training for the workforce. In community colleges, it is typically associate of applied science programs that are vocationally oriented, in contrast to associate of science or arts programs, which are oriented toward transferal to a four-year college.

**Workforce Investment Boards**   recipients and distributors of federal funds that are received by the states for job training. The Workforce Investment Boards were created as part of the Workforce Investment Act (WIA).

# ●◆ Index

AA. *See* Associate of arts
AAC&U. *See* American Association of Colleges and Universities
AACC. *See* American Association of Community Colleges
AAHE. *See* American Association of Higher Education
AAS. *See* Associate of applied science
*Abbott v. Burke*, 62, 80–81
Academic programs, 117–121
Access, 24–25, 29–30, 32, 35, 75–76
  expansion, 76
  in 21st century, 181–182
Access vs. excellence, 76–78, 83, 110–111
  challenges, 98–103
  City University of New York open admissions experience, 107–109
  and financial aid, 97–98
  and funding, 86
  international concerns, 85–86
  and market-based reforms, 96–97
  and measuring effectiveness, 86–93
  and meritocracy, 93–96
  online learning, 103–106
Accountability, 84–85, 193
Accreditation, 15–16
  agencies, 10, 16
ACCT. *See* Association of Community College Trustees
Acculturation, 50, 54–56, 65–66, 118
ACIIE. *See* American Council on International Intercultural Education
Acquisitive behavior, 149

Addams, Jane, 166
Adelman, Clifford, 32–33
Administrators. *See* Governance
Affirmative action, 186–187
AFL-CIO, 123
African Americans, 62, 205. *See also* Historically Black Colleges and Universities
Alssid, Julian, 159
Alverno College, 93, 167
American Association for Adult Education, 166
American Association of Colleges and Universities, 5, 215
American Association of Community Colleges, 7, 56, 57, 215–216
  "Access to the Baccalaureate," 140
  on financial aid, 98
  and maxims for community colleges in the 21st century, 177
  training for administrators, 192
American Association of Higher Education, 5, 215
  "Principles of Good Practice for Assessing Student Learning Outcomes," 91–93
American Association of Junior Colleges, 45, 56
American Association of State Colleges and Universities, 140
American Council on International Intercultural Education, 216
Applied knowledge, 118–121, 150
Apprenticeship programs, 123
AS. *See* Associate of science
Asians, 205

Asset development, 160
Asset Development Institute, Center
    on Hunger and Poverty, 160
Assimilation, 54–56
Associate of applied science, 9–10,
    141–143, 179
Associate of arts, 9–10
Associate of science, 9–10
Associate's degrees, 34
    increase in, 19
    as one goal of community colleges,
    20
Association of Community College
    Trustees, 7, 56, 216

Baccalaureate degrees, 34, 180–181
Bachelor's degrees, 19
Baldrige Criteria, 57
Bard High School (New York), 139
Basic Educational Opportunity
    Grants, 46
Beginning Postsecondary Students
    Longitudinal Study, 33–34
BEOG. *See* Basic Educational
    Opportunity Grants
Berg, Ivar, 133
Bergen Community College, 10, 11t.,
    102, 104–105, 177, 204
Bergen Technical High School (New
    Jersey), 138
Beverly High School (Massachusetts),
    118
Boggs, George, 177
Bourdieu, Pierre, 95, 157
BPS. *See* Beginning Postsecondary
    Students Longitudinal Study
Brandeis University, Heller School for
    Social Policy and
    Management, 160
Brown University, 103
*Building Communities: A Vision for a
    New Century,* 6–7
Bureaucratization, 58–59, 66–68
Burkham, David T., 81

Bush, George H. W., and
    administration, 27
    and lifelong learning, 162–163
Business Roundtable, 120–121
Business–Higher Education Forum,
    132

CAEL. *See* Council for Adult and
    Experiential Learning
California Institute of Technology, 6
Cambridge College, 167
Campus Compact, 103
Capella University, 152
Career pathways, 131–132, 143,
    158–160
    model, 168
Career programs, 120, 127, 137, 143
Career transcription, 129–130
Carl Perkins Vocational and Applied
    Technology Act of 1984 (and
    amendments), 46, 123, 125,
    158
Carnegie, Andrew, 68
Carnegie Classification of Institutions
    of Higher Education, 2
Carnegie Corporation, 166
Carnegie Foundation for the
    Advancement of Teaching, 68,
    184
CCLP. *See* Community College
    Leadership Program
CCRC. *See* Community College
    Research Center
CCSSE. *See* Community College
    Survey of Student
    Engagement
CED. *See* Committee for Economic
    Development
Center for Academic Transformation,
    216–217
Central High (Pennsylvania), 126
Certificate programs, 10–11, 199–200
CEUs. *See* Continuing education units
*Changing the Odds,* 108

Chavitz, Leo, 177
CHEA. *See* The Council for Higher
    Education and Accreditation
Chicago, University of, Great Books
    curriculum, 126–127
Chickering, Arthur, 88–90
Chubb, John, 96
Chubb Institute, 142, 152, 169
Church, Robert, 150
Citizenship, 25, 50, 65–66
City University of New York, 76, 101,
    107, 182
    and open admissions, 107–109
Clinton, Bill, and administration,
    131–132
    and lifelong learning, 162–163
Codes of conduct, 47
Codification, 49, 56
Coleman, James, 94, 153, 157
The College Board, 217
Columbia University, 69
Commission on the Future of
    Community Colleges, 6–7
Committee for Economic
    Development, 132, 200–201
Common schools, 43, 54–55
    as form of local control, 63
Communication, 88
Community College Leadership
    Program, 217
Community College of Vermont,
    167
Community College Research Center,
    218
Community College Survey of
    Student Engagement, 87–88
Community colleges
    categorizations, 2–3, 4 (table)
    challenges, 193–195
    and citizenship, 25
    community aspect, 5–6
    and community-building, 6–8,
        167–168
    comprehensiveness, 9–18, 195

contract training, 158
    creation of, 1, 2
    criticisms of, 28–30
    as cultural institutions, 22–23
    and democracy, 24–25
    economic impact, 23–24
    enrollment, 2, 193
    governance, 12–13, 49, 58
    growth of (1960s), 45
    growth of (twentieth century), 53t.,
        177
    hundredth anniversary, 177
    and immigration, 53–54, 55–56
    increased numbers after World
        War II, 6
    institutionalization, 58–59
    and K-12 schools, 168, 206–208
    and lifelong learning, 152–153
    and local vs. federal control, 64
    low status due to open access, 126
    as major point of entry to higher
        education, 19–20
    models of development of, 51–53
    as nonlinear cultural institutions,
        33
    open access, 24–25, 29–30, 32, 35
    organizational challenges, 197–199
    role of, 1–2
    as sites for public interactions, 178
    strong points, 28
    as teaching institutions, 98–99
    and training for entry-level work,
        120
    as workforce intermediaries, 159
    and workforce training, 22, 99–100,
        141–143, 158
    *See also* Maxims for community
        colleges in the 21st century
Compulsory schooling, 45
Computer Learning, 169
Computer Training Schools, 152
Constant Quality Initiatives Network,
    57, 197–198
Continuing education units, 151, 165

*Contradictory College,* 29
"Cooling-out" effect, 29, 31, 120
Core competencies
    Bergen Community College, 10,
        11t.
    from SCANS, 128–129
Core curriculum, 10
Core knowledge. *See* General
    education
Cornell University Leadership
    Program, 218
Corporatization, 200–201
Correspondence schools, 69, 166
Council for Adult and Experiential
        Learning, 1, 160–161, 164–165,
        180, 218
The Council for Higher Education
    and Accreditation, 219
County College of Morris, 204
*The Courage to Teach,* 197
CQIN. *See* Constant Quality Initiatives
    Network
Credentials, 199–200
Cross-functional skills, 128–130
Cultural capital, 21, 95, 157, 208–209
*The Culture of a Community College,*
    31–32
CUNY. *See* City University of New
    York
Curriculum
    academic vs. vocational, 117–126
    blending academic and vocational,
        137–140, 142
    core, 10
    and critical-thinking skills,
        139–140
    cross-functional skills, 128–130
    differentiation, 67, 68
    distributive scheme, 138
    foundational, 138
    general education, 126–127
    liberal arts, 136
    shift to applied focus, 118–120
    soft skills, 128
    structured, 137–138
    *See also* Vocational education
Cyberschools, 169, 183–184

DARPA. *See* Defense Advanced
    Research Projects Agency
Davis, Judith, 104–105
DDR&E. *See* Director of Defense
    Research and Engineering
Defense Advanced Research Projects
    Agency, 6, 18
Defense Reorganization Act, 18
Degree programs, 9–10
Detroit Public Schools, 205
Developmental education. *See*
    Learning support services
DeVry Institute, 142, 152
Dewey, John, 44, 49
Dickeson, Robert C. 161–162
Digital divide, 105–106, 186. *See also*
    Cyberschools; Information
    technology; Online learning
Director of Defense Research and
    Engineering, 18
Disabled students, 185–186
Disney, 168–169
Distance learning, 169, 189–190,
    201–203. *See also* Online
    learning
Diversity, 50, 55, 186–187, 204–205
Dougherty, Kevin J., 29
Drugs and financial aid, 47

Early childhood education, 154–155
Education Commission of the States,
    219
Education Resources Information
    Center, 219–220
Educational Alliance, 166
"Educational gospel," 151
Educational Testing Service, 220
EDUCAUSE, 220
Effective learning
    conditions for, 199

seven principles of, 88–90, 196

Effectiveness, measuring, 82–83, 86–87, 110
  baseline assessments, 91–92
  benchmarks (Goals 2000), 83–84
  Community College Survey of Student Engagement, 87–88
  as community-building process, 92–93
  contextualization, 91
  feedback, 93
  goals, 92
  high-stakes testing, 84–86
  learning as multifaceted process, 91
  outcomes assessment, 90–93
  over time, 91, 92
  seven principles of effective learning, 88–90
  triangulation of assessments, 91

Elderhostel, 170

Elementary and Secondary Education Act (ESEA). *See* No Child Left Behind Act

Eliot, Charles W., 119

Encouragement, 89

Engaged pedagogy, 195–197

English as a second language, 187–188, 204

Enrollment patterns, 161–162, 193–195

Entrepreneurialism, 203

Equality, promise of, 79–82. *See also* Access, Access vs. excellence, Inequality

*Equality of Educational Opportunity*, 153

ERIC. *See* Education Resources Information Center

ESL. *See* English as a second language

ETS. *See* Educational Testing Service

Everett, Edward, 66

Excellence. *See* Access vs. excellence; Effectiveness, measuring

Expectations, 89, 90

Extension divisions, 69

Faculty
  and governance, 14–15
  retirement, 192, 193
  status, 13–14

"Fashion process," 198

Federal Reserve Bank of Boston, 100

Financial aid, 97–98
  and drugs, 47

For-profit schools. *See* Corporatization; Market-based reforms; Proprietary schools

Full-time students, 194–195

Funding, 190
  academic pork, 191
  challenges, 193, 195–197
  formulas, 12–13
  foundations, 15, 190–191
  fund-raising, 203

The Futures Project, 221

Gamson, Zelda, 88–90

General education, 126–127

GI Bill, 16, 45, 76, 167
  and City University of New York, 107

Globalization, 48, 178

Goals 2000, 83–84
  goals, 162–163

Governance, 12–13, 49, 58
  and retirement, 192–193
  "servant leadership," 197
  shared, 14–15
  training for, 192

Graduation rate, 82, 86–87

Great Books curriculum, 126–127

Great Society, 16, 46, 76

"Great training robbery," 121, 133

Grubb, Norton, 98–99

Hand training, 150
Harper, William Rainey, 56, 68, 166
  proposal for community colleges,
    69
Harvard University
  Extension School, 17
  shift to applied focus, 119
Hayden, Tom, 138
HBCUs. *See* Historically Black
    Colleges and Universities
High schools, 206–207
  academic and vocational tracts,
    138
  comprehensive, 126
  and tracking, 125–126
Higher education
  applied (economic) focus,
    118–121, 150
  corporatization of, 200–201
  debate over whether college is for
    all, 134–136
  expanding access to, 16
  growth of, 17–18
  internal segmentation
    (departmentalization), 68
  as norm in U.S. society, 17
Higher Education Act of 1965, 16
  1998 amendment, 47
  reauthorization, 46, 98
*Higher Education for American
    Democracy*, 6, 45
Hispanics, 187, 205
Historically Black Colleges and
    Universities, 44
Honors programs, 99
Hudson Institute, 27–28, 156
Hull House, 166
Human capital, 156–157, 208–209
Hybrid courses, 191, 202–203
Hyllegard, David, 108

IDEA. *See* Individuals with Disabilities
    Education Act
IEP. *See* Individual Education Plans

Immigration
  and adult learning (early 20th
    century), 166
  and community colleges, 53–54,
    55–56
  and standardized instruction,
    48–49
*In Search of Excellence*, 57, 198
Individual Education Plans, 185–186
Individualism, 78
  and standardization, 49, 79
Individualized instructional plans,
    190, 193–195
Individuals with Disabilities
    Education Act, 185
Industrial education, 150
Industrial Revolution, 118
Industry training, 12
Inequality, 204
  and lifelong learning, 153–155
  social, 79–82, 153
  in wages, 133–134, 135–136
  *See also* Equality, promise of
*Inequality from the Starting Gate*, 81,
    154–155
Information technology, 9, 47,
    189–190
  certificate programs, 199–200
  and funding, 193
  training, 106
  *See also* Cyberschools; Digital
    divide; Online learning
Institutionalism, 58–59
International Brotherhood of
    Electrical Workers, 123
Internet. *See* Cyberschools; Digital
    divide; Information
    technology; Online learning
Internship, 168–169
Invidividual vs. society, 49, 61
IT. *See* Information technology

JFF. *See* Jobs for the Future
Jobs for the Future, 1, 160–161, 221

Johns Hopkins University, Career Transcript System, 129–130
Johnson, Lyndon B., and administration, 16, 46
Joliet Community College, 2, 44, 51

Kappa Phi Omicron, 44
Katherine Gibbs School, 152, 169
Kerr, Clark, 5–6
Kett, Joseph K., 149
Knowledge economy, 8–9, 122
  and lifelong learning, 151
  role of community colleges in, 26–28
Knowledge industry, 5–6
*The Knowledge Net*, 7–8
K-12 schools, 168, 206–208

LaGuardia Community College, 101, 190
Land-grant colleges, 44, 63–64
Lavin, David E., 108
League for Innovation in the Community College, 46, 56, 57, 101, 152, 221–222
  Executive Leadership Institute, 192
  and information technology, 106, 186
  Twenty-First Century Learning Skills, 129, 139
Learner relationship management, 192
Learning colleges, 57, 101, 184–185
  organizing principles, 101–103
Learning communities, 100–101
Learning competencies, 167
"Learning Relationship Management," 152
Learning styles, 89–90, 91
Learning support services, 77–78, 86, 103, 109-110, 181–182
"Learning swirl," 193
LEAs. *See* Local education agencies

Lee, Valerie E., 81
Levinson, David L., 177
Liberalism vs. democracy, 60–61, 78–80
Lifelong learning, 149–150, 170
  and community colleges, 152–153
  coordination between community colleges and K-12 schools, 168, 206–208
  distance learning, 169
  and economic development, 155–157
  effective adult learning, 164–165
  encroachment into all spheres of life, 152
  enrollment patterns, 161–162, 193–195
  factors inhibiting, 163
  foundation for, 162–163
  historical development of adult education programs, 165–167
  increase in adult learners, 163–164
  increasing number of educational providers, 152
  independence of time and place, 152
  and knowledge economy, 151
  lifelong learning accounts (LiLAs), 165, 179–180
  need for single academic record, 162
  noncredit adult education programs, 152
  and occupational development, 151
  and professionalization, 150–151
  proprietary and for-profit institutions, 168–169
  in retirement, 170
  small, nurturing structures, 152
  and social inequality, 153–155
  in 21st century, 179–180
  university extension programs, 165–166
  workforce training, 158–161

Livingstone, David, 133
Local control
  vs. federal control, 49, 52, 61–68
  of public schools, 43
Local education agencies, 15
London, Howard, 31
Lumina Foundation for Education,
  162, 222

Malcolm Baldrige National Quality
  Award, 198
Management, 57–58. *See also*
  Bureaucratization;
  Governance;
  Professionalization
Mann, Horace, 55, 66, 168
  on education and the economy,
  118
Manual training, 150
Manufacturing, 47
Maricopa Community Colleges, 101
Market-based reforms, 96–97. *See also*
  Politics vs. markets
Massachusetts
  and beginnings of public
  education, 44, 66
  Board of Education, 55, 66
Massachusetts Institute of
  Technology, 6
  Lincoln Laboratories, 120
Massachusetts, University of, College
  of Public and Community
  Service, 167
Maxims for community colleges in
  the 21st century, 177
  applied baccalaureate preparation,
  180–181
  competition with private
  educational providers,
  191–192
  disabled students, 185–186
  ESL instruction, 187–188
  fiscal resources, 190–191
  flexible course scheduling,
  183–184

individualized instructional plans,
  190
integrating information
  technology, 189–190
learner relationship management,
  192
learning colleges, 184–185
learning support services, 181–182
lifelong learning, 179–180
mix of traditional (didactic) and
  online learning (hybrid
  courses), 191, 202–203
noncredit offerings, 183
open access,180–181
overcoming social and technical
  inequality, 186
racial and ethnic diversity,
  186–187
remedial education, 182
responding to a rapidly changing
  world, 178–179
skill certifications, 182–183
training community college
  leaders, 192
transfer programs, 188
McDonald's University, 168
Meritocracy, 93–94
  and cultural capital, 95
  and social capital, 94–95
Miami Dade Community College,
  181
Michigan University of, Law School,
  187
The Middle College National
  Consortium, 206, 222
Middle States Commission on Higher
  Education, 10, 16, 90–91
*Milliken v. Bradley,* 205
Milliron, Mark David, 152, 177, 192
Moe, Terry, 96
Morrill Acts, 44, 63–64, 76, 118–119,
  150
Multinational corporations, 48
Multiplier effect, 23–24
Multiversity concept, 5–6

NADE. *See* National Association of
Developmental Education
NAEYC. *See* National Association for
the Education of Young
Children
*A Nation at Risk,* 26, 46, 99–100, 162
National Association for Tech Prep
Leadership, 222–223
National Association for the
Education of Young Children,
154
National Association of
Developmental Education, 57
National Association of State Student
Grant and Aid Programs,
97–98
National Center for Education and
the Economy, 1, 27, 157,
160–161, 223
National Center for Education
Statistics, 57, 223
classification system of two-year
institutions, 3, 4 (table)
*College for All?,* 134–135
on degree goals of community
college students, 82
National Center for Higher
Education Management
Systems, 162
National Center for Postsecondary
Improvement, 5
National Commission on Excellence
in Education, 26, 46, 99–100
National Commission on the High
School Senior, 207–208
National Defense Education Act of
1958, 18, 45
National Institute for Staff and
Organizational Development,
57, 223–224
National Science Foundation, 120
National Survey of Student
Engagement, 87
NCEE. *See* National Center for
Education and the Economy

NCES. *See* National Center for
Education Statistics
NCHEMS. *See* National Center for
Higher Education
Management Systems
NCLB. *See* No Child Left Behind Act
NERCHE. *See* New England Resource
Center for Higher Education
New England Association of Schools
and Colleges, 10, 16
New England Resource Center for
Higher Education, 224
New Expeditions, 7
New Jersey Transfer, 127
New Jersey Virtual Community
College Consortium, 104,
224–225
New School for Social Research, 167
New York University, School of
Continuing and Professional
Studies, 152
Ninety-Second Street Y, 152
NISOD. *See* National Institute for Staff
and Organizational
Development
No Child Left Behind Act, 62–63, 97
Noncredit programs, 23, 183
"Nontraditional" students, 18–19
North Central Association of Colleges
and Schools, 10, 16
Northwest Association of Accredited
Schools, 10, 16
Norwalk Community College, 170
NSSE. *See* National Survey of Student
Engagement

O'Banion, Terry, 57, 101–103
OECD. *See* Organization for
Economic Co-operation and
Development
Office of Scientific Research and
Development, 18
Office of Vocational and Adult
Education, 225
One-Stop Centers, 169

Online learning, 103–105, 183–184,
189–190, 201–203
and digital divide, 105–106, 186
and funding, 193
mix with traditional learning
(hybrid courses), 191, 202–203
*See also* Cyberschools; Digital
divide; Information
technology
Open enrollment, 17
and City University of New York,
107–108
Organization for Economic Co-
operation and Development
on lifelong learning, 156
Program for International Student
Assessment, 85–86
Organizational skills, 89
Organizational theory, 58
OSRD. *See* Office of Scientific
Research and Development
Outcomes assessment, 90–93
OVAE. *See* Office of Vocational and
Adult Education
Overdetermination, 50

Paideia principle, 184–185
Palmer, Parker, 197
Partnership programs, 193
Part-time students, 20
*Pathways to Getting Ahead,* 160
Pell grants, 46, 97–98
Peters, Thomas, 57, 198
Phi Theta Kappa, 44, 225
Phoenix, University of, 104, 152, 169,
177, 190, 208
PISA. *See* Program for International
Student Assessment
Policy
noncentralization of educational
and workforce policy, 120–121
and practice, 75–76
*Politics, Markets, and America's
Schools,* 96

Politics vs. markets, 59–61
Port Huron Statement, 138
Poverty, 80
President's Commission on Higher
Education, 6
"Principles of Good Practice for
Assessing Student Learning
Outcomes," 91–93
Privatization. *See* Corporatization;
Market-based reforms;
Proprietary schools
Professionalization, 150–151
defined, 150
of education, 49, 56–58
*See also* Bureaucratization
Progressive education movement, 44,
49, 67
Progressive Era, 51, 67
Proprietary schools, 122–123, 168–169
Protestant ethic, 149
Public schools
disparity in local funding, 80–81
first (Massachusetts), 44, 55, 66
and Horace Mann, 55, 66
local context, 43
and politics vs. markets, 59–61
U.S. embrace of, 65
*The Pursuit of Knowledge under
Difficult Circumstances,*
149–150

Redemption, 149
Reform efforts, 78–79
Relevance of course work, 89
Remedial education. *See* Learning
support services
Research universities, 68–69
"Re-skilling," 155
Respect for individual learning styles,
89–90
Retention, 82
*The Rise of the Meritocracy,* 94
Rockefeller, John D., and Rockefeller
Foundation, 68

Romney, Mitt, 195
Roueche, John, 177

SCANS. *See* Secretary's Commission
    on Achieving Necessary Skills
School choice, 78–79
School-to-Work Opportunities Act of
    1994, 47, 131–132
Schugert, Sanford, 197
Schultz, Theodore, 156
Secretary's Commission on Achieving
    Necessary Skills, 27
    and career transcription, 129–130
    foundational and workplace
        competencies, 128–129
Segregation, 81
Selective admissions, 76–77
Self-improvement, 149–150
Service Employees International
    Union, 123
Service learning, 103
Service sector, 28, 47
Servicemen's Readjustment Act. *See*
    GI Bill
Settlement-house movement, 166
SEVIS. *See* Student and Exchange
    Visitor Information System
Skill certifications, 182–183
Smart cards, 190
Smith-Hughes Act of 1917, 45, 123
Smith-Lever Act of 1914, 44, 63
Social capital, 21, 94–95, 157, 208–209
Social mobility, 31–32, 64–65, 66–67
    advocating for the dispossessed,
        193
Socialization, 56–57
Socioeconomic status, 81–82
    as a determinant of educational
        success, 95
Soft skills, 128, 151
Somerville School (New Jersey), 200
Southern Association of Colleges and
    Schools Commission on
    Colleges, 10, 16

Sperber, Irwin, 198
*Sputnik I*, 18
Standardization vs. individualization,
    49, 79
Standardized instruction, 48–49
Stephens College, 44
Student and Exchange Visitor
    Information System, 22, 187,
    204
Student evaluation, 89
Students
    and "at risk" factors, 21
    disadvantages of, 34–35
    as first family members in higher
        education, 20–21
    international, 21–22
    "nontraditional," 18–19
    and "occasional" use of
        community colleges, 32–33
    part-time, 20
    and self-esteem, 21, 31–32
    and social mobility, 31–32
    "traditional," 19
Supplemental instruction. *See*
    Learning support services
Symbolic analysts, 132–133, 137, 139,
    155

Tech prep, 123–125
Technological innovation, 47
Temporary Assistance for Needy
    Families Act, 159
Tenth Amendment, 43, 61
Texas, University of, at Austin, 57, 192
Thornton, Jerry Sue, 177
Tocqueville, Alexis de, 66
Total Quality Management, 57,
    197–198
*Toward a National Workforce
    Education and Training Policy*,
    1, 161
TQM. *See* Total Quality Management
Tracking, 125–126
"Traditional" students, 19

Transfer programs, 120, 127, 137, 140, 143, 188
Transfer rates, 20, 33–34
Transformation movement, 197
Transportation Security Administration, 178
Trinity College (Connecticut), 5
Truman Commission Report. *See Higher Education for American Democracy*
Trust, 198–199
"2 + 2" agreements, 123, 125

UNESCO. *See* United Nations Educational, Scientific, and Cultural Organization
Unions, 123
and adult learning, 166
United Nations Educational, Scientific, and Cultural Organization, 156
United States, twentieth-century developments, 47–50, 48t.
Upward mobility. *See* Social mobility
U.S. Constitution, Tenth Amendment, 43, 61
U.S. Department of Education, 63
Office of Vocational and Adult Education, 225
*See also* Education Resources Information Center; National Center for Education Statistics
U.S. Department of Homeland Security, 178, 187
U.S. Supreme Court, 187, 205
USA Patriot Act of 2001, 22, 204

Valencia Community College, 190, 197
Vocational clusters, 130–131
Vocational education, 50, 150
vs. academic programs, 117–121
antipathy toward, 136–137
apprenticeship programs, 123
best practices and Carl Perkins Act, 46
as focus of community colleges, 59, 136
"New Vocationalism," 136
and proprietary schools, 122–123
and Smith-Hughes Act, 45, 123
and tech prep, 123–125
technical training, 141–143
underdevelopment of in U.S., 122

Wage inequality, 133–134, 135–136
Walden University, 57, 152
Wallace, George, 62
Waterman, Robert, 57, 198
*The Way We Are*, 32–33
Wealth
as a determinant of educational success, 94, 95–96
distribution of, 80
Weber, Max, 58, 149
Western Association of Schools and Colleges, 10, 16
Western Governors University, 104, 225
WGU. *See* Western Governors University
WIA. *See* Workforce Investment Act
WIBs. *See* Workforce Investment Boards
Winn, Judith K., 177
W. K. Kellogg Foundation, 7, 192
Workforce
competencies, 128–129
and debated need for skilled workers, 132–133
development structure, 160–161
intermediaries, 159–161
and lifelong learning, 155–161
questions about shortage of skilled workers, 132–133
training, 22, 99–100, 141–143, 158
and vocational clusters, 130–131
wage inequality, 133–134, 135–136

Workforce Investment Act, 158, 159, 178

Workforce Investment Boards, 12, 117, 159, 178

Workforce Strategies, 168

Workforce Strategy Center, 158, 159–160

*Workforce 2000*, 27, 132, 139

*Workforce 2020*, 27–28, 156

World Bank, 156

World Wide Web. *See* Cyberschools; Digital divide; Information technology; Online learning

Young, Michael, 94

# •◦ About the Author

Dr. David L. Levinson is president of Norwalk Community College in Norwalk, Connecticut. Previously he served as academic vice president at Bergen Community College in Paramus, New Jersey, and dean at Massachusetts Bay Community College in Wellesley Hills, Massachusetts.

He is the general editor of *Education and Sociology: An Encyclopedia* (2002). Dr. Levinson has chaired the educational problems division of the Society for the Study of Social Problems and was editor of the American Sociological Association Sociology of Education section newsletter for ten years.

Dr. Levinson received a Distinguished Teaching Award from the University of Massachusetts at Amherst, where he received an M.A. and Ph.D. in sociology. He has taught at Bergen Community College, Massachusetts Bay Community College, Merrimack College, Tufts University, and the University of Massachusetts at Amherst. He is currently an adjunct associate professor at Teachers College, Columbia University.